Fallen Angels

CHRONICLES OF L.A. CRIME AND MYSTERY

Marvin J. Wolf and Katherine Mader

Facts On File Publications
New York, New York ● Oxford, England

FALLEN ANGELS

Chronicles of L.A. Crime and Mystery

Copyright © 1986 by Marvin J. Wolf and Katherine Mader

Library of Congress Cataloging-in-Publication Data

Wolf, Marvin J.
Fallen Angels

Bibliography: p.
1. Crime and criminals—California—Los Angeles—
History—19th century. 2. Crime and criminals—
California—Los Angeles—History—20th century.
I. Mader, Katherine. II. Title.
HV6795.L6W65 1986 364.1'0979494 86-4260
ISBN 0-8160-1171-0

Printed in the United States of America

10 9 8 7 6 5 4 3 2

For Marvin's daughter, Tomi Wolf,
a.k.a. Laura, Sunni and Anny;
and for
Katherine's family,
Norman, Julia and David Paul,
and to the memory of her parents,
Dr. Paul and Ruth Mader.

CONTENTS

PREFACE

Writing this book we were unexpectedly confronted by a character who, uninvited, elbowed her way into nearly every story. There was no way to tell the tale properly without involving or at least introducing her: La Ciudad de Nuestra Señora de la Reina de Los Angeles, as she is formally known. The City of Our Lady, Queen of Angels; the city, Los Angeles. A fictitious yet very real presence, no less palpable for being only glass and steel, concrete and macadam, thousands of streets and millions of people. Bowing to her ubiquitous presence, Los Angeles became an important character in our book. In truth, we could not do full justice to these often amazing tales without noting her presence.

There were plenty of stories—too many, we felt, to include in one volume. It was easy to agree there was no honor in including a crime or incident merely because it was violent or sensational, such as the "Bob's Big Boy Massacre," where gunmen robbed a neighborhood restaurant after closing, then shot the remaining staff, execution-style.

For the rest, we were forced to establish selection guidelines. Stories that might have been sensational when they occurred were included only if they were somehow more than that. We chose cases which set precedents, as did, for example, the accusation of rape against Alexander Pantages. We chose those which revealed an interesting or important aspect of local history, as did, for instance, the bombing of the *Los Angeles Times*. If any characters involved were celebrities, then or now, it was a reason, though not the sole one, for inclusion. If the incident or crime somehow typified the era in which it occurred, or illuminated a frequently committed crime category, it became a candidate for inclusion.

More difficult was choosing when *not* to include certain cases, though they met our other criteria. For example, much has been written about the controversial suicide of Marilyn Monroe, who is still mourned. But our research revealed little that was new, and we decided there was so much literature available that it would be redundant to include it. Following the same logic, we omitted such cases as the assassination of Robert Kennedy; the murder of Playmate Dorothy Stratten; the knife attack on actress Theresa Saldana; the trial, and eventual acquittal, of John DeLorean on cocaine trafficking charges; the swindling career of boxing promoter Harold Smith; the espionage activities of Christopher Boyce and Daulton Lee; and many other recent and widely publicized incidents.

Nor did we choose to repeat the unfounded innuendos of a few old and widely reported "mysteries." We considered, for example, the "unexplained" death of silent film director Thomas Ince, the "Wizard of Westerns." Ince discovered Tom Mix, William S. Hart and Mary Pickford, to name only a few, and established two major film studios before his untimely death at age 44 in 1924. There's a street named after him in Culver City.

For years it was rumored that Ince died at the hands of William Randolph Hearst, Sr., one of the most powerful men in American history, and that his death was the object of a vast conspiracy of silence. But looking into old allegations that Ince was shot or poisoned aboard the *Oneida*, Hearst's palatial yacht, reveals that nothing of the sort happened. Ince, despite a serious ulcer and his doctor's warnings, overindulged in food and drink, and was stricken with an ulcer attack followed by a series of coronaries. Taken from the *Oneida* to his Benedict Canyon home, he died in front of his wife, sons and brothers. But Hearst was so widely hated that his detractors seized on the incident and attempted to discredit him. Perhaps this sets the record straight.

We omitted Roman Polanski's rape conviction because the story was recently told in detail elsewhere, and because its details are far from novel. Since the passage of time has not at all increased their significance, we omitted, among other crimes, marijuana charges brought against actor Robert Mitchum; the accusations of child molesting against tennis star William Tilden; statutory rape charges lodged against actor Errol Flynn; and the paternity suit successfully, though perhaps unjustly, brought against Charlie Chaplin.

There remain a few celebrated cases about which much has been written, though not very recently, which we have included. The Charles Manson case, for example, was brilliantly dissected in *Helter Skelter*. We include an abbreviated account because the case is so important to the history of crime in Los Angeles: the bloody spectre of Manson remains part of the city's consciousness.

The Manson case may be categorized as cult killings, among several Los Angeles crimes connected with bizarre cults. But most cult crimes, such as the 1940s bombing of the Krishna Venta cult in Ventura County, have involved only members or former members of each particular cult. We saw no wisdom in recounting what were in essence the tribulations of the demented.

The principal difference among most Los Angeles serial murderers seems to be choice of victims and methods. We chose the Hillside Strangler case as representative because the convoluted actions of the convicted killers added a new dimension to serial murder. We believe there is not yet available a more detailed and objective account of these crimes than the one presented here.

There was one other criterion for selection, and we made no exceptions. We required at least one address, the location of a site important to each story. We were amazed—a few parking structures and vacant lots have replaced historically significant buildings; a few newer buildings occupy old addresses. That most intrusive and ubiquitous character, the city of Los Angeles, is more than 200 years old, but remarkably well preserved.

ACKNOWLEDGMENTS

Any project as complex and expansive as this book requires the assistance of literally dozens of people. We are greatly indebted to those who helped point the way to discovering the facts required, and equally indebted to those who helped us understand what these facts meant. Without their freely given time and effort, this book would not have been possible.

We are especially grateful to Rhonda Bright, for her dedication and cheerful attitude while she sifted through thousands of photographs in search of those we selected for publication here, and to Nick Capuano, who did yeoman duty prowling through murky microfiches in search of old newspaper and magazine articles.

For unhindered access to the Irving Wallace Library, we thank Irving and Sylvia Wallace, and especially thank David Wallechinsky. Researchers and librarians at the California Historical Society Library, Santa Monica Heritage Square Museum, the La Canada-Flintridge Historical Society, and Hollywood Heritage House went far beyond the call of duty to help us, as did Louise Gabriel of the Santa Monica Historical Society. Sue Rugge and the entire staff at *Information On Demand* were incredibly responsive and efficient in digging up long-buried facts about Caryl Chessman. Carolyn Stricker, archivist at the *Los Angeles Times*, was more than ordinarily helpful, as was Linda Arnold, a City of Los Angeles employee who helped us discover street names that had been changed since the time events in this book occurred.

Several active and retired officials were generous with their time, including LAPD Captain Arthur Sjoquist, and retired prosecutor J. Miller Leavy.

We are especially indebted to Lois Meltzer, whose magnificent mind conjured up the historical connections which ultimately became the title for this work.

Also helpful with historical insights, research hints, proofreading or constructive criticism were Jake Jacoby, *City News* reporter, Andrew Dowty of Other Times Books, Zan Thompson, Alice Greenfield McGrath, Pamela Leven, Lin Baum, Trudy Self, Laura Meyers, Robert Bortfeld, Don Clinton, Richard Sherer, Sam Smaltz, Annette Swanberg, Mary A. Fisher, Mark Day, Vincent and Andrea Cesare, Pamela Denney, Marc Wannamaker, Pug Henry, David Peterson, Fran Kaufman, Eileen Cochran, Bill Williams and Patricia Schwartz. We are also grateful to Michelle Pelland, Steve Daley and Ed Harris, rational owners of a house they believe happily haunted, for trusting us with their feelings.

For their unstinting encouragement and spiritual support, we thank Donna Haas and Michelle Bekey, our dear friends, and Katherine's husband, Norman Kulla. Most of all, we are indebted to our literary agent, Michael Hamilburg, to our editor, James Warren and associate publisher John Thornton. Their encouragement, insights and support propelled this project from concept to product.

The Avila home: The city's oldest house, it became the scene of the first Los Angeles crime to be tried under American law. Photo: Security Pacific National Bank Photographic Collection/Los Angeles Public Library.

1

THE BURGLARY
CHARGE OF THE
DRAGOONS (1847)

The proud Spanish-speaking citizens of Los Angeles called themselves *Californios* and didn't much care for the strutting, boisterous, often drunken, blue-coated army of occupation which rode in under U.S. General Stephen W. Kearny during the hot summer of 1847. Mexico and the United States were at war, from Texas to California, and a year earlier Commodore John D. Sloat had taken Monterey, the capital. Los Angeles, with only 1,500 residents, became a garrison town. But the *Californios* of Southern California kept up a sullen resistance in a hundred small, annoying ways.

The best of Kearny's troops were the First Dragoons, an elite cavalry. That regiment's Company C pitched tents or huddled in makeshift barracks behind Government House, a one-story adobe extending the length of Olvera Street between Main and Los Angeles.

The soldiers found garrison life among the snobbish *Californios* boring. They were fighting men, volunteers all, enlisted for five-year hitches and accustomed to the rigors of the march and the excitement of battle. On top of that they were at the end of a very long supply line, and even basic necessities were scarce. Company C's troopers needed blankets and uniforms. Even the paymaster's visits were behind schedule. Everyone was broke.

Among the broke was Private John Smith, a small man with what his comrades described as an "irritating personality," who could neither read nor write. He found it impossible to pass the time pleasantly without at least pocket money. And who might have some money? Some of the officers must have some, reasoned Smith, and he set out to learn which ones did. He ordered his

1

slave, a black named Peter Biggs, to find out. Biggs worked in the Avila House, "La Casa de los Avilas," a 31-room adobe near the Olvera home, which served as military headquarters and also housed some of the senior officers.

Biggs found what his master was looking for, a trunk containing $640, including $400 belonging to the U.S. government. Smith devised a plan. Biggs, who came and went from the officers' quarters without suspicion, would use an officer's key to unlock the trunk, and would leave the room door unlocked. Smith would steal the money. But he needed a confederate to ensure that he wouldn't be seen coming or going. He enlisted Private John Stokely. On the night of August 3, Stokely guarded the door while Smith slipped in and stole the money. Biggs was nowhere around.

On August 20, Smith, Biggs and Stokely were arrested, by order of their commanding officer. Later that day Smith shot himself in the chest—how he got hold of a gun was never made clear—but botched the suicide attempt. While he recovered under guard in a hospital bed, Biggs and Stokely were held in an adobe guardhouse halfway up the knoll overlooking Government House. As an extra precaution against escape, their ankles were chained to a pine log running the length of the building.

They were kept that way for a month, because their simple act of burglary created a complex legal morass that was never satisfactorily resolved. Nevertheless, Stokely and Smith became the first men in Los Angeles to be tried for a civil offense under American law.

Los Angeles was under martial law, but the offense was essentially a civil act, and the scene of the crime, "La Casa de los Avilas," was not government property but "borrowed" from its civilian owners. Under the Articles of War, the accused should have been tried in a civilian court. But the civilians, in occupied territory not yet ceded to the Union, were hostile to all American soldiers. And their laws, precedents and procedures were based on the Spanish system, quite different from the English common law of the United States. The solution was a military commission, a panel of seven officers, empowered to try essentially civil cases. But there is no federal code that deals with larceny, burglary and such matters. That is left to the states. The only state law book that could be produced was the New York statutes. So two U.S. dragoons were tried in Los Angeles under New York state laws by seven stern and unsympathetic Army combat officers.

Under oath, Biggs testified that his master, Smith, had offered him a share of the money if he'd find an officer with money and tell Smith and Stokely where it was kept. He swore that he hadn't gone along on the actual burglary, and that after the theft, Smith threatened to kill him if he told anyone about it. After Smith and Biggs were arrested, Biggs named Stokely as an accomplice. Smith paid someone to write a letter on his behalf to the court in which he confessed to the crime and begged for leniency, asserting Biggs had instigated the whole affair by suggesting he could leave the trunk and room unlocked.

Stokely testified that Smith had said Biggs had unlocked the trunk and the room, and that all Stokely had to do was come along and take the money. Stokely insisted he came no farther than the door of the house, because there were several women nearby and he feared being seen. Biggs testified that Stokely had gone into the house and stood outside the room. He also said Stokely, like Smith, had threatened his life if he told anyone about the burglary.

Later in the trial Smith and Stokely testified about events following the burglary itself. Smith, alone, had hidden the money. Stokely said he demanded his share and insisted Biggs receive a share as well, or else he would tell the authorities. Smith stalled. Stokely drew his handgun and threatened to kill him where he stood unless he came up with the money. Smith pleaded that he had become confused about the hiding place.

Smith and Stokely were convicted—and the legal quagmire became stickier. Smith, said the panel, was the instigator and should be given the harshest sentence: five years in state prison. Stokely was sentenced to two years, in consideration of the help he'd given to recover the money and because witnesses had spoken favorably of his character. But there wasn't a state prison in California, which wasn't a state. So the panel met again, and decided that the punishment should be limited to the type a person might get in any other state: a dishonorable discharge, forfeiture of all pay and allowances, and five years at hard labor with a ball and chain attached to one leg. In addition, the word "thief" was to be tattooed on their right hips with indelible ink. The commission left it to the officer reviewing the case, who was stationed in Monterey, to decide where they should be imprisoned.

The law book was an old one; the reviewing officer was not an attorney and wasn't sure if tattooing a prisoner was still legal in the United States, so that proviso was suspended. But he also said that since the theft was the result of a concerted plan between Smith and Stokely, their sentences should be equal. Both were to be confined in the guardhouse of the First Dragoons in Los Angeles, and given the same clothing and food as other prisoners in the guardhouse.

Circumstances intervened. On December 13, 1847, an explosion shook the guardhouse. Many soldiers inside were injured, and John Stokely, chained to his log, was unable to escape the fire that followed the blast and perished.

That left John Smith, who had a severe chest wound and couldn't work very hard. But he could eat. On January 9, 1848, his commanding officer, using powers at his discretion, gave Smith a dishonorable discharge and told him he was free to find his own food, if he could. Smith paid a New York Volunteers private (who was later courtmartialed for theft) $0.25 for his government-issued bed sack, and left Los Angeles. He set out alone, into the vast, arid emptiness of Southern California, into territory controlled by bandits, marauding Indians, roving bands of die-hard Mexican soldiers and wild animals. John Smith was never heard from again.

His slave fared somewhat better. After a public whipping, lashes applied to his bare back, Peter Biggs was given his freedom. He stayed in Los Angeles, opened a small barber shop and hired himself out as a gentleman's gentleman, cutting hair, washing clothes, shining shoes. And getting into all kinds of mischief.

In the rough and tumble politics of the day, office seekers used every sort of ruse or trick to get extra votes, including having men vote several times. Biggs' role was to disguise the voters, changing their hair color or style, lightening or darkening their skin, changing their clothing.

During the Gold Rush era, when San Francisco's homeowners complained of swarms of rats invading the city from deserted ships in the harbor, Biggs stole housecats in Los Angeles. He filled several crates, and caught a fast boat to San Francisco, where he auctioned the cats from a waterfront pier.

During the early years of the Civil War, Biggs, a former slave, was imprisoned at the Drumm Annex in Wilmington for "reckless secessionist" talk. He advocated the right of any state to secede from the Union. Released, he made loud boasts of his supposed importance while dining in a Los Angeles restaurant. The Mexican proprietor found his remarks personally insulting, and stabbed Peter Biggs to death with a knife.

LOCATION:
Thomas Brothers map reference: Page 44 at E 2
Exit the Hollywood Freeway (U.S. 101) southbound at Broadway, cross the freeway and turn right on Sunset to Olvera Street, opposite Union Station. La Casa de los Avilas, an L-shaped adobe of 31 rooms on Olvera Street, was built in 1818 and is the oldest surviving building in Los Angeles. As headquarters for Commodore R.F. Stockton, it was the first Los Angeles adobe to fly the Stars and Stripes, in 1846. The building still stands, though the foot of the "L" which formerly barred Olvera Street was removed. The building is open to the public; admission is free.

Vasquez & his captors: A bandit's career provided inspiration for generations of filmmakers. Photo: California Historical Society/TICOR Title Insurance (Los Angeles).

2

LAST OF HIS BREED: TIBURCIO VASQUEZ (1874)

He was a bandit. A cutthroat corsair. A brigand. A pirate who cruised California's vast and mostly empty interior on horseback. He ambushed, he laid siege, he raided, he kidnapped and ransomed. He stole cattle and horses. He stole money from bankers and from ranchers. He took gold and silver from stage lines, mule trains and miners. He emptied the pockets of travelers at gunpoint. He was the last of the great California *banditos* and the first of Hollywood's heroes. And long before Edison invented the movies, he was Hollywood's first great Latin lover.

He was Tiburcio Vasquez. He was born near Monterey in August 1835, very likely into the family of Mexican notables who had helped colonize San Francisco for Spain in 1777. He was a boy when the Bear Flag Revolt started, when California became American and he became a foreigner in the land of his birth. It was the height of the Gold Rush and he was just 15 when he first got in trouble with the law. There was a dance-hall brawl, someone was knifed, and the police came looking for Vasquez.

He fled to Mendocino, but the police still wanted to see him. They had no warrant, and the person at the dance hall had not died, but hotheaded Vasquez did not trust the *yanqui* law, and he didn't trust the lawmen. He resisted arrest. It was all very quick, a skirmish rather than a brawl; no lawmen died, but when it was over Tiburcio Vasquez was on the run. And with that act he chose a life of crime. He chose "to live off the world," as he would put it to a newspaper man, some 23 years later.

Young Vasquez took his apprenticeship in Steinbeck country, long before Steinbeck lived and wrote about the lovely area around Monterey and Salinas. Vasquez hid in the hills and stole cattle from the local ranchers, just as many of these *yanquis* had stolen the land from its Mexican owners. (The same land their grandparents stole from the Indians.) Vasquez was tutored by a man named Garcia, a renowned cattle thief. His education ended prematurely when Garcia incautiously allowed himself to be captured and was hanged. Vasquez headed inland, to greener pastures. Pastures filled with horses.

For two years he stole horses until he was caught, in 1857. Sentenced to five years at hard labor in San Quentin, he served two before the largest prison break in California history set him, along with everyone else at San Quentin, free. He was returned seven weeks later after being arrested for larceny in Amador. A year was added to his sentence for the larceny; he was released in August 1863.

He tried San Jose, but ran into some trouble there over an Italian butcher found stabbed and shot. He moved north to Contra Costa, Napa and Sonoma and began to burnish his legend as a lady killer.

He was a small, sinewy man, perhaps 5 feet, 7 inches in thick-heeled boots, and much of his face was hidden behind a mustache and a carefully groomed beard. He could read only a little, mostly numbers, and write even less. But his eyes shone with a mystical fervor, and he was phenomenally attractive to women. Young, beautiful women. Older women. Even plain women. It led him into temptation, and from temptation into action, and from action into seductions and abductions and wife stealing. And it led him into knife duels and gun fights with outraged husbands, suitors, brothers and fathers. Often they were his own men, or his benefactors.

One was named Salazar, a rancher of unblemished repute who often sheltered the bandit in his home, at some risk. Vasquez ran off with his beautiful young wife—and with Salazar's bullet in his neck. Salazar went to the law and swore out a complaint: attempted murder. He told a grand jury that Vasquez threatened his life by drawing his gun. Vasquez was indicted but never arrested.

On another occasion Vasquez took a fancy to the wife of one of his henchmen, a former blacksmith from Chile named Leiva. Vasquez sent him on a dangerous mission, hoping and expecting Leiva to be killed. He promptly took up with his wife. Leiva returned safely, but when he learned why he'd been chosen for the mission he was outraged. He surrendered to the sheriff, and gave evidence against Vasquez and his followers. Vasquez got away and took Leiva's wife along. When she was seven or eight months pregnant, he abandoned her to the elements in a lonely, desolate area without a horse, a weapon or food. She was fortuitously rescued by a passer-by.

In 1866 Vasquez tried to rustle a large herd from a Sonoma ranch. A posse tracked him down. Vasquez went to San Quentin prison for another three years and six months. He was discharged again in June 1870. Now 33 years old, he was through with stealing livestock. He was ready for the big time, ready to follow in the footsteps of Joaquin Murieta and Juan Flores, California's most famous bandits. He had a solid reputation for leadership, and among the bandit elite he had proven his abilities as a bandito beyond question. He put together a small band of toughs, and set out to terrorize Central California.

His new trademark was a row of trussed and gagged prisoners neatly laid on the ground. If his victims did not resist, they were robbed and thus laid out. But his first followers failed to demonstrate the right stuff. They did all right with defenseless storekeepers and weary travelers, and they ambushed a fair number of stagecoaches. But they failed miserably to stop trains, and in 1871 a posse caught up with them. All but Vasquez were killed or captured, and Vasquez himself was shot in the chest by a lawman.

Nevertheless he escaped, riding more than 60 miles on horseback to a hideout near Hollister. There he recuperated. As he gathered strength he recruited a new band of followers, a somewhat hardier bunch. He staged a series of robberies, perfecting his techniques and his strategies. They raided the general store at Firebaugh's Ferry in the San Joaquin Valley, expecting a $30,000 payroll for cattle king Henry Miller but settling for small change and what supplies they could carry off. They went after other general stores, isolated roadside inns, travelers, stagecoaches and the Southern Pacific Railroad.

And in August 1873, Vasquez and six followers called on Andrew Snyder's store in Tres Pinos. What followed, though more than a robbery, was less than the massacre it became in legend. Vasquez rode off with cash, clothing, tobacco, food, liquor, the personal valuables of several customers and seven of the town's best horses. He left three men dead and two people unconscious after brutally pistol-whipping them. One of them was a small boy.

Emboldened by his success at Tres Pinos, Vasquez swooped down on Kingston, a small town near Fresno. He and his followers plundered the hotel and two stores, and rode off with $2,000 in coin, and the watches and jewelry of the 35 men and women he left face down in the street.

These raids were the last straw. Californians would no longer tolerate such banditry. Just as they had tracked down and destroyed the other great *banditos,*they would stop Vasquez.

But first they had to find him. Harry Morse, sheriff of Alameda County, had been keeping an eye on the exploits of Vasquez for years. In a strange way he had come to admire Vasquez and had learned to see things as Vasquez saw them. Morse had established a statewide reputation as a premier tracker and manhunter. California Governor Newton Booth put a price on Vasquez's head: $8,000 alive, $6,000 dead. And he pushed through the legislature a special appropriation to fund Morse in forming an expeditionary posse with the sole purpose of finding and capturing Tiburcio Vasquez.

Vasquez decided that Central California was no longer safe. He took his band south, stopping en route at Owens Valley. There he stormed the stage depot at

Coyote Holes and took the occupants hostage. He stripped the valuables from half a dozen mule skinners and the wife of the station manager and left them tied up in the sagebrush while his band waited for the real prize: the stagecoach from San Francisco.

On the coach were several passengers and a strongbox. The passengers had a silver watch and $25 between them. But Mortimer Belshaw, Inyo County's mining king, was also on the coach, and he was carrying $10,000—in mining stock certificates. Not much use to a band on the run. The strongbox contained only the ledgers and accounting documents for a gold mine. In disgust, Vasquez commanded Belshaw to give him his new boots, and, putting them on, he prepared to ride off. Moments later an unscheduled arrival brought the bandits a second chance. Into the station came a train of mule teams, but, as luck would have it, their wagons contained only trail dust. Vasquez emptied the skinners' pockets and left 16 men trussed up face down in the dust.

Vasquez drifted further south, looking for the big score. To gain the sympathy of the area's mostly Mexican population, he let it be known that he was no longer merely a *bandito*. He was instead their liberator, their leader. He would lead a revolt against the *yanquis* who had stolen their country. He would return California, at least the southern part, to Mexican control. But first he needed money for arms.

Vasquez holed up in the mesquite canyons and arid arroyos near Soledad Canyon. In this rock-strewn wilderness of cliffs and caves and small villages he was sheltered by the locals. In Soledad Canyon he was safe from the posses. But he was also lonely. There were few women, and fewer cantinas. There were only poor Mexican peasants.

So from time to time, Vasquez went to Hollywood. Of course there was no Hollywood at the time. There were only the crumbling granite and mesquite canyons of the range of low hills a few miles northwest of the Los Angeles pueblo. They were called the Cahuengas. There were Laurel, Alison and Nichols Canyons, and Rancho La Brea.

Rancho La Brea sat at the foot of the Cahuengas. Near its northern edge was the adobe hut of a man who called himself George Allen, and was widely known as Greek George. George may possibly have been Greek, but his birthplace was Smyrna, otherwise known as Izmir, in Turkey. And there George the Greek Turk had learned to handle camels, before immigrating to America in 1865. When the U.S. Army decided, after the Civil War, that a camel corps would be useful to help tame the great deserts of the Southwest, they hired George as a drover. The camels were for a time pastured on Rancho La Brea, but soon proved difficult, tiresome and expensive and so were phased out. George became the regular driver for the stage that ran between Los Angeles and Tejon, at the summit of the pass over the Tehachipi Mountains to the north. When, in 1874, Vasquez tired of the sagebrush and safety of Soledad Canyon, when he fancied a little feminine companionship or a few drinks, he came to stay at Greek George's adobe, where the camel driver welcomed him.

By the spring of 1874 the pickings north of Los Angeles were slim, and Vasquez was getting desperate for money. On April 24, with great guile and planning, he raided the sheep ranch of Alexandro Repetto, an Italian who had settled near El Monte, in what is today East Los Angeles. At sheep shearing time, he and his men secreted their pistols under their shirts and rode up. They told Repetto they were shearers, looking for work. When he invited them into his shaded, cool home, they pulled their pistols.

All Repetto had was $80 in cash, and he gave it to them. Vasquez was not satisfied. He knew that the rancher had recently sold some $10,000 worth of sheep. Repetto would show them where he'd hidden the money, or they would kill him. The rancher took out his books, explaining that most of the money had gone to buy land, and the rest was in the Temple & Workman Bank in Los Angeles. Vasquez, who knew figures, examined the books.

Vasquez offered Repetto a choice. He could send his small nephew to the bank for $800, or he could die at the end of a rope hung from one of his sturdy olive trees. As a demonstration of sincerity, the bandits tied Repetto to a tree, and shoved a pistol in each of his ears. Repetto decided he'd write a check. The boy left in a hurry, while Vasquez, prideful of his cooking, scurried about the kitchen making breakfast for his men.

At the bank, six miles away, tellers examined the check they took from the youngster, and decided to call the sheriff, Billy Rowland. The boy soon told Rowland who was holding his uncle, and what they'd do if he didn't return with the money. The bankers gave the boy a sack with $500 in gold coin.

While he rode back, Rowland hurriedly rounded up a posse. He dispatched one third of it to El Monte, to the east of the Repetto spread. They were to cut off the bandits' retreat and to summon help from El Monte. He sent another group north along the dry Los Angeles River to block their escape toward Soledad Canyon. He led seven men with rifles.

Vasquez was pleased with the $500 in gold. As the bandits were dividing their booty, the posse arrived, shooting. Vasquez and company rode off on their fresh horses, the posse pursuing them on tired mounts. They chose not the eastern route toward El Monte nor the northern route of the Los Angeles River but instead the Arroyo Seco leading through Pasadena. Once again luck was on the side of the bandits, and they eluded the posse.

But Sheriff Harry Morse of Alameda was determined to end that luck. By May he and his men had carefully searched all of Central California down to the Tehachipis. Near Tejon they ran into a Mexican who knew Greek George. For a small consideration, he shared what he knew of Vasquez's comings and goings from George's adobe in Alison Canyon.

Harry Morse could have had Vasquez then and there, but he was a prudent and politically sensitive man. He would not invade Sheriff Billy Rowland's turf without permission. Besides, the wily Vasquez had eluded capture longer than any bandit in the state's history. There was no such thing as too many men in the posse. If he and Rowland were to join forces, it would be much safer for all. Morse quietly approached Rowland.

But Billy Rowland, son of a prominent rancher, wouldn't hear of it. He didn't need any Northern California help to police his territory. Harry Morse and his men turned around and headed north the way they'd come.

Now that Tiburcio Vasquez had a few dollars in his pockets, he was spending more time than ever at Greek George's place. He had his eye on George's pretty young wife, and George was enjoying it less. One of Rowland's men managed to get George off by himself for a few minutes and inform him of how much money the local merchants had raised as a bounty on Vasquez. George was astonished to learn it was $15,000. And interested. Very interested.

George told Vasquez about a dance in neighboring Nichols Canyon which all the pretty *senoritas* would attend. Vasquez, always the womanizer, fell for it. On the night of May 13 he went dancing with only one bodyguard. Knowing Vasquez would return very late and tired, George went downtown to see Billy Rowland and Rowland started rounding up a few good men.

At 1:30 in the morning they moved out from the sheriff's corral at Seventh and Spring, led by Undersheriff Albert Johnson, with City Detective Emil Harris, five deputized citizens—and George Beers, correspondent of the *San Francisco Chronicle*. At four the following morning the posse, hidden by a dense fog, surrounded the ranch house. Inside were Vasquez, his lone *compadre* and Greek George's wife and infant son. But the leader of the posse had no way of being sure Vasquez was there so they waited for daylight.

About midmorning the fog burned off and Johnson spotted Vasquez's distinctive silver-studded saddle on a horse tethered to a tree. Through the open kitchen door they saw a young woman moving around, making breakfast. And at the table sat Vasquez. But how to get close enough?

Just then a wagon driven by two Mexican-Americans came down the canyon. Johnson commandeered it. The posse hid beneath the firewood behind the drivers, who leisurely drove into the front yard. A hundred yards from the house the posse materialized. The woman screamed. All hell broke loose as two men charged the front door. George's wife slammed it, but not before Emil Harris had poked his rifle barrel inside. He pushed the door wide and entered the kitchen.

Vasquez dove through the window and fled, a lawman firing his shotgun at him. But Vasquez, who seemed to have nine lives, fell down just before the load of buckshot went by. Quickly on his feet he sprinted toward his waiting horse and ran into newsman George Beers, whose shotgun was ready. His shot hit Vasquez in the shoulder and it was followed by a fusillade from the others. Vasquez went down and stayed down.

But his wounds were not serious. He surrendered, claiming his name was Alejandro Martinez. But had they really got him? None of the posse had ever seen Vasquez, and some half wondered if this was he. But Johnson had, over the years, seen many pictures of Vasquez, and he was sure he had the right man. Vasquez denied it until the pain from his many wounds broke down his resolve. As they bandaged his wounds, Vasquez gently reminded the posse that he was worth $8,000 alive, but only $6,000 dead.

An hour later he was in the city jail with Sheriff Billy Rowland and a bottle of good whisky. He was poured a glass, and then he proposed a toast: "To the President of the United States!" Vasquez was out of business, he was shot full of holes, he was in jail, but even if he was a murderer and a thief he was also as charming a guest as the jail had ever held.

And as enterprising. In need of cash, the man who had robbed storekeepers up and down the state sold the only thing he had—his name. Sold it to Mendell Meyer, a storekeeper, whose display advertisement ran in the evening edition the same day Vasquez went behind bars:

VASQUEZ SAYS THAT MENDELL MEYER
HAS THE FINEST AND MOST COMPLETE
STOCK OF DRY GOODS AND CLOTHING.

And Los Angeles had its first celebrity bandit. He held court as though his cell, filled to overflowing with baskets of fruit and flowers from the adoring ladies of Los Angeles, were not a cell at all, but a sitting room. Finally Sheriff Rowland ordered a stop to it, but not before the state controller telegraphed $8,000 to Rowland's bank account.

Tiburcio Vasquez was charged with the murder of two of the three men killed at Tres Pinos. He denied it. Vasquez went to his death denying he'd ever killed anyone. Rowlands wanted Vasquez tried in Los Angeles, but the city had no proper prison facilities for such an important prisoner—and Northern Californians remembered Rowlands' rude reply to Sheriff Morse's offer. Noting how Los Angeles had taken this charming bandit to its bosom and wondering how long he'd stay in jail, the governor ordered Vasquez taken north to San Jose for trial. For security, he traveled aboard the sidewheel steamer *Senator*.

Vasquez raised a defense fund among his supporters and engaged two able attorneys. But they failed to sway the jury, which convicted Vasquez of murder on January 5, 1875. On January 23 the judge told Vasquez that his name "was a synonym for all that was wicked and infamous," and that his life had been an unbroken record of lawlessness and outrage, "a career of pillage and murder."

Though the Santa Clara County sheriff issued hundreds of printed invitations to the bandit's execution on March 16, 1875, Vasquez went with dignity to his death on the hangman's scaffold. His last word, with the noose already around his neck, and deputies buckling straps to bind his arms and legs to his sides, was "pronto." Make it fast.

Thus ended the life of California's last great bandit. And thus began the movie stereotype of the handsome, charming, utterly amoral Mexican bandit, the basis for dozens of Hollywood film characters, from the silent era to the present. All because of a nearly illiterate—but charming—cutthroat who eluded capture longer than any of his equally famous predecessors. And who was finally betrayed by his friend—for money. In Hollywood. Close to where, a few decades later, the film industry set up shop.

LOCATIONS:

Thomas Brothers map reference: Page 33 at E3
Greek George's adobe was situated up what was formerly known as Alison Canyon. Go west on Sunset Boulevard from Crescent Heights; turn right up Kings Road, and follow the canyon to Franklin Avenue, now a traffic circle. The adobe where Tiburcio Vasquez was captured was near the center of the circle.

Thomas Brothers map reference: Page 33 at E4
The Rancho La Brea's main building formerly occupied the area around the intersection of Kings Road and Santa Monica Boulevard.

Thomas Brothers map reference: Page 125 at A2
Vasquez Canyon is part of the vast Soledad Canyon area. Take the Golden State Freeway (I-5) north toward Magic Mountain. Turn off at Antelope Valley Freeway (State 14) and go north to the first exit. Exit there, go under the freeway and take the Sierra Highway north. Vasquez Canyon Road is a left turn about five miles up the road. Take Vasquez Canyon Road north through the canyon. The road ends in an area of fractured fault lines and giant rocks. An enormous rock near the mouth of the canyon is a state historical point called Vasquez Rock. Vasquez and his band hid out here for several months in 1873 and 1874.

Earl Rogers: He knew more about anatomy and alcohol than most doctors of his era; still he drank himself to death. Photo: Security Pacific National Bank Photographic Collection/Los Angeles Public Library.

3

A VISCERAL ISSUE: THE SHOOTING OF JAY HUNTER (1899)

He was the aristocratic darling of Gay Nineties society, a scion of the defeated impoverished Southern oligarchy who came to Los Angeles to make his fortune. He did. And he quickly became admired. A tall, well-dressed, handsome, cultured, charming attorney who for years topped the city's list of eligible bachelors, his name was Jay E. Hunter. In addition to all his virtues, he was on occasion a stubborn, miserly, self-righteous, cane-wielding bully. The day came when he lived just long enough to regret these flaws.

William Alford was also a Southerner by birth, but born to the sharecropper's shanty. In Los Angeles he became a handyman, known to his neighbors as an honest and hard worker. Late in 1898, Hunter hired him to repair some plumbing. Alford did the work, and sent his eminent customer a bill for $102.

Hunter neglected to pay. Alford sent him another bill. Hunter refused it, as well as several others sent in quick succession. Alford sued in municipal court, but Hunter never deigned even to show up. The court awarded Alford judgment for the full amount. Of course, he still had to collect the money from Hunter, and Hunter was denying he owed the money at all.

Alford knew that the rich Hunter could well afford to pay. Frustrated and near desperation, he decided to embarass his debtor into settling. In the South such situations were often handled in a direct manner. Alford had handbills printed headlined: "*Jay E. Hunter Does Not Pay His Debts.*" The text explained the repairs, the court judgment and Hunter's refusal to pay.

Alford planned to post the bills all over Los Angeles. But first he would show them to Hunter, and give him one last chance to pay. On February 18, 1899, he went to the fourth-floor of the Stimson Block, an office building in downtown Los Angeles, where Hunter had his offices.

Hunter and Alford met in a fourth-floor corridor. Alford demanded his money at once. If he did not receive it, he would paper the city with damning handbills. Hunter refused, and soon the argument became physical. Hunter's office neighbors heard the sounds of men struggling. And then a shot.

Those first on the scene found Alford standing over Hunter, who still clutched a heavy cane in his hand. It was shattered. Hunter was carried to a hospital with a bullet wound in his belly. Though conscious, coherent and able to speak, he died two days later. Cause of death: peritonitis, an acute infection of the abdominal organs, caused by the matter that had oozed from the five holes where Alford's bullet had perforated his intestines. Had antibiotics been available, he might have survived.

Alford was charged with murder in the first degree. There were no witnesses to the shooting, but several people had heard Alford threaten Hunter, and others had heard their quarrel in the corridor. So popular was Hunter that the leading citizens of Los Angeles named a special prosecutor, former Senator Stephen M. White, to handle the case.

White, a former professor of law, was by long repute the most able of California attorneys. With him assisting the district attorney there could be no question of a conviction.

Alford had little money, no important friends, and no witnesses to back up his story. The public was howling for his blood. One of Stephen White's former law students, the young, handsome and inexperienced Earl Rogers, volunteered to defend Alford. His fee: $100.

Rogers promptly spent $40 of it on a new suit, and set out to study the evidence and prepare a strategy.

The first prosecution witness was the coroner, who described the condition of Hunter's body and offered his expert opinion of where Hunter had been shot. Since the bullet had traveled downward through his body, the coroner's opinion was that Alford was standing over his victim. In cross-examination, Rogers was unable to shake this testimony. But he did manage to get the jury's mind off its implications by forcing the coroner to admit that he had refused to perform the autopsy until the body was transferred from one undertaker's establishment to another owned by the coroner's good friend.

Later in the trial, Rogers questioned the chief autopsy surgeon at great length, establishing that Hunter's cane had been used to savagely beat Alford's head—so hard that the cane had shattered while inflicting long lacerations to Alford's head. Rogers planted the suggestion that Hunter's cane had been wielded offensively, not defensively.

He next called as witness F.A. Stephenson, an attorney whose offices were next door to Hunter's. Stephenson hadn't seen the fight, but he had heard it.

He had disarmed an unresisting Alford seconds after the single shot was fired. Under oath, Stephenson admitted that he knew Hunter had used his heavy cane to strike people on the head on previous occasions.

Then a surgeon took the stand. Dr. C.W. Pierce had operated on Hunter, trying to save his life. His testimony also affirmed that the fatal bullet had traveled downward through the intestines. Rogers was unperturbed. In cross-examination he had Dr. Pierce describe the bullet holes in Hunter's clothing; based on powder burns and the way fibers were torn, it appeared the bullet had entered the body after piercing the front of his trousers below the navel, and subsequently exited from the rear.

As Rogers saw it, the chief obstacle to an acquittal was the formidable and distinguished White. White left much of the prosecution's case, and all of the minutiae, to the deputy district attorney, Johnstone Jones. Jones, usually addressed as "General Jones," was pompous, vain and self-important, slow of mind and short on courtroom experience. The General was a man trying to operate beyond his level of competence.

Rogers set out to humble him before the jury. He baited Jones at every opportunity, drawing laughs from the spectators, grins from the jury, and now and then an admonishment from the bench. This strategy forced Senator White to spend most of his time protecting Jones from Rogers' thinly veiled ridicule. It portrayed to the jury a prosecution that was trying much too hard.

Rogers knew that White was brilliant on cross-examinations. Many times he had shattered previously unflappable witnesses with brilliant insights and relentless questioning. Rogers hoped to find a way to deny White any opportunity to question Alford. And after several days, he found it.

As the trial proceeded day by day, White's lunch hour grew longer and longer. At first, out of courtesy to White, the judge delayed starting the afternoon session for 5 or 10 minutes, until White arrived. But after a week, White was coming in 15 or 20 minutes late, and the judge gaveled the courtroom to order without him.

There was a custom then—still practiced by many defense attorneys—that a defendant called as witness in his own case is the last witness to testify. For good reason: the defendant will then have had the advantage of hearing all previous witnesses, and will be able to tell his story to his best advantage.

On the day Alford was scheduled to testify, Rogers hurried from the courtroom at noon recess. He wanted several minutes alone with his client to rehearse his testimony. Then he rushed to a nearby saloon favored by local attorneys and other courthouse types. White was at the bar, enjoying an ample free lunch along with several glasses of whisky. He invited Rogers to join him. Rogers hinted that Alford would take the stand late in the day, when everyone was tired. White hinted that he'd tear his testimony to pieces. The seed planted, Rogers declined a second drink, pleading an office appointment. He hurried off.

When the judge entered the courtroom at 2:00, Rogers was in his chair. Senator White was still taking lunch. And when court came to order, Rogers called his first witness: William Alford.

Quickly and clearly, Alford told how Hunter had attacked him with a weighted cane, knocked him down, and continued to beat his head and shoulders, gripping the heavy cane near its ornate head, wielding it mercilessly until Alford began to fear he would be killed. Then—but only then—he'd worked his gun from its holster, pointed it up at Hunter, who was bent almost double as he struck at Alford on the floor, and pulled the trigger.

"Take the witness," said Rogers, and as he'd hoped, the General was unprepared. The prosecution's plan was for White to cross-examine the witness, and Jones was clearly unwilling to start without him.

Eyeing the doorway for the compact figure of Senator White, Jones tried to delay. Admonished by the judge to proceed, he stumbled through a few perfunctory questions, the effect of which strengthened Alford's bare-bones testimony. Unable to think of anything further, he mumbled "No more questions."

Just then White elbowed his way through the crowd, and quickly grasped the situation. "No redirect examination," chanted Rogers, which meant that Alford could not be questioned by White. The defendant left the stand.

White was nearly beside himself. He raged. He spouted. He eventually calmed. Rogers called a few character witnesses, men who vouched for Alford's standing in the community. And then he asked the coroner to bring the intestines of the late Jay Hunter into court as evidence. The spectators' gasp filled the room, followed by a hubbub of excitement.

White jumped to his feet, objecting: there was no foundation for presenting such an unusual piece of evidence.

Rogers answered: the foundation had been laid by the special prosecutor himself, who had brought the coroner to the stand and elicited testimony that Alford's bullet "had ranged *downward* through the intestines." Rogers would prove that the shot had been fired up—but he needed the guts to do it.

It might be in bad taste, but it was legal, ruled the judge. And for the first time in Western criminal law, the bowels of the deceased were brought into court. A bailiff gingerly carried a large glass jar filled with alcohol and the viscera of the late Jay Hunter. An unbroken seal and the testimony of the coroner and autopsy surgeon verified their authenticity.

Dr. Edward Pallete, 25, a year out of medical school, was called as expert witness. He produced a colored chart of the intestines, and with calm answers to Rogers' questions, proved that the bullet had indeed passed downward through the intestines.

And the only way this could have happened was if Hunter were doubled over at the waist, the intestines folded over upon themselves. In his fury, Hunter had shattered his cane. He then continued to wield the shorter remnant, using it as a short club. Alford on the ground had shot *up* at Hunter but the bullet had traveled *down* through Hunter's body while his shoulders were below his hips.

The jury took only minutes to bring in a verdict: Alford had acted in self-defense. He was not guilty.

Rogers went on to become the most famous trial lawyer in the West, the man chosen to defend Clarence Darrow. (See chapter 6.)

LOCATIONS:

Thomas Brothers map reference: Page A at D3
The Stimson block where Hunter was slain in self-defense was at the southeast corner of Third and Spring at 129 West Third. It's now a parking lot. Take the Hollywood Freeway (US 101) to Spring, cross the freeway south, and go four short blocks to Third.

Thomas Brothers map reference: Page A at B5
William Alford lived at 134 West 14th Street. From Third and Spring, go south to 14th Street, turn right. The vacant lot on the south side, the next-to-last property before the corner, was the site of Alford's home.

Col. Griffith J. Griffith: While under the influence, he fantasized papist plots, then shot his wife's eye out. Photo: Courtesy UCLA Library Special Collections.

4

GREEK THEATER: ATTEMPTED MURDER BY COLONEL GRIFFITH (1903)

Like his name, Griffith J. Griffith was almost a parody of himself. Vain and pompous, he was a grotesque, roly-poly, almost gnomelike creature who from young adulthood habitually strutted about like a barnyard fowl, usually swinging an ornate cane. He had an unquenchable thirst for alcohol and was almost constantly in a state of inebriation, which distorted his perception of reality. Nevertheless Griffith was an astute mining engineer and businessman who made a fortune in mining. He enlarged it considerably by dealing in Los Angeles real estate around the turn of the century. His political cronies in the California National Guard made him a "colonel," a courtesy title that became a permanent part of his name.

In 1896, Griffith presented the City of Los Angeles with a gift: more than 4,100 acres of forested hills, valleys, streams and meadows, which became Griffith Park. It is the second-largest city park in the country, a lush, verdant enclave of leisure and recreation in the middle of a booming metropolis. Griffith had lived and ranched on the land for a dozen years before he gave it to the city; some cynically declared that the "gift" was more a bribe to help settle some tax problems.

Christina Griffith, Griffith's wife, was a Los Angeles blueblood, who traced her roots to the Verdugos, the titled landholders of Spanish ancestry who first put the city on the map. The Colonel was a man of strong prejudices and often peculiar opinions; in his later years he developed an almost rabid fear of the Roman Catholic Church. Though Griffith disapproved, Christina remained active in many social causes connected with the Catholic Church.

In 1903, Griffith asked Christina to deed to him a piece of her own land as collateral for a complex business transaction. She dutifully obliged her husband, but when the deal was concluded and Griffith had pocketed a healthy profit, Christina asked him to return the property, which had been in her family for generations. When he didn't comply, she asked him for it again. And again. But Griffith was long past rational behavior.

Perhaps due to his alcoholism, he began to believe that Christina was attempting to poison him. She was trying to kill him, he thought, at the order of the pope in Rome, so the church could get its hands on his millions. Griffith concealed this paranoia from his wife, but all the while he was forming a convoluted and demented plan. It hatched on a fine summer day at the elegant old Arcadia Hotel, overlooking Santa Monica Bay, where the Griffiths were vacationing. Without warning the Colonel handed Christina a prayer book, and took out a loaded pistol.

He commanded her to kneel before him and to open the book. As she did so, he cocked the pistol. In his pocket Griffith had a slip of paper on which were written a series of questions. He took out the paper, told Christina to close her eyes, and began to read.

Christina begged for her life. They had a 12-year-old son, she sobbed, and he needed his mother. Griffith was undeterred. She begged for time to pray. He told her she might have a few moments to prepare her soul to meet its maker. Almost crazed with fear, she prayed out loud.

Abruptly, Griffith interrupted. "Have you ever been unfaithful to me?" he asked.

"Oh Papa, you know I have always been true to you," she cried.

But Griffith was unmoved by her avowals of chastity. He asked her if she knew who had poisoned their neighbor, Mr. Briswalter, who months earlier had cut his leg, then died from the resulting infection. Now utterly terrified, Christina was wailing and crying, trying to speak, but only capable of making incoherent sounds. She opened her eyes.

Christina reflexively jerked away from the gun barrel, the mouth of which was almost resting on her temple. Jerked, just as Griffith pulled the trigger.

The bullet went through her left eye, which disintegrated.

Screaming in terror, Christina jumped through the open window before Griffith could recock and aim the pistol. She tumbled two stories to the roof of the veranda below, and landed in a bloody heap.

Her leg was broken, but adrenaline generated by fear coursed through her veins. Christina dragged herself off the roof through a window leading to a second-story room. There she found a towel. Holding it over the wound that opened where her eye had been, she screamed for help.

The Arcadia's owner, a man named Wright, answered her call. On his heels was Colonel Griffith. "Please, Mr. Wright, don't let him come in," she screamed. "He shot me! He's crazy!"

Griffith calmly denied that he'd fired the shot. Christina had accidentally shot herself, he declared. The sheriff was summoned.

Colonel Griffith was so rich and eminent a personage—and so well connected to the sources of local power—that many of the city's leading citizens were inclined to let the matter pass as a domestic dispute. But not Christina's family, who wanted Griffith punished. They hired three of Southern California's most respected lawyers to act as special prosecutors under the aegis of the district attorney. Chief among them was former California Governor Henry T. Gage.

Griffith was initially represented by his usual firm, Works and Silent. After spending several weeks preparing a defense, these two former judges surveyed the formidable legal talent assembled by the prosecution and decided they didn't like the odds. They brought in an additional colleague, a young but colorfully unconventional lawyer who was already more expert in the lore of physiology, anatomy and the budding field of psychiatry than most physicians in the West. His name was Earl Rogers, and he was destined to redefine the role of the defense attorney in California.

Rogers' first move was to ask for a continuance. He needed two weeks, he said, in order to prepare an adequate defense.

The prosecution argued that Rogers was stalling. Works and Silent had had sufficient time to prepare Griffith's defense, they said. Though the judge refused to change the trial date, he said he would hear arguments for and against a continuance on the first day of trial.

Special prosecutor Gage was known throughout the West as a spellbinding orator and one of the best prosecutors the state ever produced. He was a tall, imposing figure with a great mass of steel-gray hair, a man who always wore cowboy boots beneath his elegant suit trousers. He came into court with a gaggle of witnesses prepared to swear that Griffith's defense team had been given time enough. Armed with dozens of precedents and a strategy for forcing Rogers to begin at once, Gage came ready to spend the whole day and the next, if necessary, arguing that the trial should begin whether Rogers was prepared or not.

But instead of preparing for a postponement, Rogers had spent most of the 36 hours since he accepted the case preparing a defense strategy. And preparing to take old Henry Gage by surprise. When the court was gaveled to order, the young attorney stood up and announced that the defense was ready to begin the trial.

Gage and the other prosecuting attorneys were dumbfounded. They were not quite ready to go to trial, because they had planned to spend this day arguing against postponement. They had intended to conduct their last-minute strategy

council later in the day, or perhaps in the evening. Now, as the judge impatient-
ly urged them to begin, they were confused.

Rogers' line of defense was obvious from the character of the witnesses he had
brought into court. He had brewmasters and bartenders, common drunks and
distinguished alcoholics, doctors expert in mental illnesses—they were called
"alienists" as the term "psychiatrist" hadn't yet been coined—and doctors who
treated alcoholism. He had bellboys and barbers, and an undertaker. And he
had himself, a man quite intimately acquainted with the contents of all manner
of kegs, bottles and flasks. For Rogers, like the man he was defending, had a
lifelong problem with alcohol.

As jury selection commenced, it became apparent that neither Gage nor
Rogers would permit a Catholic on the jury. They questioned prospective jurors
("veniremen") carefully about their religion and about their attitudes toward
booze. "From the questioning of veniremen it was evident that Rogers was going
to attempt to prove that Mrs. Griffith had too much religion, and the Colonel
too much champagne," wrote a reporter for the *Los Angeles Times*.

The first witness was Christina Griffith, who, to the gasps of a packed
courtroom, lifted her veil to show the ugly scar and gaping socket that was all
that remained of her eye.

On cross-examination Rogers was softspoken, deferential—and he tried to
trap Mrs. Griffith. He displayed a scrap of paper, which he said was the same
the Colonel had held as he questioned her at the Arcadia Hotel. Rogers read
each question, then asked Christina if it was the same as Griffith had asked. To
each she answered that it seemed substantially the same. Then he read the final
question: "Will you swear on your sacred honor and by all the Gods you have
been taught to worship that you will be true to me and find no further fault with
the Hollywood Monument?"

"No," said Christina. "That wasn't one of his questions."

The bogus question was an attempt by Rogers to show that Griffith was in-
coherently drunk when he wrote the question, and still drunk when he read it.
It was part of Rogers' strategy to portray Griffith as a man long unhinged by the
effects of alcohol. Rogers introduced as evidence some of Griffith's most
preposterous public statements. Since about 1890, Griffith had on different
occasions:

> Claimed that Bishop Conaty of the Los Angeles archdiocese
> wanted him killed so that the church could get his land holdings;

> Said that he slept in a bath house to escape his wife and killers hired
> by the pope;

> Told friends that soon after their marriage, Christina and a nun had
> tried to poison him while they were lodged in a hotel;

Mentioned his belief that soon after the late Senator Stephen M. White, in an alcoholic haze, had told Griffith that priests should be expelled from the Philippines, that White was poisoned by Catholics and died.

As all this was introduced, Rogers kept repeating that Griffith was drunk when he made these wild accusations.

As further support for his theory of alcohol-induced paranoia, Rogers brought to the stand Louis Garrett, son of one of Griffith's closest friends. Garrett testified that Griffith had long been mentally unstable. He said that Griffith was invited to serve as a pallbearer at his late father's funeral. But the Colonel refused to attend the funeral because he feared assassination by Catholics. Griffith was obviously of unsound mind, said Garrett.

On cross-examination Gage laid his own trap. He asked Garrett if there had been other incidents when Griffith seemed irrational. There had been several, said Garrett. Rogers looked down the road of Gage's questions and saw the destination. He scowled at his witness. He cleared his throat. He launched a string of objections. He tried to pick a fight with Gage, but Gage smiled it away. Though Garrett was also a lawyer, Rogers did not succeed in conveying the warning.

Gage asked Garrett if the incidents he referred to had taken place before or after the funeral. "Before," answered Garrett.

"You were absolutely convinced by the defendant's delusions concerning religious persecution, his delusions of grandeur, and other abnormal mental symptoms, that he was not sane at the time of your father's death?" asked Gage.

"Absolutely . . . any reasonable man would have realized he was crazy," said Garrett.

As his trap snapped shut, Gage's voice was full of sad wonder: "And yet, Mr. Garrett, knowing this, you nevertheless tried to get an insane man to act as pallbearer for your dear father's funeral?" Garrett had no answer and, thus discredited, left the stand in embarrassment.

But he was only one man. Rogers presented a parade of witnesses who testified to the cumulative, deleterious effects of alcohol upon reason: It was all part of his carefully constructed case that chronic abuse of alcohol rendered Griffith incapable of a rational act.

The prosecution, of course, had their own witnesses. But one aspect of Rogers' genius lay in knowing more about his subject than most "expert" witnesses. As each prosecution alienist and specialist in *delirium tremens*—acute alcohol poisoning—testified, Rogers called increasingly upon his own phenomenal memory and his encyclopedic knowledge of medical subjects. And each prosecution medical expert was subject, on cross-examination, to Rogers' pet hypothetical question.

It was a question of such magnificent phrase, esoteric connotation and stultifying length—about 20 minutes—that none were able to answer satisfactorily. Neither Gates, nor any of his distinguished associates, nor the presiding judge himself were able to make sense out of either the question or any of the attempted answers. And when Rogers asked his question for the third time, when he asked the third expert witness to wrestle with a reply, the spectators got up almost as one body and emptied the room. They were soon followed by most of the prosecution staff, except for Gage and his most junior associate.

Down to his last expert medical witness, and nearly desperate, Gage put a Dr. Campbell on the stand, and tried his own version of a 20-minute hypothetical question. But by the time he got it all out over Rogers' repeated objections, no one in the court, including Gage himself, understood what was being asked. So Gage withdrew the question, and Campbell left the stand without testifying that he thought Griffith was sane.

Rogers hoped to clinch his case when he called Dr. E.M. Butler, who ran the city's most widely admired hospital for chronic alcoholism. He asked Butler if Griffith was sane or insane. Butler obliged with straightforward testimony that Griffith suffered from a classic case of chronic alcoholic insanity.

Arrayed against Griffith was a mountain of incriminating evidence; there was little doubt he had pulled the trigger of the gun that destroyed his wife's eye. His only out was if Rogers could convince the jury that he was insane and therefore not responsible for the act. So the final element of Rogers' defense strategy was to concentrate on psychologically bending the jury to his premise, while virtually ignoring what prosecution witnesses said on the stand.

Gage understood Rogers' approach, and with the craft born of many years' experience, he offered an eloquent summary in which he dismissed Rogers' tactics as "brazen attempts to confuse the real issues." He then concluded with an even more brazen call to equally irrelevant issues:

> Griffith's vicious assault upon the loving wife who had borne him a son has done far more than destroy forever one of her eyes, with all the physical suffering, all the mental anguish such disfigurement means to a beautiful and sensitive woman; it has left forever an awful scar upon her soul, that of her outraged love, the destruction of the beautiful romance a good woman weaves about her husband and motherhood. But what does it matter? No *rich* man has ever been punished for such a crime in this part of the United States.

This sad fact weighing on their souls, the jury found Griffith guilty, and sentenced him to two years in prison. Rogers, who undoubtedly succeeded in lightening his client's sentence but nevertheless suffered his first loss of an important case, was probably more disheartened than Griffith. For a time he contemplated suicide.

Griffith served one year in prison, then was let out on good behavior. He promptly made a splendid second gift to the city, donating additional property adjacent to Griffith Park for the magnificent, 6,000-seat, open-air amphitheater called The Greek Theater, and designing the theater itself in exquisite detail. After his death in 1919 at age 67, Griffith willed even more land and later a building fund for the observatory that crowns the park's peak, Mt. Hollywood. The will also created a permanent endowment to help maintain the theater and the park grounds. In 1985 it yielded a six-figure sum that was used to refurbish the observatory's copper dome.

Griffith's gifts were not without strings; they were conditioned on the park property *always* remaining as a free public recreation area. Over the years Griffith's descendants have come forward to defend these strictures. During World War II the federal government tried to build veterans' housing in Griffith Park. But Griffith's son, police commissioner during Mayor Byron's administration, led a protest movement to preserve the park. In 1981 the Los Angeles Parks & Recreation Department began levying a parking fee—and grandson Harold Griffith sued to stop the practice. He lost, but in 1984 the parking fees were ended.

Earl Rogers went on to win many more important cases, and he heavily influenced succeeding generations of Los Angeles lawyers. But, like Griffith, Rogers had an unquenchable thirst. He spent years drying out in expensive sanitaria. His first wife left him because of his drinking. He remarried, but his new wife, Teddy, whom he adored, died of influenza in 1919.

In 1922, Rogers was asked to defend Fatty Arbuckle against rape and murder charges in connection with the death of starlet Virginia Rappe. Rogers, still drinking heavily, told Arbuckle, "Not a chance, I'm through." (Though Arbuckle was eventually acquitted, the charges ruined his film career.)

A few weeks later, Rogers died in a cheap rooming house. The great attorney died alone. His body was discovered by his law clerk on February 22, 1922, three years to the day after Teddy's death.

A daughter by his first marriage, Adela Rogers St. John, became a noted author, whose books remain standard chronicles of the City of Los Angeles in its boisterous youth.

LOCATIONS:
Thomas Brothers map reference: Page 49 at A2
The Arcadia Hotel was at 1661 Appian Way, Santa Monica. Take the Santa Monica Freeway (I-10) to Lincoln Avenue; cross back over the freeway to Pico, and turn right to Ocean Avenue. Go right again to Sea View Terrace. Walk down a long flight of steps to a two-story turquoise apartment building. All that remains of the Arcadia Hotel are two red bricks, one each at the front corners of the building. They are noted by modest markers.

Thomas Brothers map reference: Page 34 at F1
The Greek Theater in the middle of Griffith Park remains one of Los Angeles' most famous landmarks. Was Griffith inspired to name and donate this wonderful facility because the incident that marred his life was reminiscent of a Greek tragedy? Many thought so; others said it was simply Griffith trying to buy back his shattered reputation.

Thomas Brothers map reference: Page A at D2
The final residence of Earl Rogers was a rooming house at 211 W. Temple. The house was pulled down a few years after his death. Rogers would have been pleased to know that the building erected on the site was the Los Angeles Hall of Justice. Exit the northbound Hollywood Freeway (U.S. 101) at Spring; cross back over the freeway to the first street, Temple, and turn right. The Hall of Justice is on the corner of Broadway.

Thomas Brothers map reference: Page 44 at D3
During most of his career, Earl Rogers' offices were in the California Building at 107 S. Broadway. From the Hall of Justice, go south on Broadway to First. The present structure was built shortly after Rogers' death.

The brothers McNamara: John (left) and James planted bombs and reaped mindless destruction. Photo: Security Pacific National Bank Photographic Collection/Los Angeles Public Library.

5

ORGANIZED TERROR: THE BOMBING OF THE *LOS ANGELES TIMES* (1910)

The blast came at 1:00 on the morning of October 1, 1910, a gigantic explosion that ripped through Ink Alley, the narrow walkway connecting the press and stereotyping buildings occupied by the *Los Angeles Times*. The dynamite bomb badly damaged the pressrooms south of the alley and ignited huge barrels of ink. The viscous fluid soaked down through the building, spreading the fire throughout the structure. By daylight the building was totally gutted; the fire had burned itself out. Twenty *Times* employees—copy boys, reporters, editors, clerks, typesetters, and scrubwomen—were dead. As many more were seriously injured. But beyond the carnage, the death and the destruction, the dynamite blast also forced the budding American labor movement to choke on the ashes of the *Los Angeles Times*.

Within hours of the bombing, the management of *Times* publisher General Harrison Gray Otis, Civil War and Spanish American War hero, civic leader and virulent anti-unionist, had put out a four-page bulldog edition on an antiquated letterpress borrowed from a competing newspaper. Publisher Otis was out of town at the moment, en route home from Mexico, but his feelings were well known and his staff loyal to them. The bombing was the lead story, and the headline fulminated Otis' rage: *Unionist Bombs Wreck* The Times. The text unabashedly referred to the incident as "the crime of the century."

On the day following the blast more bombs were found. One of them was at Otis' home. Another was found at the home of the secretary to the Merchant's & Manufacturer's Association, an anti-union group organized by Otis. A third bomb was defused at the *Times* auxiliary plant.

Otis returned on the afternoon of the 1st. Surveying the smoking ruins of his buildings at First and Broadway, he affirmed his newspaper's accusation. Though he had no proof, he had ample cause to believe that labor union organizers were behind the attack. Labor leaders had termed Los Angeles "the scabbiest town on earth." Indeed, for years Otis had seized every opportunity to malign, attack and discredit unions. The unions responded by redoubling their efforts to organize. The Typographical Union had recently tried to organize *Times* linotype operators. The local of the structural iron workers' union was out on strike; and now the bombing. The General had picked his enemy; now he found himself at war.

The local unions, however, wanted peace. They denied responsibility for the blast. Instead they pointed to reports that the odor of leaking gas had been frequently detected at the *Times'* buildings in the weeks prior to the blast. In fact, a Typographical Union official, Ben Robinson, had demanded an investigation during his tenure on the Board of Fire Commissioners, to no avail.

National labor leaders were unwilling to let unionists take the rap for the bombing. Samuel Gompers, head of the American Federation of Labor, denied that unionists were responsible.

To find the bombers, Otis hired the noted private investigator, William J. Burns, who had reorganized the U.S. Secret Service before starting his own detective agency. Burns determined that the dynamite from the unexploded bombs, an especially powerful type, had been made by a San Francisco company, Giant Powder Works, as a special order. The men who ordered it were quickly identified: the brothers John and James McNamara, and Ortie McManigal. John McNamara was secretary-treasurer of the International Union of Bridge and Structural Iron Workers. A coast-to-coast manhunt was launched.

Meanwhile two other investigations of the bombing were proceeding, both with Otis' close cooperation. The District Attorney's detective Samuel Browne was looking for leads in Los Angeles, while the city's leading criminal attorney, Earl Rogers*, conducted extensive investigations in San Francisco. Late in the year, Rogers was named special prosecutor to a special grand jury. On the basis of what Rogers, Browne and Burns had uncovered, the panel returned indictments on 23 people.

It took six months, but in April 1911, Burns tracked McManigal, a resident of Indianapolis, to Detroit. He sent his grown son, Raymond, along with Detroit and Chicago police, to arrest McManigal and James McNamara at the Oxford Hotel where they were staying under assumed names. In their luggage were six clock batteries identical to those found on the unexploded Los Angeles bombs. They also had three pistols, one of them with a silencer affixed.

Otis wanted Burns to nail John McNamara, especially because he was a high union official. But he needed a witness against him. Burns threatened his two captives with bank robbery charges. They then agreed not to fight extradition if Michigan would drop the bank robbery issue. The bombers were taken to Chicago, and, to maintain secrecy, sequestered in the home of a Chicago policeman. When Burns arrived, he told McManigal that under conspiracy laws, all three bombers were equally guilty. But, said the detective, unionist John McNamara would have the support and financial backing of organized labor. His brother James could expect no less. Which meant that the brunt of the punishment would ultimately be borne by McManigal.

His only hope was to help Burns catch and convict John McNamara. McManigal hesitated, but Burns was convincing. McManigal dictated a complete confession, also naming two other conspirators, anarchists David Caplan and Matthew A. Schmidt.

On April 22, armed with extradition papers signed by the governor of Indiana, Burns and Indianapolis policemen stalked into the iron workers' headquarters to interrupt an executive board meeting and arrest John McNamara. The three prisoners were returned to Los Angeles on April 26.

The arrests sparked nationwide protests by organized labor. American Federation of Labor president Samuel Gompers hired Clarence Darrow, who had recently won acquittals for two other noted labor leaders, Eugene V. Debs of the Railroad Brotherhoods, and the International Workers of The World's Big Bill Hayward. Darrow was promised $50,000 as a fee, and a $200,000 defense fund.

The McNamara brothers, Jim, 27, and John, 28, were nice-looking fellows, clean-cut in appearance, with no prior criminal involvement. The national labor movement united behind them, staging a series of torchlight parades and distributing lapel buttons. Labor also made use of the new medium of film for the first time, producing a one-reel motion picture in support of the accused. Eugene Debs made a stirring oration in which he called for a general strike over the entire West Coast. "Let the striking toilers of the Pacific coast raise the red standard of revolt, and the workers in other states fall in line and swell the hosts of American freemen in their fight to rescue their kidnapped brothers from the clutches of a murderous plutocracy," he shouted. Soon a great many Americans—including many who had no love for organized labor—were inclined to believe the McNamaras had been framed by General Otis because of his implacable hatred of unions.

Otis felt that more evidence than the confession of McManigal was needed to assure not only a conviction but also the appearance of a fair trial. Burns had assured him that the required incriminating evidence could be found in the vaults of the iron workers' union in Indianapolis. But the union had strong political support in Indiana, and powerful allies in the state government. So on October 17, 1911, Otis, along with Oscar Lawler, attorney for Merchant's and Manufacturer's, met secretly in a private Los Angeles home with William

Howard Taft, President of the United States. Taft, who was on a political tour of the West, was there and then convinced that the bombing of the *Times* was part of a vast national conspiracy. He ordered federal agents to help.

On the next day, the U.S. Attorney General's investigators swarmed over the iron workers' offices. They confiscated a mound of dynamite hidden in the basement, as well as incriminating letters and other documents. The case against the brothers McNamara now seemed airtight. Burns offered to meet with Samuel Gompers. "If Mr. Gompers will just sit down with me, at his convenience, I am certain I can convince him this is strictly a criminal case, and does not concern organized labor. If need be, I will even show him evidence that cannot be made public as yet," said Burns. Gompers countered by telling reporters that private detectives in the employ of industrial concerns had frequently manufactured evidence and bought false confessions to discredit union leaders. He was convinced that the McNamaras were innocent.

But as the trial date drew closer, Clarence Darrow came to the opposite conclusion. The more he investigated, the more convinced of their guilt he became. He found himself on the horns of a dilemma. The American Federation of Labor was his client, and was to pay his fee and expenses. The leaders of the labor movement wanted to see the McNamaras freed, but if that were to prove impossible, they would settle for the public outrage that was sure to erupt if they were convicted and martyred—for in the heated atmosphere of Los Angeles, it seemed certain judge and jury would insist on hanging the McNamaras. On the other hand, if the accused bombers were to plead guilty, it might save their lives.

Deciding his first duty lay to the accused, Darrow made the painful decision to enter a "guilty" plea. But first he would have to convince the brothers McNamara. Darrow was assisted in this by a colleague, LeCompte Davis, who used a bit of strategy: He suggested to the McNamaras that probably the goals of the labor movement would best be served if they were hanged, and could then become martyrs. This had its desired effect; the bombers instead insisted on being allowed to plead guilty if they would be spared the hangman's noose.

Now Darrow had the more difficult task of convincing General Otis to make a deal. He was helped by the crusading journalist, Lincoln Steffens, who thought that a guilty plea and long sentences would be a compromise that would help heal the breach between labor and management. Through intermediaries, including E.W. Scripps, the powerful San Diego publisher, Darrow approached General Otis, and a bargain was struck. Just as the trial began, the McNamaras rose in the dock to plead guilty, and to make a brief statement: They had placed the bombs for reasons of principle, they said.

The presiding judge received hundreds of telegrams from labor organizations all over the country, most urging that *no* leniency be shown. James got life imprisonment. There was no direct evidence linking John to the *Times* bombing, but he admitted taking part in an earlier bombing of the Llewellyn Iron Works in Los Angeles, where one man had been injured. He was sentenced to

15 years in San Quentin. Caplan and Schmidt were apprehended in 1915, and received life sentences. Ortie McManigal, who had turned state's evidence, was freed.

But by far the most severe sentence was meted out to the West Coast labor movement, which was widely discredited by its enthusiastic support of the McNamara brothers. Labor did not recover from this until the start of World War II.

LOCATIONS:

Thomas Brothers map reference: Page A at D3
Ink Alley is no more, but there remains in the same location a narrow walkway between the front and back parts of the modern *Los Angeles Times* complex on the southwest corner of First and Broadway. In the lobby of the *Times* building (enter from First Street) is a statue of General Otis, and a plaque to the victims of the bombing. The present head of the Times-Mirror Corporation, the holding company that controls the newspaper, is Otis Chandler, great-grandson of the general. Take the Spring Street exit from the Hollywood Freeway, go west to First, then right to Broadway.

Thomas Brothers map reference: Page 44 at 2A
The Otis home was at 2401 Wilshire. Otis called it The "Bivouac." (He called his house staff "The Phalanx.") The building was torn down in the 1950s and the land became the Otis Art Institute after it was donated to the Parsons School of Design by the publisher's descendants. It's on the northwest corner of Wilshire and Carondolet. From the Harbor Freeway (I-110) exit at Wilshire and go west to the first street past MacArthur Park.

*See Chapter 3, *A Visceral Issue: The Shooting of Jay Hunter (1899)* and Chapter 4, *Greek Theater: Attempted Murder by Colonel Griffith (1903)*.

Clarence Darrow (L) with Arthur G. Hays: General Otis wanted him ruined. Photo: Courtesy of the Hearst Collection, USC Library.

6

DID CLARENCE DARROW BRIBE JURORS? (1912)

When Clarence Darrow saved the lives of the McNamara brothers by making a deal with the powerful publisher of the *Times* (see previous chapter), Samuel Gompers and other labor leaders were outraged. They called Darrow a traitor, and refused to pay his $50,000 fee. Darrow, never a rich man, was heading for a financial crisis.

Even more trouble was headed Darrow's way from the other side of the McNamara case. Having triumphed over the labor movement, General Harrison Gray Otis, publisher of the *Times*, might have sat back in satisfaction. Instead he set out to destroy Darrow. Otis, who virtually controlled the district attorney, brought charges against Darrow: two counts of jury tampering in the recently concluded bombing case.

The bribery issue was rooted in the jury selection process. Prosecution and defense were given a publication called a "venire list," a roster of eligible jurors. It was each side's privilege to determine attitudes or biases of prospective jurors through interviews or other means. This began before the trial was formally convened. To carry out these interviews Darrow had hired a shrewd, experienced and resourceful investigator, Bert Franklin, formerly associated with the U.S. marshal and with the Los Angeles district attorney.

On October 6, 1911, Franklin interviewed Mrs. Robert Bain, wife of an elderly carpenter. Robert wasn't home when Franklin called. In the course of their conversation, Mrs. Bain complained of being heavily in debt. Franklin offered a way out of debt. He would pay an overdue note if Bain would vote for acquittal.

39

Mrs. Bain conveyed the offer to her husband. Robert Bain was poor but honest. He at once declared that he would report the incident to authorities. When Mrs. Bain told Franklin of her husband's intentions, he persuaded her that her husband might go to prison if he were to mention the matter. Franklin, who had friends at the district attorney's office, would say that Bain had solicited the bribe. Bain was silenced, for the moment.

By early November, the jury selection process seemed stalled, with neither side willing to accept the other's choice of jurors. On November 4, Franklin spoke with prospective juror George Lockwood. He offered $500 cash in advance, and $3,500 more if Lockwood succeeded in getting on the jury and voted for the McNamaras' acquittal. And he needn't feel alone, said Franklin, because Robert Bain would also be voting for acquittal. Lockwood said he'd think it over.

But Lockwood had already made up his mind. He was a former prison guard, police officer and undercover investigator, and he promptly went to the district attorney's office.

On the morning of November 28, Lockwood approached the corner of Third and Los Angeles Streets, not far from—but out of sight of—the courthouse. Staked out around the area of boarding houses and factories were police detectives. A friend of Franklin's, C.E. White, showed up on schedule. He handed Lockwood an envelope with a $500 bill inside. White told Lockwood that he had the remaining $3,500, and after an acquittal he would get it. The two men strolled down the street, conversing like two ordinary businessmen.

They kept going until they were stopped by Samuel Browne, chief detective of the district attorney. As Browne made the arrest, an incredible coincidence occurred: Clarence Darrow, on a personal errand, crossed the street nearby. He saw White's arrest take place, but at that moment had no idea who Lockwood or White were. A few minutes later Franklin was also taken into custody.

The next day the papers—especially the *Times*—trumpeted the story of Franklin's arrest. Mrs. Robert Bain then took it upon herself to report Franklin's bribery offer to the district attorney.

The trial of the McNamara brothers ended on December 1, the day it began, with the sudden guilty plea of the bombing brothers. Late in January Bert Franklin pleaded guilty to bribing Lockwood and, in exchange for giving evidence against Darrow, was fined $4,000, the amount of the bribe. However, the bribe money taken from White and Lockwood had come from a check Franklin drew on the McNamaras' defense fund, and the cash from this check, already in the possession of authorities, was used to pay this fine, so the fine cost Franklin nothing.

Franklin proceeded to testify before the grand jury. He told a tale of duplicity. The whole notion of bribery had been Darrow's idea, and he, Franklin, was only a messenger boy. The grand jury returned twin indictments against Darrow for attempting to bribe Lockwood and Bain. Darrow turned himself in to authorities and, after posting $20,000 cash bond, was released. Newspaper photographers swarmed all over the scene, taking photo after photo of America's most famous criminal defense attorney.

Darrow retained as counsel his former adversary, Earl Rogers. The two operated in striking contrast. Darrow, practically a teetotaler, was a mountainous shamble of wrinkled clothing, who came into court with day-old stubble and a folksy, humble, aw-shucks demeanor. Rogers was a confirmed alcoholic, a fashionable, cultured, impressively handsome man who had a way of making juries feel his equal in civility. In court Darrow relied on homilies and down-home witticisms; Rogers was a crafty showman who might bring in unusual, even shocking, exhibits to dazzle a jury. Darrow, at the height of his powers, had a reputation as champion of the poor and oppressed. Rogers, though past his zenith, was still the most effective criminal defense attorney in the West.

They would need each other in the days to come. Otis was determined to make Darrow pay for saving the lives of the *Times* bombers—even though he'd been a party to the deal. And Otis could be an incredibly tough adversary. His strategy was to exacerbate the attorney's money woes by stringing the trial out as long as possible. It lasted 13 weeks. Darrow swung between the extremes of optimistic hope and hellish despair. Though he had hired Rogers, as the trial went on he took over more and more of his defense, perhaps because he felt Rogers believed him guilty and was incapable of giving his best effort.

It was a strange trial. Practically every witness was called a liar by another. There was enough conflicting testimony under oath to fuel a dozen perjury trials—but no one was ever indicted. Attorneys filled the courtroom, and all of them heaped egregious oaths upon their opposite numbers. At times the opposing lawyers almost came to blows. At one point, a prosecutor, Chief Deputy District Attorney Joseph Ford, hoisted a heavy bottle of ink to toss at Horace Appel, a Rogers associate. On another occasion District Attorney Fredericks took an inkwell in hand, but was restrained just before he could toss it at Rogers.

Toward the end of the trial, Darrow got up and gave an eloquent two-day summary of his innocence that moved the court reporter and many on the jury to tears. "I am not on trial for having sought to bribe a man named Lockwood. I am on trial because I have been a lover of the poor, a friend of the oppressed, because I have stood by Labor for all these years," said Darrow. "If you believe me innocent and return a verdict of not guilty in this case, I know that from thousands and tens of thousands and yea, perhaps of the weak and the poor and the helpless throughout the world, will come thanks to this jury for saving my liberty and my name."

Nevertheless Earl Rogers earned his fee. He subjected the enigmatic Franklin to a scathing cross-examination, eliciting many contradictory statements. Franklin, claimed Rogers, had actually been the district attorney's agent all the time he worked for Darrow. Rogers was a superb actor. He was respectful and gentle with George Lockwood on the stand, and tough as nails on the popularly detested William Burns, the detective who masterminded the investigation of the *Times* bombing for Otis.

When Darrow had used emotion, Rogers opted for logic. He brought into court a huge chart, which he hung from the judge's bench so that the jury could see. On it he listed the prosecution's witnesses, and, holding a long pointer, attacked each witness' testimony in turn suggesting that together they formed the elements of a conspiracy against Darrow. And then he said: "Will you tell me how any sane, sensible man who knows anything about the law business—and this defendant has been in it for 35 years—could make himself go to a detective and say to him: 'Just buy all the jurors you want. I put my whole life, my reputation, I put everything I have in your two hands. I trust you absolutely. I never knew you until two or three months ago and I don't know much about you now. But there you are. Go to it!'"

Instructed by the judge that it wasn't the obligation of the defendant to prove who, if anyone, gave the bribe money to Franklin, the jury left the room. They returned in 30 minutes with a verdict: not guilty.

Darrow was promptly arrested on the second charge, the attempted bribery of Robert Bain. That trial began in November. Rogers became ill early in the proceedings, and dropped out. Darrow then put on the defense he'd wanted to use in his first trial. It amounted to a general condoning of the bombing of the *Times* as a crime of social passion and a denial that it was the mass murder that Otis had termed it. An attorney who defends himself in court has a fool for a client. When the trial was over, the jury voted eight to four for Darrow's conviction.

But conviction required a unanimous verdict. Though the charges were dropped, Otis had accomplished his objective: Darrow was broke. Clarence Darrow received $1,000 from an anonymous benefactor, and returned home to Chicago, announcing that he was through with the practice of law. His psychic wounds healed in a few years, however, and he returned to defending criminal cases. But either because he never forgave organized labor for abandoning him to the ferocious Harrison Gray Otis, or because he feared the power of the industrialists, Clarence Darrow never again took a labor case.

LOCATION:
Thomas Brothers map reference: Page A at D3
Third and Los Angeles looks somewhat as it did in 1911, when Darrow walked across the street just as his employee was arrested. It sits at the bottom of a shallow depression, an intersection on the edge of Little Tokyo, fronted by worn warehouses, cheap hotels and weed-strewn vacant lots. From the Hollywood Freeway (US 101) northbound, exit at Los Angeles and turn left to Third.

Roscoe "Fatty" Arbuckle: A jury found him not guilty of murder, but the scandal ended his silent film career. Photo: Marc Wannamaker Bison Archives.

7

A HEAVY CRUSH RUINS FATTY ARBUCKLE (1921)

Roscoe "Fatty" Arbuckle was 34, weighed almost 300 pounds, and was second only to Charlie Chaplin at comedy box offices. Fatty gave new dimension to the Lost Generation's endless search for mind-numbing diversion. As Hollywood's star party animal, he had no equal.

He bought his first Los Angeles home from silent film vamp Theda Bara, an ostentatious house in one of the city's best neighborhoods. Soon his outrageous lifestyle and wild, weeklong parties stretched the sensibilities of his backyard neighbors, the oil- and real estate-wealthy but staidly conventional Doheny family. E.L. Doheny offered to buy Fatty's place—at any price. Fatty named an outrageous figure, and Doheny accepted without quibbling.

Fatty took his profit and built an even larger home a few miles away on West Adams. Always something of a momma's boy, he built still another huge house nearby for his mother.

A man of prodigious appetites, Fatty ate hugely and drank endless quantities of bathtub gin—or whatever his bootlegger could provide. But his true passion was sex. Fatty regarded women the way most people regarded facial tissue: something to be used, then discarded. "All girls got the same round heels, no matter who they are," he told one friend. Fabulously rich from his movies, famous worldwide, Fatty had little trouble finding plenty of beautiful young women. Until he fixed a bloodshot eye on Virginia Rappe. She looked away. Virginia Rappe was a delicate brunette of 25, whose lovely face was chosen to ornament the sheet music to the top musical hit of the era, *Let Me Call You Sweetheart*. Her face became her fortune as a leading lady in the silent films of the Roaring Twenties. Ultimately, her face was a fatal attraction.

Despite her Madonna-like features, Virginia had a checkered past. Her father, a scampish English noble of cloudy title, never bothered to marry her alcoholic mother. Virginia shared her mother's fondness for gin, as well as for other worldly pleasures. While still in her teens, the young beauty had already generously sampled the sexual delights offered by assorted rogues in Paris, New York, Buenos Aires and Rio. Indeed, she enjoyed most men as much as they enjoyed her. The trouble was, Fatty wasn't like most men.

Virginia's eyes were on a dashing film director, Harry Lehrman, who shared her bed but seemed unwilling to set a wedding date. He entrained for New York just before Labor Day, 1921, leaving Virginia behind. Perhaps to fill the void, she agreed to join a couple, friends from Hollywood, who had been invited to a Labor Day party in San Francisco. The host, who had craftily connived her second-hand invitation, was Fatty Arbuckle.

Accompanied by actor friend Lowell Sherman, Fatty drove to San Franciso in his $25,000 Rolls, a custom-made auto with a built-in backseat toilet, checking into the St. Francis Hotel 2:00 Sunday morning. He spent the rest of the night drinking. Just before noon on Labor Day, his San Francisco friends, their friends and the usual crowd of hangers-on arrived to party. Fatty telephoned his friends from Hollywood, temporarily ensconced at the nearby Palace Hotel, and with Virginia Rappe in tow, they too joined the party. By midafternoon, the three-room suite on the 12th floor of the staid St. Francis was on the brink of an orgy.

While Virginia seemed to avoid contact or conversation with Fatty, she drank glass after glass of gin and orange juice. From time to time she got up to use the toilet in the bathroom, but found the bathroom constantly occupied. Finally it was empty. But as she steered an unsteady course toward its open door, Virginia was intercepted by Fatty. He wore pajamas and bathrobe. And lust in his eye. "This is the chance I've been waiting for for a long time," he cried. He took her by the hand and steered her into the bedroom. The door closed and locked.

For 20 minutes there was only silence from the room. What follows is shrouded in mystery and conflicting accounts. Some guests reported they heard Virginia screaming. Others insisted they heard nothing. Those who heard screaming said they tried to open the locked door, and that failing to do so they summoned hotel management, who demanded Fatty open the door. They said that when Fatty emerged, grinning outrageously, sporting Virginia's hat, his pajamas torn, Virginia was writhing on the rumpled bed, moaning, "I'm dying . . . he hurt me . . ."

And they said Fatty insisted she was only drunk, that she was carried away with the moment, that she was unharmed. One account has Fatty threatening to throw her from the window if she didn't stop screaming. She didn't stop and soon Fatty told all his guests to leave.

But everyone agreed Virginia was hurting. She was carried to another room. A pair of chorus girls gave her a cold bath. She was examined by the hotel's doctor and on the next day hospitalized. She told a nurse, "Fatty Arbuckle did this to me . . . Please see that he doesn't get away with it." On the next day Virginia Rappe died.

The cause of death was peritonitis, an infection of the membrane lining the abdominal cavity. The source of the infection was the urine in her bladder, which had burst. The San Francisco coroner's report opined this had happened because it was overly full and Fatty's immense bulk had crushed it while in the act of sexual intercourse. And he further argued that the intercourse was forcible. Fingerprints on the bedroom door bore this out, indicating a struggle. Dr. T.B.W. Leland, the coroner, said Virginia Rappe died because Fatty Arbuckle had raped her.

Fatty was rich and famous, and his studio stood to lose a bundle if he was convicted of murder. A lot of money began to change hands in San Francisco, some of it Fatty's. Some witnesses developed sudden and temporary amnesia. Others took extended vacations abroad. But some remained. Fatty stood trial for murder. Stood trial three times. The first two juries were unable to reach a decision. The third came back with "not guilty." The foreman apologized to Fatty, saying it was obvious a great injustice had been done.

But Fatty was also tried in the court of public opinion, the lurid accounts printed by newspapers across the country serving as indictment. The moviegoing public found Fatty guilty of gross misconduct, and stopped going to see his films. The studio cancelled his three-year, $3 million contract. For 12 years Fatty Arbuckle was Hollywood's living ghost, vastly talented but totally unemployable. Using pseudonyms, he directed a few films, but the public found out and boycotted them. He tried to return to the vaudeville stage, but after the city of Minneapolis refused to let him appear, other cities followed suit. Fatty lapsed into obscurity.

By 1933 the country, writhing in the agony of the Great Depression, badly needed something to laugh at. Some in the movie industry believed the public might be willing to forgive Fatty. He starred in a new comedy, shot in New York. To celebrate its completion, and the first anniversary of his third wedding, he threw a modest party. He died in his sleep that night, victim of a heart attack at age 46.

Fatty's unlikely legacy was the film industry's morals clause and the industry's decision to police itself. With former Postmaster General Will Hays as its head, the studios created the Motion Picture Producers and Distributors of America, Inc. Studios held their talent responsible for their off-screen conduct, and more than one promising performer was quietly dismissed for activities Hays—and Hays alone—felt were potentially embarrassing to the industry.

LOCATIONS:

Thomas Brothers map reference: Page 44 at 5A
Fatty's first Los Angeles house is at 649 West Adams Avenue. From downtown Los Angeles take Figueroa Street south to Adams. Turn west; it's the third house west of Figueroa on the north side of the street.

Thomas Brothers map reference: Page 43 at B5
After selling out to the Dohenys, Fatty had another house built at 3424 Adams, near the corner of Fifth Avenue, a few miles west of his first home. The house, still in original condition, is now called the Polish Parish and owned by the Los Angeles Roman Catholic Archdiocese. It's a unique—some say outrageous—example of period architecture. One house west is the former home of choreographer and film director Busby Berkeley.

Thomas Brothers map reference: Page 43 at 4D
During the height of his popularity, Fatty built a three-story mansion for his mother. The Rappe scandal cost him his career and most of his income. Among the properties he had to sell was this one. From the Polish Parish, go east seven short blocks on Adams, turn north on Arlington, cross the Santa Monica Freeway; turn right on 20th to Gramercy. It's the white Victorian on the northwest corner.

Otto Sanhuber: Was he Walburga's love slave or merely one of her lovers? Photo: AP/Wide World.

8

LOVE IN THE ATTIC: OTTO SANHUBER & WALBURGA OESTERREICH (1918-1930)

Her name was Walburga Oesterreich, but despite the cold Teutonic sound of it, her passions of the flesh were hot, consuming, often overwhelming. She was 36 in 1903, but she looked much younger. A woman of average height and a trim yet voluptuous build, she had a sultry smile and her eyes sometimes flamed with desires that no one would surmise from her *gemutlich* dress and demeanor. When her story became known, she was called, perhaps accurately, a nymphomaniac. Mrs. Oesterreich often attributed her desires to some Spanish ancestors, whose blood, she claimed, still coursed through her veins.

But she had few such passions for her husband, Fred, a Milwaukee apron manufacturer. Fred, a few years older than Walburga, was almost the stereotype of a solid German businessman. Transplanted in early adulthood to Milwaukee, he became wealthy. By 1903 he was worth about $250,000, in an era without inflation or income tax. Fred prospered by watching every penny, by devoting nearly every waking moment to his business, by pushing his fearful employees to work ever harder.

One of these employees was a small, sickly looking young man, Otto Sanhuber. He was barely five feet tall, with a sallow complexion, receding hair and chin, weak blue eyes staring out through cheap spectacles, and 105 pounds clinging to the scrawny physique of an abandoned housecat. As an infant, he'd been left at a foundling home. Otto didn't know his parents and wasn't sure of his birthdate. But in the summer of 1903 he said he was 17, and applied for a job as an apprentice sewing-machine repairman at Oesterreich's factory.

Young Otto soon caught Walburga's eye. He reminded her, she said, of her late and lamented son Raymond, who would have been about Otto's age. At first she displayed a motherly interest in the youth. He came to admire her spunk, the way she stood up to her browbeating husband. Soon he began to think of her as more than a motherly figure. For her part, Walburga detected in young Sanhuber latent hungers that might complement her own.

One day she called her husband from home, complaining that her sewing machine didn't work. Fred dutifully dispatched Sanhuber to fix it. When he arrived, Walburga led him to the jammed machine in her bedroom. She was wearing a silk robe, silk stockings, and little else but a fetching perfume.

Little Otto soon serviced the machine. Then he serviced Walburga. She discovered, as she had hoped, that in a certain way this scrawny little boy was much more of a man than her hard-driving husband.

Their affair continued as constant "breakdowns" of her sewing machine required his repeated visits to their home. After almost three years, neighbors began to gossip. The lovers took a "weekend" trip to St. Louis, but were unwilling to leave their hotel bed. It was nine days before they returned to Milwaukee. Still not satisfied, Walburga took to visiting Otto's own boardinghouse room, but she began to fear discovery.

Fred Oesterreich had heard whispers of his cuckolding and one day in 1907 he confronted his wife. She denied everything, looked him in the eye, and put on a wonderfully convincing display of wounded outrage. Stared down, Fred retreated, sorry he'd ever brought it up. And he started hitting the bottle a little harder than he'd been hitting it, which was very hard indeed.

Walburga was torn. She couldn't bear to give up Otto and she couldn't chance Fred hearing more whispers. So she decided to find Otto a place to stay where they could couple conveniently. A place where he could come and go and nobody would ever see him. And she found such a place. Otto moved into the Oesterreichs' house.

He moved into the attic, into a small space directly above the master bedroom. It was really just a cubbyhole barely big enough for tiny Otto and a cot, a table and chair, and a chamberpot. And so Otto Sanhuber lived under the same roof with his lover and her husband. By day he helped Walburga around the house, making beds, sweeping floors, peeling vegetables—and seeing that her sexual needs were met. By night he huddled in his airless garret, reading, by candlelight, adventure novels provided by Walburga from the public library. And directly below him, she shared her bed with Fred. Despite a number of close calls, this astonishing arrangement continued for almost four years.

After reading hundreds of pulp magazines and cheap novels, Otto decided to try his own hand as a writer. Walburga got him a post-office box, and, using a pen name, he began to submit handwritten stories of excitement, adventure and lust, often set in the Orient. After a time, his stories began to sell and Walburga opened a bank account for him. He soon earned enough to buy a typewriter, and he pecked away on it during days when he wasn't cleaning house or bedding his mistress.

Then Sanhuber got careless. Walburga had warned him about going near the tiny, dust-covered window that overlooked the Oesterreichs' backyard, but one day he peered out just as Fred looked up. The older man went running for his wife, screaming about a face in the attic window.

Walburga was unruffled. The only entrance to the attic was over their bed. She let Fred try the trap door. Since Otto had locked it on the other side it wouldn't budge. It must be stuck, said Walburga. But no one had been in there for years. Walburga suggested that Fred was losing his mind. Too much drink, or too much work, or both. Perhaps he should see a doctor. Fred refused. But thereafter, when he heard a cough from above the rafters, or noticed that little remained of the previous evening's dinner leftovers, or that his cigar humidors seemed to empty faster than he could fill them, he kept silent.

But he started looking around for a new house, and when he found one, with Walburga's help, the Oesterreichs moved. Otto moved as well, into a more securely hidden part of the new attic. Fred's hallucinations continued in the new house: soft noises in the night, the disappearance of food, the smell of cigar smoke in rooms he never frequented.

In 1913, they moved again. Otto Sanhuber came along, to Walburga's relief and delight. And the three of them might have remained in Milwaukee until death parted their strange relationship, except that one day in 1918 Sanhuber again got careless. While Fred and Walburga were out for an evening of cards and schnapps, Otto had dinner. In his underwear. In the kitchen. But Fred and Walburga returned unexpectedly early.

Fortunately for Otto, Fred was thoroughly drunk. The little fellow escaped with only a severe beating before Oesterreich tumbled off to bed, sure he had surprised a burglar, though a most peculiarly attired one. Otto, still wearing only underwear, found himself locked out of the only home he had. He hid in a park and returned the following day, after Fred departed for work.

Worried that Fred would finally realize what had been going on for nearly 15 years, a tearful Walburga told her diminutive lover that he would have to go away. World War I was on and Otto told Walburga he would join the Army and serve his country. Walburga insisted she needed his services more. Eventually Otto agreed to her plan: He would go to Los Angeles, and she would soon follow. She gave Otto the money he'd earned from his writing, about $1,500, and he entrained for California. He became a hotel porter and stayed in touch through his old post office box in Milwaukee.

And in a few months, true to her word, Walburga persuaded her husband to sell his Milwaukee holdings and move to Los Angeles. She wrote to Sanhuber, advising him of their train's scheduled arrival at Union Station. He stationed himself on the Elysian Street bridge, overlooking the railroad depot, and with binoculars watched the Oesterreichs' arrival. At a discrete distance, he followed them to their hotel.

While Fred looked around for a new factory site, Walburga found them a home on posh Andrews Boulevard. A nice, two-story frame house on a small hill overlooking Sunset Boulevard. A home with an attic. Otto worked nights for two weeks creating a comfortable and secure spot for himself. Then the rest of the strange family of three moved in. Life went on, much as it had in Milwaukee.

Until the night of August 22, 1922. Late that night the Oesterreichs returned home from an evening out and promptly fell to arguing. As usual. But this time their argument was louder than usual. So loud and so abusive was Fred that Otto felt compelled to come down from his attic hideaway. To come down toting his pair of .25 caliber revolvers. While still upstairs, he heard the crash and thump of Walburga hitting the polished hardwood floor of the living room.

In fact, she had merely slipped on a throw rug, but Sanhuber didn't know. He thought Fred had knocked her down and with this belief he entered the Oesterreichs' living room. It had been a long time since Fred had laid sober eyes on him, nevertheless he called out his name and seemed to understand, all at once, what had been going on in five different houses for more than 15 years. He let out a bellow of rage and advanced on the pale apparition that had so suddenly appeared.

Fred was big and strong and enraged. Otto was small and frail. In his hands he clutched the guns he had bought to make himself feel safer during his occasional nocturnal strolls around the neighborhood. Two men who knew the same woman in very different ways grappled for a brief moment. But then the right-hand gun spoke, and again, and a third and fourth time, and Fred Oesterreich fell to the floor with a bullet in his head and two more in his chest.

The report of the pistol was so loud that Sanhuber knew the neighbors would hear it. He hustled Walburga into the hall closet, locked it, removed the big, old-fashioned key, and dropped it on the floor near the front door. Then he scurried up to his attic hideaway, and bolted himself in.

Responding to a neighbor's telephone call, the police soon arrived. They heard loud knocking and wailing emanating from the hall closet, and when they opened it found Walburga, unhurt. She told a curious story about a burglar. He must have broken into the house, said Walburga, just as one had, in truth, some weeks earlier—and the Oesterreichs surprised him when they returned from their evening out. The widow Walburga claimed the burglar had shot Fred, taken his expensive wristwatch, and then, after locking her in the closet, he had fled.

She seemed very upset over the death of her husband, and the cops took this as proper. Then she volunteered to the senior officer, Detective Captain Herman Cline, that in more than 30 years of marriage, she and Fred had never quarreled.

That little white lie pricked up Cline's ears. That and the gap between the bottom of the closet door and floor. A gap easily wide enough to accommodate a large key, like the one on the floor several feet in front of the locked door when the cops arrived. In Cline's suspicion-ridden mind, he saw Walburga shooting her husband, locking herself in the closet, and shoving the key back under the door. As for motive, considered Cline, there was the apronmaker's estate, valued at nearly a million dollars.

Cline hadn't enough hard evidence for an arrest, but he had his suspicions. He went back to Milwaukee, where dozens of witnesses swore that Walburga and Fred quarreled, bickered, fought and argued constantly. That still wasn't enough for an arrest, but Cline kept the strange murder in mind for the next year.

Meanwhile, Walburga had Fred's complicated estate to settle. She chose Herman Shapiro, a leading estate attorney, to sort things out. After a time, Walburga presented Shapiro with a token of her esteem: an expensive, diamond-studded wristwatch. Shapiro knew enough about the case to recognize this as the very watch the burglar took from Fred Oesterreich the night he was killed. Walburga claimed that she had found the watch under some living-room cushions a few months after the shooting, but had been too distraught to inform the police.

Shortly afterward, Walburga moved from her large house on Andrews to a smaller but still elegant home on Beachwood Drive. It had an attic. In the attic, Otto Sanhuber took up residence, just as though Fred Oesterreich were still the man of the house.

Walburga, worried about the police finding the gun that killed Fred, asked Otto to break his two guns up into small pieces with a hammer. She wrapped the pieces in handkerchiefs, and knotted them up tightly. Not long after that, Walburga began to date a man some years her junior, an actor named Bellows. As their relationship ripened, Walburga begged a favor from him. She had this pistol, she said, and it was the same caliber as the one that had killed her husband. She had kept it for protection, but now she was worried that the police might find it and suspect her of murder. Could he dispose of the little gun and let her sleep easier?

Bellows took the knotted handkerchief to the La Brea Tar Pits, a vast ooze that bubbled up near Wilshire Boulevard and something of a local tourist attraction for the thousands of bones of extinct animals that archaeologists had dug out. In the dark of night he tossed the handkerchief over the fence toward the sticky, apparently bottomless tarpit.

Now Walburga had one more pistol. She told a similar story to another male friend and he buried the handkerchief beneath a bush in his yard.

About a year after Fred's death, Chief Detective Herman Cline happened to run into Herman Shapiro. He noticed Shapiro's wristwatch and asked him about it. Shapiro explained that Walburga had given it to him, repeating the story Walburga had told him about discovering the watch where the burglar had stashed it. Cline filed that fact away for future reference.

He thought of it a few weeks later when Bellows came forward. He and Walburga had quarreled, and she had broken off the relationship. So he now felt obliged to tell the police about the package he'd thrown into the La Brea Tar Pits. Police made a careful search along the pit perimeter. By incredible chance, the handkerchief had landed a few inches short of the tar. The contents were rusted but recognizable. Cline made a beeline for the home on Beachwood Drive and ordered Walburga arrested for the murder of her husband. The story made all the newspapers and the next day another man walked into the police station carrying a knotted handkerchief with still another smashed .25 caliber revolver inside.

In jail Walburga tearfully stuck to her story. But she also stuck by Otto, whom she feared might starve if no one brought him food. So she asked Shapiro to go to the bedroom closet of her new home, find the trap door in the ceiling leading to the attic and knock softly three times. Then, she said, her retarded half-brother would come out. Shapiro should then give him some groceries.

Shapiro, though bewildered, did as he was asked. A pale and wizened Otto answered the knock. He seemed to welcome what may have been his first conversation with anyone except Walburga in several years. He told Shapiro that she had often spoken of him fondly, and so he felt he knew and could trust the attorney. Otto said he was sorry that she was in jail. Sorry, because her only crime was in protecting her attic dweller from the consequences of accidentally killing Fred.

Once he started talking, Sanhuber couldn't stop. While Shapiro sat in astonished silence on the floor of Walburga's closet, staring up at the unlikely bespectacled resident of six Oesterreich attics, Otto poured out the details of his 20 years of secret sex with Walburga.

Shapiro was fascinated. He kept this secret to himself, and worked to secure Walburga's release. After 18 months without trial, she was released. The pistols were so corroded that no match could be made between the fatal bullets and their barrels.

Out of jail, her relationship with Shapiro became more than professional. They became friends, then lovers. Whereupon Shapiro told her that he knew all about Otto. And he delivered an ultimatum: the little man must go, and at once. Though upset, Walburga agreed, on condition that Shapiro take him to San Francisco and find him a job. So ended Otto Sanhuber's decades in the Oesterreichs' attics. Shapiro found him a job as a janitor. From there he went to Vancouver, Canada, where he worked as a porter. He soon married a Canadian woman. After a time he returned to Los Angeles with his wife. He found another hotel porter's job, one where he worked nights and retired to sleep before the sun rose. He made no contact with his former lover.

As time wore on, Shapiro's relationship with Walburga became rather stormy. The more intimate they became, the more fiercely they quarreled. And finally, in the spring of 1930, after a particularly angry episode, Shapiro broke with Walburga. He went straight to District Attorney Buron Fitts and filed an affidavit concerning the death of Fred Oesterreich. A second warrant for Walburga's arrest was served. Soon the police took Sanhuber into custody as well.

Before the grand jury, Walburga took the Fifth Amendment, but was nevertheless indicted for murder. She was defended by Jerry Giesler, who sought and got separate trials for the former lovers.

Sanhuber was tried first. In a wavering, reedy voice, he detailed the incredible story of 20 years with Walburga. He said he was her love slave. He said that during the first years of their relationship, she had forced him to have sex with her. That she had often threatened him with physical punishment, or with reporting his presence to her husband. That there had been periods when he was too sick to perform sexually, and times when he wanted to leave. On these occasions Walburga had starved him until he agreed to continue giving her sex. When he wasn't making love to Walburga he was working very hard as the household's only servant and many of his duties included cleaning up after Fred. All of this was delivered in a childish, often sobbing voice. Jurors strained forward to hear every delicious word.

Otto was charged with murder, which had no statute of limitations. The jury returned their verdict: guilty. Guilty, not of murder, but of manslaughter. The statute on manslaughter was three years; nearly eight had expired since the night of Fred's death in August 1922. Otto Sanhuber was 43 years old and free to resume his life. Or almost.

There remained the matter of testifying at Walburga's trial. The district attorney couldn't try her for murder; he charged her with conspiracy. The principal witness against her was Sanhuber. But during Giesler's relentless cross-examination Otto was forced to admit that far from being a love "slave," in the beginning he had sought sex with Walburga. His credibility undermined, the trial ended in a hung jury, the majority voting for acquittal. The district attorney elected not to try again, and there the matter rested.

Walburga had lost most of her money in the stock market plunge of October 1929. With what remained she opened Beverly Hills' first supermarket on Wilshire Boulevard. She had a small apartment built for herself in the loft over the store. Rarely seen, Walburga passed her last years living in a sort of attic.

LOCATIONS:
Thomas Brothers map reference: Page 35 at B5
The Oesterreichs bought their home at 858 Andrews Boulevard. The street and the house remain, but in the 1930s the street was renamed. Today it is La Fayette Park Place. From the Hollywood Freeway (US 101) exit at Rampart Boulevard, go north to Sunset Boulevard, then go left until the second street, La Fayette Park

Place. Go up the hill to the first house on the left. No longer a single family residence, it's now an apartment building with nine small units. One of them is in the attic.

Thomas Brothers map reference: Page 42 at F1
The gun used to shoot Fred Oesterreich was thrown into La Brea Tar Pits (sometimes called the La Brea Fossil Pits). They are in Hancock Park, at the corner of Wilshire and Curson. From the former Oesterreich residence, go northwest on Sunset to Silver Lake, then south under the freeway to Virgil, then left to Wilshire, and right to Hancock Park.

Clara Phillips: A dancer, she killed her husband's lover, then fled to Tegucigalpa. Photo: Security Pacific National Bank Photographic Collection/Los Angeles Public Library.

9

ON THE TRAIL OF THE TIGER WOMAN: CLARA PHILLIPS (1922)

In Southern California, some words seem to take on extraordinary powers. Images, descriptions, notions—even illusions—seem to spring from conversation to cold print to full-blooded life in scarcely more than the tic of a true believer's eye. So it was during the oil boom of 1922. Wildcatters drilled everywhere. Derricks sprang up like mushrooms after a spring cloudburst. Magnates—would-be, has-been and a few of the real McCoy—were starting oil companies in what are now Long Beach, Venice, Culver City, Santa Fe Springs and a dozen other Los Angeles locales. Black Gold Fever, always contagious, spread like an epidemic throughout the city. Anyone with a lick of sense was going to get rich. If you couldn't drill for oil, you could buy land. If you couldn't do either, you could find a few bucks to buy oil stocks. And anybody could see what was going to happen. From oil came gasoline, and gasoline fueled automobiles. And already a hundred thousand cars were cruising around the basin, though *smog* and *freeway* were words that hadn't yet been invented.

Big, charming, handsome young Armour L. Phillips, a believer in the power of words, started calling himself an oil stock salesman. He bought himself the requisite fine clothing, and he bought a big house for his wife, 23-year-old Clara. Clara was poised, shapely, dimpled and dark-haired. A former vaudeville hoofer, she flashed a captivating, toothpaste-ad smile. Armour furnished the place in opulent taste, including three sets of silver. He did all this mostly on the expectation that there was still much undiscovered oil, that more new companies would float more new stock issues, that more and more people would buy these oil stocks, and that he would soon be rolling in money. So he bought on credit. Easy credit.

61

But most of the prospects he courted seemed immune to Black Gold Fever. Armour was living on dwindling credit, making excuses to creditors while trying to keep up appearances, and watching his dreams begin to unravel. Perhaps seeking distraction, Armour turned his attentions to a tall, stylish, wealthy and seductively beautiful young widow named Alberta Meadows. In the spring of 1922 he began to spend most of his evenings with her. And his weekends. He could do that without arousing Clara's suspicions, he knew, because oil stock salesmen kept strange hours. They were always chasing around town, out to prospects' homes. Or they were fetching investors out to tomorrow's oilfields to see their money going downhole. So Clara, although she might not enjoy Armour's absences, would surely understand.

But Clara was a suspicious sort and she was not timid about protecting her own interests. In her show-business days she'd more than once come to blows with women who infringed on her territory. Clara spent most of June eavesdropping on Armour's late-night calls from the upstairs extension, following him around in taxicabs, and otherwise prying into her husband's affairs. She quickly developed a state of intense loathing for Alberta Meadows. By July 5th she had some notion of how to handle the matter. She bought a claw hammer at a dime store.

The next day, Thursday, Clara told her best friend, the exquisitely formed former chorine, Mrs. Peggy Caffee, about Armour's infidelities. And about the detestable, gorgeous Mrs. Meadows. The ladies repaired to a Long Beach speakeasy to soak their outrage in bathtub gin.

And found themselves—a bit unsteady of balance, a trifle thick of tongue, but otherwise presentable—in the parking lot of the Los Angeles bank that employed young Mrs. Meadows. The time was half past four in the afternoon, quitting time. So when Alberta Meadows appeared to claim her Ford, Clara greeted her with a tight little smile and cooly asked for a lift for herself and Peggy. Over to her sister Etta's place, in Montecito Heights.

On the way over, Clara complimented Alberta on her nice car, commiserated on the unfortunate death of her departed husband, commented favorably on her dress, and commended the fine weather they were enjoying.

Montecito was a new subdivision with a few grand homes near the top of the winding road leading from an arroyo toward the rumpled green and largely vacant hilltop. Near the end of the road, below the summit of the hill, at the last bend, out of human sight, Clara asked Alberta to stop. Clara confessed that she felt troubled by the new tires on Alberta's car and her lovely new gold wristwatch. Wasn't it true that her husband, Armour, had bought them for Alberta? Alberta denied it. Clara insisted. She became visibly angry. She punched Alberta—and knocked her out of the open car. Hatless, Alberta fled down the hill, with Clara in pursuit and Peggy trying to wedge between them. Then the high heel of Alberta's shoe broke and the chase ended. Clara took the hammer out of her purse. She pushed Peggy aside, screaming and shouting at her to get out of the way. She raised the hammer and brought it down squarely into Alberta's face. And then again and again.

While Peggy hysterically vomited into the grass, Clara rained hammer blows on the now lifeless Alberta. She beat her face to a bloody pulp, disemboweled her with the claw end of the hammer, and then bashed her broken bloody head some more. Finally the wooden hammer handle broke, but the head remained imbedded in Alberta's skull. Clara looked around for a big rock. She rolled and dragged and pushed it on top of Alberta's corpse.

Clara had broken a finger on the hand she used to wield the hammer, but Clara was unaware of it as she removed her bloody wedding rings, and dropped them into Alberta's purse. She got into Alberta's car, leaving blood stains everywhere. She opened a door for Peggy to enter and, smiling strangely, said, "It's all right now, dear, get inside. Time to go home."

Clara dropped Peggy at her home in Long Beach then drove to her own place. Her waiting husband was shaken when she drove up in Alberta's car. He began to panic when he saw her bloody hands. "I guess it's murder," she said. "I killed your lover, Alberta." Clara poured herself a drink. She was going to bed, she announced. She'd surrender to the police in the morning.

Armour Phillips wouldn't hear of it. "You've got to escape, get out," he said. Soon he was in his own car, following Clara in Alberta's, over the hills to Pomona, a 30-mile, two-hour jaunt.

There they abandoned the Ford. It might be months, if ever, before anyone reported it, or investigated, or linked it to Alberta Meadows. Southern Californians were always abandoning their cars when they couldn't keep up the payments or afford to fix them. And the state automobile bureaucracy was incapable of keeping up with them all.

Returning to Los Angeles, Armour borrowed more money to put Clara on the next train to El Paso. There she would cross the border to Mexico, which was still torn by bandits and insurrection and revolution, still smarting from John "Black Jack" Pershing's 1917 expedition, and had no extradition treaty with the United States.

Up on Montecito Heights the police made a grisly discovery. "It looked like she'd been attacked by a tiger," ventured one of the cops who saw Alberta's disemboweled corpse. Even veteran reporters, who rushed to the scene, were sick to their stomachs. But it was midsummer, when newspapermen wonder how they will fill their front pages. A brutal murder was serendipitous this time of year. What sort of monster was loose in Los Angeles, attacking beautiful young women? And whose corpse was this, in silk underwear, with no identification and no face to photograph? The newspapers had their headlines, and the city shuddered with delicious fear.

Meanwhile, Armour was dissolving into jello. His lover was gone. His killer wife was escaping. He found his attorney, John Haas, unsympathetic. Haas called the sheriff. Undersheriff Gene Biscailuz, a legendary figure in Los

Angeles law enforcement, went to see his old friend Haas. And there sat pathetically trembling Armour Phillips. He had decided not to become an accessory to murder, and he told Biscailuz what he knew about Clara's crime.

Arizona police took Clara Phillips off the train at Tucson. She was held two nights in a filthy, airless, verminous cell, sleeping without blanket or mattress on a rusty iron cot, and barely fed. But back in Los Angeles, the newspapers were creating her legend. Who was the beast that had mauled Alberta Meadows, had crushed her skull and ripped out her guts? Why, it was the Tiger Woman! It was Clara Phillips, the Tiger Woman!

The Tiger Woman rode back to Los Angeles in style, accompanied by Sheriff Bill Traeger himself. Mrs. Traeger shared a Pullman compartment with Clara. En route she was confronted by a distraught Peggy Caffee, in the protective custody of a plainclothesman. Peggy identified Clara as the person she saw strike Mrs. Meadows with a hammer. Clara cooly ignored her and went about applying her makeup.

Clara consented to be interviewed en route, disclosing to reporters that she enjoyed driving cars, riding bicycles, motorcycles and horses, and she knew nothing about murder. A smartly tailored suit displayed her stunning figure to advantage as she posed for a crowd of photographers while getting off the train at Union Station. She showed her wonderful teeth and a broad smile showcased her dimples. The city of Los Angeles took the Tiger Woman to its heart. Scores of letters, boxes of candy, and dozens of bouquets of flowers were delivered to her cell. The Los Angeles public scorned her cad of a husband, who had cheated and then ratted on her. Nevertheless, Armour borrowed more money to pay for her lawyers.

Her trial created a sensation. Peggy arrived to give testimony in a very lowcut green blouse and a short skirt. Stuttering and stammering she eventually mumbled her story, naming Clara as Alberta's killer.

Clara denied it cooly. She had had words with Alberta, had called her a few names there on Montecito Drive. "Alberta, you're just as dirty as a dog," she yelled. Alberta, who was taller and heavier, then slapped Clara. They had struggled. Clara broke her finger. And it was then *Peggy* who lost her head, *Peggy* who had brought the hammer, *Peggy* who had used it to strike down Alberta.

The jury found Clara guilty of murder in the first degree. The judge sentenced her to from 10 years to life, to be served at San Quentin. Nine days later her attorney filed an appeal.

During the trial Clara had made the very slight and public acquaintance of a spectator, Jesse Carson. Unable to get a seat in the packed courtroom, he had watched her being taken daily from her cell at the county jail to the courtroom. And he had announced to her, very cooly, that if she had the misfortune to be convicted, he would get her out. He would take her from her cell to freedom. Clara's attorney knew a crackpot when he saw one, and he laughed off the whole affair.

He wasn't laughing, however, on December 5th, when at dawn a jail matron came to Clara's third-floor cell to bring her breakfast. Clara was dining out. Jesse Carson, soldier of fortune, gun runner and smuggler had engineered a classic escape. He had smuggled her a hacksaw blade. Over the space of three nights she used it to cut the iron bars on the window. Chewing gum held them in place until late on the night of December 4th. Then Clara slipped her slender shoulders through an opening 10 by 13 inches. Perched on the narrow window ledge, she reached up and grasped a cornice on the roof above. Hand over hand she inched along the building, around a corner and to a vent pipe. She shinnied down the pipe 50 feet to a rooftop. Carson's rope hung over the edge, and she went down it to the alley below, another 50 feet. Then she climbed over a steel fence barring the mouth of the alley and into Carson's car. And she was free.

Carson had been with her every step of the way. Carson himself had taken the escape route on December 2 to bring her the hacksaw blade. He came for her again on December 4, and helped her over the wall. And the two of them went to ground underneath a house near Pomona, not far from where she had abandoned Alberta's Ford.

And there they stayed, cold and damp, while the manhunt unfolded, while the newspapers ran her picture, with rehashes of the Tiger Woman's derring-do. Then Clara came down with tonsilitis.

Carson found a warm apartment in Redlands, 30 miles to the east, in a duplex that they shared with a kindly old woman who couldn't read or write and who therefore never looked at newspapers. By the fourth of January Clara was fit to travel again.

She bleached her hair blonde, put on a pair of dark glasses, changed her hat—but wore the same torn dress she'd escaped in. She spotted a plainclothes cop on the train to St. Louis, but he never noticed her. In St. Louis their taxi skidded into another on the rain-slicked streets. The police took witnesses' names and addresses. Clara was inventive, and no one guessed the Tiger Woman had passed through St. Louis.

In New Orleans they rented rooms in the home of an amiable couple. Clara was then to sail to Vera Cruz—alone. Before the ship disembarked, this couple came aboard to wish her bon voyage, a wonderful cover that dispelled any suspicions that a lovely young woman traveling alone to Mexico might have engendered. The steamship sailed on schedule, and Clara was able to relax for the first time in months.

The day she escaped Clara's attorney had a heart attack and died. The questions raised by her flight remained unanswered. How did Clara do it? Was she alone? Where was she now? Nobody had a clue. Except Morris Lavine. Lavine, an *Examiner* reporter, was a thinker. He went up on the roof of the decaying county jail and saw two sets of footprints. His and hers. And Lavine sat down on the roof and thought about what the Tiger Woman needed once she got out of jail. Money. If she went to her friends or relatives in Los Angeles, the police would know. But if she left the area, perhaps someone would *send* her money. And money never disappears. It just moves around. And it often leaves tracks.

Lavine remembered that Mrs. Meadows had worked in a bank. He found a friendly banker to share the secrets of the Armour Phillips account and learned that Armour had been borrowing heavily and making withdrawals. On January 1, he took out $570; on the 30th, $119.50; the next day, $140. But there were no money orders or checks drawn on his account. Where was the money going? Lavine knew that most of the financial transactions between U.S. and Mexican firms were handled, during this period of official antagonism, by the Bank of Montreal's Mexican branch or by the Mexico City Banking Corporation. So he wrote to his paper's Mexico City correspondent, Julio Trens. Trens poked around a bit. He spread some *gringo* dollars here and there and learned that money from Los Angeles was going to Galveston, Texas, through the Bank of Montreal. And from Galveston it went to Jesse Carson in Mexico, in an envelope bearing the return address of a local church. A church where the sister of Armour Phillips taught Sunday school.

Lavine shared his information with the authorities. They telegraphed Mexico, asking for cooperation, asking police to hold the Tiger Woman. But she had gone to Guatemala. They wired Guatemala City. Too late again. Lavine picked up her trail in Honduras, a nation that had an extradition treaty with the United States and a consulate in Los Angeles. Consul General Dr. Rodriguez cabled Tegucigalpa. The Hondurans took Clara into custody, and with her, Etta May Jackson, her younger sister. Undersheriff Biscailuz, his wife and another deputy set sail aboard the S.S. *Venezuela* for San Salvador, the nearest port to Tegucigalpa.

The situation in Tegucigalpa was complicated and unstable. In fact, it was much like Gilbert and Sullivan. Honduras was on the brink of revolution. As usual. Jesse Carson was presently in a local prison, for the crime of having smuggled guns to his good friends, the revolutionaries. As usual. Since it was customary during these revolutions that all jails were emptied, he wouldn't be behind bars much longer. Nor would Clara. And in the meantime, Clara had excited the machismo of some very important locals, including the chief of police. They were smitten with her considerable charms. The dimples, again. And the populace held her in high esteem. The prevailing sentiment seemed to be that what Clara had done to Mrs. Meadows with a hammer was no more than Mrs. Meadows deserved, no more than many of them would have done in the same situation.

With both an election and a possible revolution pending, the issue of Clara's extradition became a political cause celebre. Should this small, poor, backward country simply turn Clara over to the Colossus of the North just because the *yanqui* government demanded it? Was not Honduras an independent nation? Had they not their pride? Clara was meanwhile being held at the jail in spacious second-story rooms, without bars on the windows. And the citizens of Tegucigalpa, anxious to play a part in this international melodrama, were slipping her ropes.

Into this delicate situation rode Morris Lavine. He paid a call on Franklin Morales, the American ambassador. There was to be a special session of the Chamber of Deputies. It seemed likely that this body would repudiate the extradition treaty. But Morales had his resources. He let Honduran President Gutierrez know that a certain large American firm might pay a substantial advance on their taxes—but only if the extradition treaty was *not* discussed in the Chamber of Deputies. This had a certain appeal to Gutierrez.

At this point of the stalemate Eugene Biscailuz and company arrived. The undersheriff conducted negotiations in his excellent Spanish. All parties, revolutionaries excepted, were consulted, and in a few days it was agreed to remove Clara from Tegucigalpa and transport her overland to Puerto Cortez, on the north coast. Here they would catch a ship for New Orleans. The party could depart as soon as the extradition request, the formal documents, arrived from Washington.

A mounted messenger was dispatched a hundred miles to pick up the diplomatic pouch. When it was unsealed in Tegucigalpa, there were no extradition papers inside. It was at least another week until the next pouch. But one of those enamored of the Tiger Woman, a powerful man, pointed out that Honduras had already held Clara longer than the treaty required. If there were no papers, she must be let go. Biscailuz and Morales went to President Gutierrez's palatial country estate. The cabinet met in extraordinary session. Undoubtedly some dollars moved around. The cabinet voted to move Clara from Tegucigalpa to Puerto Cortez, two days journey distant, and to keep her on Honduran soil until the extradition papers arrived. After they were examined, the extradition request would be formally considered by the Chamber of Deputies and voted upon. Gutierrez would ensure it was promptly honored.

Clara was spirited out of Tegucigalpa in the middle of the night, without a chance to use the telephone to speak to Carson. Biscailuz and his party motored out of town, crossed a vast lake in dugout log canoes, and stopped to make camp in the jungle at the edge of a tiny town, Jaral. Lavine sat down for the first time to interview the Tiger Woman. She insisted she was innocent, that she was convicted by newspaper headlines, that she'd never had a chance to tell her story to the public. Lavine mentally filed that away for future use.

The next morning the party arrived in San Pedro by narrow gauge railroad. They were met by the local military commander, who demanded Clara's freedom, on authority of orders from Tegucigalpa. Further negotiations ensued. More cash changed hands. The party left for Puerto Cortez where the S.S. *Copan*, a banana boat, a tramp steamer, lay at anchor with steam up.

They were greeted by a wire from the capital: The extradition papers had arrived—and were worthless. There was a technical matter: The language was incorrect. Words have power in Central America, too. The Honduran Supreme Court would on the morrow order Clara's freedom. Biscailuz called a council of war. He had only $40 left. Lavine had only a little more. They were of a mind to bundle Clara onto the tramp steamer *Copan* and let the governments decide who was right at a later date. Except for three nasty little gunboats, flying Honduran colors in the harbor. Was Biscailuz willing to get his country involved in a war over Clara Phillips?

Before making that decision, Biscailuz asked Lavine to try persuading Clara to come back voluntarily, to waive her extradition rights. Lavine agreed to have a go at it. He asked Clara why, if she were innocent, had she been convicted? And Clara said that no one in authority had bothered to learn who had bought the hammer that killed Alberta. But if they did, said Clara, they would find that Peggy bought it. So she had been convicted in court, but she was innocent.

Lavine argued that she should come back and clear her name. "Set the record straight," he told her. New evidence was a good basis for a new trial, he told her, and her attorney should be able to find the salesclerk who sold Peggy the hammer. The attorney, he reminded her, had already filed an appeal. (He didn't mention that Harrington, her attorney, had died the day she escaped from jail.)

Clara hesitated. Lavine, to Clara an emissary of the mighty Hearst newspaper chain, appealed to her vanity. If she were truly innocent, she should come back. But if she were really the Tiger Woman, if she had brained and dis-emboweled Alberta, then she should flee at once, before the Hondurans changed their minds.

Clara voluntarily boarded the *Copan* in the early hours of the next morning. In New Orleans the party of captive and captors caught the train to Los Angeles. And when it stopped at Colton, near San Bernardino, Los Angeles District Attorney Asa Keyes boarded. With him were Sheriff Traeger and John Richardson, Clara's new attorney. They had bad news.

California law required that appeals be filed within five days of sentencing. But Harrington, Clara's original attorney, had inexplicably waited nine. The words of the law were very clear, and the power of those words put Clara in jail without another trial. The train stopped in Los Angeles, but Clara stayed on it. It took her to San Francisco and then to San Quentin. She was transferred to the new women's prison at Tehachipi in 1933 and paroled in June 1935. Hundreds greeted her as she left the prison; they were all chanting, "Tiger Woman, Tiger Woman." Clara Phillips practiced dentistry in the San Diego area until 1961, when she moved to Texas.

In 1930, reporter Morris Lavine was sentenced to prison after his conviction on an extortion charge. Lavine was apparently acting as a bag man for a trio of racketeers when he accepted $75,000 in cash from Charles Crawford, * a realtor and political kingmaker. At the trial, Crawford testified that the money was intended to buy silence about his connections with the 1927 Julian Pete stock scandal. **

LOCATIONS:
Thomas Brothers map reference: Page 35 at F3
In the Tiger Woman's time, Montecito Heights included the area now known as Mt. Washington. The body of Alberta Meadows was found on a then-vacant lot now known as 815 W. Avenue 37. Exit the northbound Santa Ana Freeway (I-5) at Avenue 26. Turn left to Figueroa, then left again on Cypress. Take a right on Pepper to Isabel, then left to Roseview and right up the hill to Avenue 37. Turn right to near the very top of the street, where the road ends. The Tiger Woman killed her prey in the space between the road and the hilltop.

Thomas Brothers map reference: Page 44 at E2
Eugene Biscailuz succeeded Bill Traeger as Los Angeles County Sheriff. His roots went deep into the community-his grandfather, William C. Warren, was the first Los Angeles City Marshall-and he was a powerful influence on Los Angeles for decades. His family's business office was on Olvera Street, in the oldest part of the city. The building remains in use as the Consulate for the Republic of Mexico. (See Chapter 1 for directions to Olvera St.)

* See Chapter 16, *Justifiable Homicide by David Clark (1931).*

** See Chapter 12, *Motley Flint and the Julian Pete Scandal (1927).*

W.D. Taylor: He never came out of the closet.
Photo: Marc Wannamaker Bison Archives.

10

ENIGMA: THE UNSOLVED MURDER OF WILLIAM DESMOND TAYLOR (1922)

William Desmond Taylor departed Hollywood as mysteriously as he had arrived. He came from nowhere, in 1910, an elegantly handsome, well-mannered and affluent Englishman, an urbane and witty intellectual among the rough-edged former glove salesmen, truck drivers and boiler makers who pioneered the new film industry. He left after appearing in a few films, but turned up again in 1919, claiming to be a director. Taylor had nothing to support this claim, but in those early years of the silent film era, talent and *chutzpah* made almost anything possible.

He was hired to direct segments of a serial, *Diamond from The Sky*, and soon proved himself. Then it was on to features: *Anne of Green Gables*, *A Tale of Two Cities*, *Tom Sawyer* and *The Top of New York*, all big box-office successes. He followed with several films starring "America's Sweetheart," the incomparable Mary Pickford. By 1922 Taylor was one of the most respected dramatic directors in the industry, and president of the Director's Guild to prove it.

A bachelor, Taylor lived in a bungalow court on fashionable Alvarado Street. The bungalow court, a narrow but deep lot lined with small free-standing houses surrounding a central walkway, was a peculiarly local invention. Taylor's unit was of two floors, with the bedroom above. His neighbors included actor Douglas MacLean and his wife Faith, and buxom, blonde Edna Purviance, Charlie Chaplin's leading lady and close friend.

Perhaps befitting a leading figure in an industry that created elaborate fantasies for popular consumption, William Desmond Taylor wasn't at all the man he seemed to be. His real name was William Cunningham Deane-Tanner. He gave his birth year as 1887—but if so, he would have been 15 years old in 1902 when he married a New York woman. He claimed to be an Englishman but was really born in Ireland. As Deane-Tanner he had acquired a reputation in New York as an art connoisseur, and operated a New York business successful to the tune of about $25,000 annually, a considerable sum in 1908.

That was the year Deane-Tanner vanished. Just disappeared one day, leaving a bewildered wife and a young daughter, taking with him $500 and some clothes and personal things from a hotel room he'd long kept in Manhattan. Four years later, in exactly the same manner, his younger brother, Dennis, performed an almost identical vanishing act, leaving a wife and two children.

William apparently went looking for gold in Alaska. After that he came to Hollywood, acted in a few films, faded out of sight, joined the Canadian Army and served as a captain during World War I. He returned to Hollywood accompanied by his valet of many years, Edward Sands, and began his second Hollywood career as film director. Soon he was making important friends, making movies, making quite a lot of money—much more than his modest bungalow home would indicate—and making love with an astonishing number of film actresses and aspirants.

But in 1921 things began to unravel. While Taylor was vacationing in Europe, valet Sands began to forge Taylor's name to checks. He stole jewelry and other small valuables. He smashed up Taylor's car. He bought his girlfriends lingerie and clothing at department stores, charging the purchases to Taylor's account. When Taylor returned he fired Sands. Later he hired a new valet, Henry Peavey.

Other incidents followed: mysterious phone call hangups at odd hours; an unidentified nocturnal intruder, whom Taylor chased off by brandishing his gun; a succession of prowlers leaving their spoor where Taylor would be sure to find it. Then someone burglarized his home, not just once but repeatedly, stealing none of the cash he usually kept about, but instead valuable jewelry and some of the specially made gold-tipped filter cigarettes he favored. The burglar then pawned the jewelry—and mailed the pawn tickets back to Taylor. The tickets bore the name of William Deane-Tanner.

While there were many women in Taylor's life, by the start of 1922 there were two with whom he was very close: stunning, angelic, virginal Mary Miles Minter, and lovely, sometimes bawdy Mabel Normand. Both were complex women; with each Taylor enjoyed a complicated relationship.

Mary Minter was 20, claimed to be 17, and in long blonde curls looked 15 on camera. She'd been appearing in films since the age of seven; her considerable box-office appeal rested on a combination of saintly demeanor and sanitary sex appeal. Mary's mother, Charlotte Selby, a quintessential stage mother, enjoyed a long sexual relationship with Taylor. Perhaps she was in love with him, as many women were. Or maybe her objective was to advance her daughter's career. If so, she was successful. But when Taylor began an affair with Mary, an angry Selby turned against him, demanding that the studio bar him from directing pictures in which Mary appeared. She may have been jealous of Mary, but she was also apprehensive about bad publicity. Mary's screen roles always involved pointed choices between good and evil, with good always triumphing in the end. If the public learned that virginal Mary had taken up with a middle-aged lover, it might ruin her career.

Comedienne Mabel Normand was 28, a glamorous star whose only box-office rival was Mary Pickford. She and Taylor were close. At one point they announced their engagement, but never set a date. Normand's one big love had been director Mack Sennett, to whom she had also been engaged. But Sennett repeatedly postponed the wedding date, pleading business pressures, while simultaneously seeing several other women. Disgruntled and disillusioned, Mabel broke off the relationship.

She became involved with the most hedonistic element in Hollywood, a demented demiworld of orgiastic parties, casual sex, bootleg booze, and drugs. Soon Mabel Normand was using cocaine. Lots of cocaine. By early 1922 she had an ugly gorilla on her back: a $2,000-a-week cocaine habit. Her coke dealer used a neighborhood peanut vendor as a distributor. Some of the peanut shells contained toot instead of nuts. Mabel came to love peanuts almost as much as she craved cocaine. She had her chauffeur stop at the peanut vendor every day on the way to the studio. The back seat of her limousine was usually littered with shells from the peanuts she munched all day long.

Taylor was outraged at Mabel's cocaine addiction—but not at her. He wanted the sources dealt with and went to the U.S. attorney with information about a dealer. The police dutifully rounded up several addicts and some minor pushers, but nothing ever came of it. According to some accounts, Taylor also personally confronted a leading cocaine dealer and told him that he was never again to sell drugs to Mabel Normand. The dealer just laughed at him.

Early on the evening of February 1, 1922, Taylor telephoned Mabel and asked her to stop by. He wanted to see her—it had been about two months since her last visit—and he also had two books he wished to share. One was by Sigmund Freud—in 1922, the father of psychoanalysis and his revolutionary concepts were almost unknown in the United States—and the other a work by Friedrich Nietzsche.

Taylor had spent the late afternoon working on his income tax return at a downstairs desk. He had earned $37,000 in 1921, and would have to pay the maximum rate on net income: four percent. His work was interrupted by a telephone call at about 6:30; about 15 minutes later, while he was speaking, Normand's chauffeured limousine pulled up. Peavey, the new valet, met Mabel at the door; Taylor waved her in, abruptly ending his telephone conversation.

Normand hadn't yet eaten dinner; Taylor had already done so. She nibbled on some of her peanuts, carelessly dropping empty husks on the rug. The couple chatted. They enjoyed a cocktail, and then another. Taylor dismissed Peavey at 7:20, about 10 minutes before his usual quitting time. Peavey spent most of that time talking with Normand's driver at curbside. At about 7:45, Normand left, clutching her borrowed books. Taylor said he would telephone about 9:00 to see how she was enjoying Freud. He left the door of his bungalow open while walking her to the car. She waved farewell, eating peanuts as the car pulled away.

At about 8:00, neighbor Faith MacLean heard a loud noise, perhaps a car backfiring in the street. She looked out her window but saw nothing. A little later, she saw someone standing under the light in front of Taylor's door. He was leaving, but turned back to say something over his shoulder as he left. He was of about average height and seemed well built. Faith thought he was young, perhaps about 26 or so. He spotted her peering out the window, but she couldn't see his face clearly. His cap was pulled down over his eyes and a scarf covered his nose and mouth, perhaps as protection against the bitter cold evening. He wore no overcoat. MacLean thought he walked oddly for a man—almost like a woman. Then she put him out of her mind.

Howard Fellows, Taylor's driver, telephoned his employer at about 7:55, but got no answer. He came over at about 8:15 and rang the bell. Again there was no answer. Fellows garaged Taylor's car and went home.

The following morning at 7:30, Taylor's valet, Henry Peavey, arrived to start the day as usual, by making breakfast. Peavey let himself in and found Taylor stretched out on the living room floor. He was fully clothed, in trousers, shirt, suit jacket and shoes. His hair was neatly combed. He lay on his back, his arms at his sides. William Desmond Taylor—or William Deane-Tanner—was dead. His death turned Hollywood upside down and inside out.

Upon discovering the body, Peavey was beside himself. He ran out into the court yelling "Massa Taylor is dead," over and over, tears streaming down his face. Across the court Edna Purviance, still in bed, was shocked into action. She instantly telephoned Mabel Normand with the news, warning her that if there was anything she didn't want the police to find in Taylor's home, she'd better come immediately. Purviance hung up and immediately dialed Mary Minter's number. She gave Mary the same instructions.

By now Peavey had regained his composure. He called Taylor's doctor, who surmised the death was from natural causes, perhaps from a chronic stomach ailment Taylor suffered. The studio doctor called Charles Eyton, a top executive at Taylor's studio, Famous Players-Lasky (later Paramount). Hollywood was still reeling from the aftershocks of the Fatty Arbuckle case, and Eyton, knowing Taylor had a very long list of bedroom playmates, wanted no more scandal. He took a couple of his most trusted assistants and set out for Taylor's bungalow. His objective: sanitize the death scene before police arrived.

Doctor and studio executives arrived together. In that Prohibition year of 1922, the first thing they did was cart off Taylor's ample supply of bootleg whisky. While they were rifling through his papers, occasionally finding one they burned on the spot, Purviance and Mabel Normand went looking for Normand's love letters. In the middle of this incredible scene the coroner arrived. He rolled Taylor's corpse over, and noticed a stain, dried blood, on the carpet. Taylor had been murdered. Under his left arm was a single bullet hole. In his back, an exit wound. A distinctly old-fashioned type of .38 caliber bullet had passed through his heart.

The coroner called the police. They arrived almost immediately—and on their heels were Mary Miles Minter and her mother. Both wanted to find *their* love letters. But the police refused to let them in, though Mary dropped her virginal role, screaming and pounding her fists on the broad chests of policemen barring her from even a glimpse of her departed lover.

The police had little difficulty finding Mary's letters. And Mabel's. And those of Mary's mother, as well as the letters of dozens of other women. They made very juicy reading, especially the gushy, sophomoric notes penned by Mary. Police found a cache of her missives written in a secret, but decipherable, code, tucked into the toe of Taylor's riding boot. And they found what Mary had been desperate to recover: a lacy nightgown bearing the initials MMM, and with it a note:

Dearest, I love you—I love you—I love you! X X X X X X X ! Yours always, Mary.

Eight days after Taylor's death, a more thorough search of his bungalow bedroom revealed a locked secret compartment within a locked chest. In it were dozens of women's undergarments—panties, bras, nightgowns—scandalous trophies of the hunt, souvenirs from an almost incredibly large number of women.

Police conducted a crime scene investigation that became the focus of much subsequent controversy. There were few clues, and those more tantalizing than informative. A pile of cigarette butts on the back steps testified to someone waiting a long time before entering the apartment. Upstairs in plain sight was almost $1,000 in cash, and another $78 was in Taylor's pocket. Clearly, robbery was not the motive.

Someone had laid the body out on the floor. Taylor couldn't have been shot where he was found, nor could he have fallen quite so tidily in what looked like a burial pose. Mysteriously, the bullet holes in his jacket didn't correspond with those in his shirt and in his body. Some theorized Taylor had his arms raised when he was shot. This posture pulled the jacket higher, and when his arms were lowered in death, the holes didn't match up. Mystery author Erle Stanley Gardner, writing decades after the event, theorized that Taylor had been seated at his desk, leaning forward and writing with his right hand while his left arm was extended to secure the paper. The killer, suggested Gardner, was an expert shot who waited until Taylor's signature was affixed and then drilled him precisely through the heart with a single shot.

There were other mysterious clues. According to Frank Bryson, the public administrator who served as executor of Taylor's estate and hence had access to all his financial records, on January 31, Taylor withdrew $2,500 in cash from his bank account. The next day, the same day he died, he deposited the same sum into exactly the same account. However, this statement was subsequently challenged by certain unnamed "high officials" in leaks to newspaper reporters—which may or may not have been an indication of its significance.

A mysterious pink silk nightie with a butterfly on the back was said to be in the bungalow when police arrived, but later disappeared from a locked evidence box in the district attorney's office.

As officials pored over Taylor's papers his true identity became known, creating a public sensation. It was revealed that his ex-wife had tracked him down in Hollywood after she saw him in an early film. When she confronted him, he stonily denied being her absent husband—but had ever since sent her a monthly stipend as child support. His sister-in-law also found him after seeing pictures in newspapers. Again he denied his identity, but started sending regular checks to help support his brother's wife.

A logical suspect in Taylor's murder was the thieving valet, Sands. Many people came forward to assert that Sands was in fact William's long-vanished brother, Dennis. An intriguing theory, but without any hard evidence to support it. Nevertheless, Taylor's fury at his former valet seemed all out of proportion to the man's crimes. Taylor, a reserved person who didn't often engage in hyperbole, told his close friend and secretary, "If I ever lay my hands on Sands, I'll kill him." He told police, after hearing that Sands had likely fled the state, "I would go to any trouble or expense to extradite him, not only from a neighboring state but from any country in the world. All I want is five minutes alone with him." Sands was never found, nor was Dennis.

There was another mysterious figure, a soldier from Taylor's wartime Canadian regiment. According to the statement of a British officer who had been with Taylor in London after the war, Taylor once pointed out a soldier in the mess, saying "That man is going to get me if it takes 1,000 years to do it. I had him court-martialed for the theft of army property."

A Santa Ana rancher picked up a hitchhiker who closely matched the soldier described by the British officer. Police later found him in Tijuana; he admitted to being a former Canadian serviceman, and was carrying bullets in his suitcase for an obsolete .38, but no gun. Los Angeles police knew him as "Slim" or "Whitey" Kirby, a sometime chauffeur and full-time drug addict who might have once worked for Taylor. He had an airtight alibi for his whereabouts on the night Taylor was killed. Released by police, he vanished. His decomposed body was found near Calexico in an Imperial Valley swamp by two rabbit-hunting youngsters in May 1922. Some of his Mexicali friends, questioned by police, said he'd feared for his life for several months. The cause of his death was never established.

Within two months of Taylor's death, more than 300 people, some of them in Europe and South America, had confessed to his murder. Police investigated each confession to the degree they thought it plausible. And came up empty. All they had was a jigsaw puzzle of contradictory accounts.

A man matching the description of the one Faith MacLean saw leaving Taylor's apartment about 8:00 was seen again when he boarded an Alvarado streetcar at Maryland, the stop nearest Taylor's bungalow. The conductor wasn't sure whether he'd got on at 7:54 p.m. or 8:27 p.m. If the former, it was minutes before MacLean and other neighbors heard the loud noise, very likely the shot that killed Taylor. If the latter, it was just after Taylor died, and long enough afterward for the killer to have laid his victim out, made a casual exit out the front door, and strolled unhurriedly to the street corner without an undue wait for the next streetcar. This led some officials and reporters to a "hired gun" theory. Someone had paid for a professional hit.

But who? Surely not Mary Miles Minter, whose career was utterly destroyed by the publicity about her affair with Taylor. Surely not her mother. She may have been jealous of her daughter, but she'd worked a lifetime to advance her career and she must have known that the scandal would taint her daughter. But this still left many other women. One with at least three reasons to want Taylor dead was Mabel Normand. She might have been jealous of his attentions to Mary. She might have feared exposure of her drug habit—she was already paying weekly blackmail to one small-time hood—if Taylor pushed his one-man drug crusade too far. Or maybe the severe paranoia that usually accompanies prolonged cocaine addiction, combined with the first two factors, caused Mabel to fear Taylor.

And some evidence pointed to Normand. Months after the murder, a Detroit desperado with a long record was arrested by police on unrelated charges. He offered that he'd been paid $900 to drive a car with two men and a woman in it to Taylor's house on the night of his death. One of the men was San Francisco narcotics kingpin Harry "the Chink" Fields. The driver said he'd been hired by a woman, who had come along in the car. Fields was connected to Mabel Normand through the cocaine he peddled; the drug dealer Taylor had threatened was an associate of his. Fields was arrested with a big supply of cocaine and a vintage .38, but never indicted for anything relating to Taylor's death.

E.C. King, a district attorney's office investigator, claimed he knew who killed Taylor: a killer hired by a rich, powerful, cunning and shrewd woman who had mentioned Taylor's death to her chauffeur at least half an hour before Peavey discovered the body. Why then was there no arrest? King maintained there was no physical evidence, nothing to base an indictment on, and the woman had refused even to discuss the case with investigators. Or perhaps, as

King did *not* say, it was because someone had been able to buy the disappearance of what physical evidence there was. Someone in a position to do that was an assistant district attorney, Asa Keyes. Several years later, after he became district attorney, he was convicted of taking a bribe in another famous case.

The Taylor scandal immediately ruined Mabel Normand's career. Her funniest picture was released in 1923, and played coast to coast to empty houses. As the movie moguls feared, people wouldn't pay to watch a notorious drug addict. Normand experimented with other drugs, ruined her health and died of tuberculosis in 1930.

Four years after Taylor's death it was made public that police had found—and preserved—two long strands of hair taken from the coat worn by his corpse. They were blonde. Normand had dark brown hair. Mary Miles Minter's long blonde locks were a more likely source. Some have speculated that Mary was hiding upstairs during Normand's brief visit and that she may still have been upstairs when Taylor was killed and so might have seen or heard the killer. Police found handkerchiefs with her monogram in the bedroom. Might she have come downstairs after the killer left, found Taylor's body in a chair, and out of grief laid him gently on the floor before leaving via the back door? Or had she dressed in man's clothing and gone out the front? Does this explain the "odd manner of walking for a man" observed by Faith MacLean?

Minter was so overcome at Taylor's funeral that in view of hundreds of mourners she passionately kissed his embalmed corpse full on the mouth for several minutes. She then fainted, claiming later that she'd heard the painted corpse whisper, "I shall love you always, Mary." The Taylor murder put an abrupt end to her career. Mary's mother, Charlotte, went to Europe and stayed three years, but even after she returned it was a while before they spoke to each other.

They reconciled a few years before Charlotte Selby died in her daughter's Santa Monica home, where Mary had lived in retirement for several years amid rumors that she had gained some 50 pounds. Mary emerged in the 1940's as a respected interior decorator, catering to an upscale Beverly Hills clientele from a Santa Monica Boulevard shop. She married wealthy land developer Brandon O'Hildebrant in 1958; he died in 1965. Mary was brutally beaten and robbed of jewelry and antiques valued at $300,000 in 1981. She died of heart failure on August 4, 1984. With her died the last link to Hollywood's greatest unsolved mystery.

In 1967, however, noted director King Vidor, apparently intent on developing the Taylor mystery into a film, conducted his own investigation. What he learned—or the people he learned it from—caused him to abandon the project and to conceal the fruits of his research.

After Vidor's death in 1982, his biographer, Sidney Kirkpatrick, discovered the Taylor files in a locked metal box concealed behind a water heater in a guest cottage on Vidor's Hollywood estate.

Vidor's conclusion was that Charlotte Selby killed Taylor, apparently because he had refused to marry her daughter, Mary Miles Minter. Vidor also learned that Taylor was bisexual, but seemed to prefer homosexual relationships.

According to Vidor's notes, these facts had been suppressed by top Paramount executives, some of whom were Vidor's contemporaries and colleagues. The reason: Taylor's death came only a few months after the Fatty Arbuckle scandal and the studio heads were unwilling to chance public opprobrium from yet another sex scandal.*

So, using their power to create illusion, and their considerable wealth, top studio executives invented a plausible scenario for Taylor's death, a dramatic set that included drawers filled with his paramours' lingerie, intimate love notes, titillating photos of undraped leading ladies, etc., along with clues pointing to mysterious strangers. Kirkpatrick learned that Shelby had bribed police investigators to suppress their own investigation, while the studio encouraged officials to leak bits of the fabricated story to the newspapers.

LOCATION:
Thomas Brothers map reference: Page 44 at B2
Take Sixth Street west from downtown; turn right on Alvarado to Maryland. The bungalow court where Taylor died was at 404 1/2 South Alvarado, near the corner of Maryland. It is now a supermarket parking lot.

*See Chapter 7, A *Heavy Crush Ruins Fatty Arbuckle* (1921).

Norman "Kid McCoy" Selby: After nine wives and two world boxing titles, he went down for the count on murder charges. Photo: UPI/Bettmann Newsphotos.

11

THE REAL MCCOY (1924)

His real name was Norman Selby, but he was the real McCoy. He fought as Kid McCoy, a cheerful brawler who won the world middleweight and welterweight championships in 1895 and 1897. Won them as much by guile and strategy as by punching prowess. Before his title bout against welterweight champ Tommy Ryan, he sent Ryan a letter begging him to "take it easy" on him, to carry him a few rounds. McCoy wrote that he hoped not to be embarrassed by his showing against Ryan, conceding that the champ was far out of his class. Sure of a victory over a weakling like McCoy, Ryan cut back his training schedule. In the ring he was carelessly confident. So Kid McCoy had him just where he wanted him. He kept at Ryan for 15 brutal rounds and took a unanimous decision. "The bastard played possum," croaked ex-champ Ryan as he was led from the ring, his face a mass of cuts, bruises and welts.

McCoy was famous for his "corkscrew" punch. In his heyday, around the turn of the century, he was just as famous for being an easy touch for an old friend, a slight acquaintance, or even a total stranger. McCoy was good for a few bucks to most anyone with a hard-luck story. He was famous for his amorous attachments, 10 of which ended in marriage. And McCoy was equally famous for his boozing.

So it was only natural that his name entered the lexicon of American slang because of a woman, a bar, and a punch. But let him tell it:

> "I'm in a saloon with a charming young lady, as usual," he recounted. "A drunk is making passes at her. I try to brush him off without too much fuss. 'Beat it,' I says. 'I'm Kid McCoy.' He laughs and says, 'Yeah? Well I'm

George Washington.' I have to clip him a short one and down he goes. He wakes up 10 minutes later, rubs his jaw, and says, 'Jeez, it *was* the real McCoy!'"

The tale of his encounter was repeated in his own broadway cabaret and spread by newsmen like Damon Runyon. In short order everyone was calling a genuine article "the real McCoy."

McCoy retired from the ring as the reigning welterweight in 1897. He was 24 years old, worth about a half-million, preinflation dollars. He opened a New York cabaret. For years he rubbed elbows with and carried tabs for the celebrated figures of Times Square and the Broadway stage. He came out of retirement in 1900 for one more fight—against "Gentleman Jim" Corbett, who beat him easily.

By 1924 McCoy was a flabby 51, his fortune vanished into nine divorce settlements, month-long benders, flashy, forgotten wardrobes and innumerable handouts. He came to Los Angeles, where his many friends helped him get bit parts in movies. He landed a job as a security guard in an aircraft factory, which enabled him to carry a sidearm. His pal, the dashing aerial stuntman Hub Kittle, former cop—and frequent burglary suspect—gave him a 32 caliber revolver. McCoy took to carrying it everywhere he went.

He soon found himself in a dangerous situation. He had taken up with another woman, planning to make her his wife. But Theresa Mors was married to wealthy art and antique dealer Albert Mors, a nasty and vindictive man. She filed for a divorce and moved with McCoy into an apartment near Hoover and Seventh. For a time McCoy thought he was in Seventh Heaven. Theresa was *the* love of his life, the ex-champ told her. Theresa happily agreed to his marriage proposal.

But first there was the divorce. An enraged Albert Mors filed a countersuit, naming McCoy as co-respondent. He sent a few toughs to threaten Theresa into reconsidering. He tipped U.S. Treasury agents that Theresa was involved in smuggling diamonds. The Kid countered by warning Albert to stop bothering Theresa. He got so angry that Albert called the police to remove McCoy from his Hollywood Hills house.

Then Theresa seemed to waver on the subject of marriage. When the divorce was final she would be worth about $125,000 in cash, jewelry and an antique store. Her friends whispered that McCoy was out for her money. Mr. and Mrs. Sam Schapps, owners of the millinery shop next to the Mors' antique store, counseled that McCoy was a punch-drunk opportunist. They encouraged Theresa to leave him, to go back to New York, to family and friends, and to start a new life for herself. Theresa listened to her friends, and seemed torn.

Albert began to be bothersome. He broke into a store she had opened after leaving him and took some valuable items. Theresa called the police. Albert was arrested but he posted bail and was released. And on the torrid night of

August 12, Albert Mors inexplicably moved out of his home in the Hollywood Hills to take a room at the Westgate Hotel, near Fifth Street and Western Avenue, not far from his shop. He did not use his own name when he signed the guest register.

His room, near the back of the hotel, was close to a rear exit and stairs leading to an alley. It was an easy walk from there to the fashionable apartment Theresa shared with McCoy at Leeward and Hoover. About midnight of August 12, the lady living on the first floor, in apartment 112, heard something go bump above her ceiling. Something heavy fell on the floor of the apartment above, apartment 212, where McCoy and Theresa lived. Then she heard someone descending the rear stairs. She looked out the window and saw a man emerging from the stairwell. She later told police it was Albert Mors.

Sometime later that night, perhaps as late as two in the morning, Kid McCoy walked into the Hollywood police station and demanded to see a certain officer, the cop who had forcibly removed him from Albert Mors' home. But this officer wasn't on duty that night. "It's a lucky thing for him he's not here," snarled McCoy.

"And why was that," asked an officer named Griffin. McCoy told him to read the newspapers in the morning, and then he'd know. "Hell, I'll be in the can tomorrow," he said. Griffin and his partner smiled knowingly. They were aware of McCoy's reputation and his penchant for drink. Since he was drunk and obviously a menace on the road, they insisted on driving him home. They took him to the door of his apartment.

Inside McCoy resumed swilling whisky and started writing his will. He left everything he owned, an estate worth perhaps $300, to his mother.
About three in the morning on August 13, a few hours after the downstairs neighbor had heard the bump on the floor of McCoy's apartment, Kid McCoy was scratching on the bedroom window screens at the home of his sister, Jennie Thomas. He was drunk, very drunk, and he carried a box containing Theresa's jewelry, which he gave to Jennie. "I just had to kill that woman!" he told his sister.

"Did you kill that man, too?" she asked. She meant Albert Mors.

"Yeah, I got him too," said Kid McCoy, then lurched drunkenly away into the night.

But he hadn't gotten to Albert yet. He continued his drinking, and at dawn went to the antique store. When the young janitor showed up he brandished his .32 and forced him to let him in the store. Then he amused himself by playing tunes from an antique music box while the terrified boy sat quietly. When Albert Mors arrived with his clerk, McCoy ordered them to take off their trousers. As customers entered, McCoy decided if he liked them or not. If not, he made the men remove their trousers and sit on the floor to one side of the store. He demanded their money; he gave it to other customers, to those he liked. He made them sit on the *other* side of the store.

At midmorning a customer came in, quickly saw what was going on and fled. McCoy shot him. He fell, not seriously hurt. McCoy decided it was time to leave. Going out the door he ran into the Schapps from the millinery store. "My God, what are you doing?" shouted Sam Schapp. McCoy shot him. As he fell, McCoy took aim at Mrs. Schapp and shot her too. He ran into the street and jumped on the running board of a passing car. The frightened driver wove back and forth up Seventh Street. A beat cop took pursuit by commandeering another car. McCoy abandoned the car at what is now MacArthur Park, and ran. Years out of shape, badly hungover from a night of steady drinking, he was quickly brought to earth by the young cop.

Police escorted McCoy home, where the building janitor had discovered the body of Theresa Mors on the floor of apartment 212. She lay covered by a bedsheet. Beneath it, next to her breast, was a picture of Kid McCoy. She had been stabbed, not seriously, in the breast. The cause of death was a gunshot wound to the back of the left side of her head.

McCoy, still a little under the weather, chose this occasion to confess to her murder. He was adamant. He repeated his confession several times. The cops took him downtown and locked him in the city jail. Before dinner time, Detective Captain Herman Cline went to see McCoy. He let him out of his cell and took him to eat a good meal in a Mexican restaurant.

Drinking glass after glass of water, and eating *frijoles*, rice and spicy food, McCoy seemed to sober. Now he recanted his confessions. He had not killed Theresa, he said. She had committed suicide—taken her own life because Albert had tried to frame her on smuggling charges, because Albert had sent thugs around to beat her, because Albert had made her life a living hell.

And then he told Cline in detail how it happened. After returning from an automobile ride around 8:00 p.m., they both began to drink. Theresa was very depressed. At length Theresa said, "I'm going to end it all." She tried to stab herself with a butcher knife, but he knocked the blade away before it penetrated deeply. She grabbed his pistol from the table, where he customarily left it when it wasn't on his hip. He struggled with her, but she shot herself before he could stop her. McCoy, in shock, put her favorite picture of himself on her breast, covered her with a sheet, and set out to drink himself to death. He succeeded in passing out. Regaining consciousness—but still drunk—he was sure he had killed her. So he went out to tell the police, but lost his nerve.

Kid McCoy was tried for murder, armed robbery and three counts of assault with a deadly weapon. Damon Runyon, the legendary columnist and sports writer, appeared as his character witness, one among many. The Schapps testified Theresa had told them she had decided not to become the tenth Mrs. Kid McCoy. She was going to leave him and return to New York soon. That was why McCoy had killed her, suggested the prosecutor.

McCoy was defended by Jerry Giesler, just beginning what would be a brilliant career as attorney to the stars. Giesler put Albert Mors on the stand, but couldn't get him to give a straight answer about why he had checked into the

Westgate Hotel under an assumed name the night of his wife's death, a mystery that remains unsolved. Giesler demonstrated how Theresa had tried to stab herself with a butcher knife, how McCoy had stopped her. But he had a problem making the jury believe she had shot herself. The wound was situated in such a way that she could only have used the thumb of her left hand to pull the trigger.

This fact on top of McCoy's confessions before sobering up gave Giesler a mountain to climb. The jury was inclined to be sympathetic; McCoy's mother died during the trial, and most of the jury remembered the glory that had once been the real McCoy. Giesler persuaded the jury it wasn't murder, but manslaughter, the verdict they brought in after 99 hours of deliberation. McCoy was sentenced to one to ten years on that charge and from one to fourteen years on each of the assault charges.

During McCoy's eight years in San Quentin, such notables as General Douglas MacArthur, Sophie Tucker, Lionel Barrymore, New York Governor Al Smith, U.S. Vice President Charles Curtis and six senators and six congressmen, as well as numerous businessmen and celebrities, petitioned for his release. Even the warden was sympathetic. McCoy showed a flash of his mettle while working on a road gang near San Simeon. A small plane crashed nearby and burst into flames. McCoy raced to the wreckage and pulled the pilot to safety.

In 1931 Henry Ford offered to hire McCoy to teach physical conditioning to his workers, if the State of California would parole him to Ford's custody. McCoy got out of jail in 1932, and soon afterward married his tenth and last wife.

In 1940, when he was 66, he told a friend, "It's no fun telling people you're Kid McCoy if they've heard of you before." A few days later he swallowed a bottle of sleeping pills in a Detroit hotel room. His epitaph might well be the warning he gave a posturing young tough who had just arrived at San Quentin. "Remember that the bright lights go out the quickest. Kid McCoy knows."

LOCATION:
Thomas Brothers map reference: Page 44 at A2
From Wilshire and Hoover, go south on Hoover to the fourth street, turn right to 2819. This is a multicolored brick, Baroque, three-story apartment building. Parts of the building go back to the era when Kid McCoy lived there with Theresa Mors.

Thomas Brothers map reference: Page 43 at E1
The Westgate Hotel is on Western, just north of Fifth. Most of its rooms now seem to rent by the hour. From Wilshire and Hoover, go west to Western, then north to Fifth. The hotel is on the west side of the street.

Motley Flint: Suave and politically well connected, a rascal or a victim, his day in court ended in tragedy. Photo: Courtesy of the Hearst Collection, USC Library.

12

MOTLEY FLINT AND THE JULIAN PETE SCANDAL (1927)

In the early 1920s, Los Angeles became a boomtown, a brawling, sprawling El Dorado of new oil and real estate fortunes, cheek-by-jowl with the madcap world of the silent-movie studios. It was finally easy to get to Los Angeles, the last stop on the new transcontinental blacktop, and tens of thousands of new immigrants poured in, looking for wealth.

Among them was Canadian-born Courtney Chauncey ("Call me C.C.") Julian, a penniless Texas oilfield roughneck. He had a silver tongue and a golden touch. In 1921 C.C. found work as a derrick rigger in oil baron Edward Doheny's oil fields. He saved most of his pay. He found a manicurist. He bought spiffy clothing. He swung a loan on a Pierce-Arrow. And he got lucky. In June of 1922 he somehow got title to 10 acres of scrub near oil-rich Santa Fe Springs. And on June 19, C.C. Julian brought in a gusher. In the next few months he hit three more on the same property.

As an oilman C.C. was just lucky. But as a pitchman, promoter and publicist, he had few equals after P.T. Barnum. He began a steady drumbeat of publicity and ballyhoo, buying ad space in local newspapers, courting reporters and editors. And investors. Especially investors.

He founded the Julian Petroleum Corporation, which he took to calling "Julian Pete," and invited everyone to get rich with him. He wrote his own ad copy, a judicious mixture of down-home homilies and sensational pie-in-the-sky. He was very persuasive. He took a third-floor suite of offices in the posh Loews State Theater Building and sat back and waited for investors to come begging him to take their money.

C.C. took their money. He built a hollow empire founded on promising oil leases with refineries, pipelines and service stations to handle the expected gushers. But all this—and the huge salary and perks he paid himself and his staff—took even more money than could be pried from the hands of small Los Angeles investors. C.C. went to the local banks for more working capital.

The bankers turned up their noses. C.C. called them crooks and con men. They demanded collateral. He called them pawnbrokers. He turned to Eastern bankers. They all but laughed in his face. C.C. bought a local radio station so he could harangue bankers—and appeal to the masses.

But C.C. was no longer *of* the masses. He soaked in a gold-lined bathtub. He spent $25,000 on a weeklong bender. He tipped a taxi driver $1,500. He traded punches with Charlie Chaplin in a Hollywood cabaret. He had a high old time of it. Until 1924.

Two years after he started, C.C. pulled out. After the first four gushers there had been no more. But his leases seemed promising. He turned everything over to S.C. Lewis and Jacob Bennett Berman. They agreed to pay him half a million dollars which "he was owed against his personal advances to the company."

Lewis and Berman were a polished pair of midwestern sharpies. Like Julian they'd turned up in Los Angeles next to broke. Unlike him there was no grease under their fingernails. Using their considerable charm to the limit, Lewis and Berman succeeded where C.C. had failed and borrowed $10 million from Los Angeles banks. Berman went round to the business community to organize stock pools. And many leading businessmen and executives in the Los Angeles financial community rushed forward with tens of thousands of dollars and the same eager expectations as the widows and orphans who had pressed well-worn bills on C.C. only a couple of years earlier.

One of these business leaders was Motley H. Flint, a Boston-born banker and one of the most respected men in California. He was the brother of U.S. Senator Frank Flint of California, and executive vice president of Pacific Southwest Trust & Savings Bank. When Motley Flint spoke, people believed. He promised them cash dividends. He promised them unheard-of interest rates on their investments. He promised them stock bonuses. He soon put together a stock pool of $1 million from the city's elite: real estate tycoons, bankers, attorneys—even movie magnates Louis B. Mayer and Cecil B. DeMille invested. Administrator of the pool was Henry MacKay, not coincidentally Senator Flint's law partner and son-in-law.

And at first Julian Pete's investors did well. In a few weeks the original $1 million had earned $670,000 for its investors, among them C.C. Julian himself. The smell of easy money wafted quickly through Los Angeles. Tens of thousands of investors clamored to get money into Julian Pete. In their swank new offices on the ninth floor of the Pershing Square Building, Lewis, Berman and their right-hand man, Edward Rosenberg, had dozens of office girls signing names to stock certificates.

But these were worthless stock certificates. The original and properly under-written issue had long since been exhausted. Office girls were signing blank forms with names taken at random from telephone directories. They created some five million shares of worthless stock. And as these were sold, some of the proceeds went to pay off earlier investors.

But such Ponzi schemes inevitably collapse of their own weight; at some point there are too many old investors and not enough new ones. And on May 7, 1927, the Julian bubble burst. More than 40,000 investors were left hanging. Some of the insiders, those who bought-in early, scrambled frantically to sell out at the end. Some of them bailed out in time. Among the latter was Motley Flint.

In June a grand jury summoned Motley Flint and other key figures to testify. He, Lewis, Berman and several others were indicted: conspiracy to obtain money under false pretenses; conspiracy to violate securities laws; conspiracy to violate state usury acts; forgery; and embezzlement.

The task of prosecuting the alleged swindlers fell to District Attorney Asa Keyes. But Keyes did not bring to this task his usual zeal and energy. In fact he turned his back on the whole affair. He left his subordinates to uncover evidence, to piece together a very complicated mosaic of crass fraud, ineptitude and calculating conspiracy, and to present all this to a jury. His staff succeeded only in confusing the jurors. To the amazement and fury of 40,000 outraged investors, all the accused were acquitted.

Presiding Judge William Doran was aghast. "I feel that diligence [on the part of District Attorney Asa Keyes] would have brought about a different verdict, at least in the case of some of the defendants who were responsible for one of the most deplorable, unfortunate and reprehensible episodes in the history of the country," he told a newsman.

But how did it happen? Lewis and Berman, facing 14-year jail terms for each of six or seven counts, were not about to let events take their course. They had right-hand man Edward Rosenberg find a fixer, a man of many parts named Ben Getzoff. Getzoff was an intimate of District Attorney Keyes. It was rumored that Keyes had been bribed by a bunco artist, "Big Hutch," in 1925 and rumored anew that he had taken $30,000 to withdraw a perjury charge against evangelist Aimee Semple McPherson in 1926. Perhaps he could be bribed in 1927.

Rosenberg told Getzoff he had a budget of $125,000 for "expenses." How much of this would Keyes need to "take it easy" on the indicted? Keyes struggled with his conscience. After some alcoholic persuasion, he agreed to $27,500. A slightly lesser figure bought the cooperation of Chief Deputy District Attorney Harold Davis. Rosenberg and Getzoff divided the rest. A tailor named Milton Pike was employed as bag man.

But Pike was fearful. He kept a diary, detailing payouts and dates. As public fury focused on Keyes, the diary fell into the hands of newspapermen and was published. Getzoff decided he hadn't been paid enough to take the whole rap.

In exchange for leniency, he described the roles of Berman and Rosenberg in secret testimony before the grand jury.

Keyes and Davis were indicted, tried, convicted and sentenced to one-to-14-year terms in San Quentin. It was a terrible and terrifying time for Keyes, who was personally responsible for prosecuting and convicting at least a third of San Quentin's inmate population. But after 19 months, Keyes, who never admitted his guilt, was pardoned by California Governor James Rolph. Out of prison, he returned home to Beverly Hills and set a new standard for notorious ex-convicts by launching a successful career selling expensive automobiles.

Some of those who had profited by getting in and out early hoped to avoid prosecution and so voluntarily repaid their profits to Julian Pete, which had gone into receivership. Former State Corporation Commissioner H.L. Carnahan and Joseph Scott, a leading attorney, were appointed as trustees. Their first move was to give all Julian stockholders equal standing, whether their stock certificates were genuine or not. The company had some assets. These were sold to a newly created corporation, Sunset Pacific Oil, in exchange for the outstanding shares of Julian Pete. In the end most of the 40,000 stockholders got at least some of their money back. A few ultimately turned a profit.

Lewis and Berman couldn't be tried again for their part in the Julian affair. But they were convicted in federal court of stock fraud in connection with another company, Lewis Corporation. Each got seven years in prison.

Motley Flint was indicted by the grand jury five times. Four times the indictments were dismissed. The fifth indictment—conspiracy to violate the state corporate securities act—was scheduled for trial in July 1930. On July 14 he gave testimony in a related case, David Selznick's suit against Security First National Bank.

His testimony completed, Flint stepped from the witness stand. A courtroom spectator named Keaton leaned forward and shot Flint three times. Then he threw the revolver at the crumpled body and sank back in his chair. Superior Court Judge Collier came off the bench to seize Keaton, who offered no resistance.

While there is no record that Keaton, an Inglewood real estate broker, ever bought Julian stock, police found a pamphlet, *Julian Thieves*, in his pocket. Keaton's wife said he'd lost his entire fortune of $35,000 after investing in bank stocks on Flint's advice.

Flint's will left two-thirds of his $750,000 estate to charitable organizations for "poor children, the aged in want, and young men and women in need of help to start them well in life."

While he was never indicted, Senator Frank Flint was so bedeviled by the scandal and by his many close connections to Julian Pete that he needed to get away for a while. In early 1929, he took ship for a lengthy ocean cruise. At sea he died in his sleep, apparently of natural causes.

And what of C.C. Julian, the man who started it all? No one could touch him on Julian Pete, and for years he used his radio station to castigate bankers and hawk shares of Inyo County gold and silver mines and Oklahoma oil wells. He filed insanity charges against his wife in 1928. She promptly divorced him and sold off their mansion with its gold-lined tub. In 1933 C.C. was indicted on a mail fraud charge. He posted bail, then vanished.

He turned up the following year in Shanghai, China, accompanied by a nubile 19-year-old whom he introduced as his secretary. On March 25, 1934, while attending a chic dinner party at the Shanghai Astor Hotel, C.C. took poison before dessert and died at the table. Since he was utterly without an estate, his fellow Americans observed local tradition and passed the hat to come up with $46 to pay for a proper pauper's burial.

LOCATIONS:
Thomas Brothers map reference: Page A at 3D
Senator Frank Flint's friends bought and installed a huge white marble drinking fountain on the lawn behind City Hall at First and Spring Streets. It's adorned with a black bust of Flint on either side. But the fountain, like Julian Pete, is purely decorative. It hasn't gushed anything for years.

Thomas Brothers map reference: Page A at 4C
The Pershing Square Building where Lewis, Berman and Rosenberg produced millions of phony stock certificates is at 448 S. Hill. Exit the Harbor Freeway at Sixth Street, follow Sixth east to Pershing Square, and turn left on Hill. The ornate, 13-story building is two doors north of Fifth Street, on the right side. Real and mythical beasts—phoenixes and griffins, eagles and rams—in bas-relief decorate cornices. The street entrance is recent black marble with elaborate gilded bronze scroll work dating from the pre-Depression era.

Thomas Brothers map reference: Page 19 at 5C
The Flint brothers, especially Frank, were noted land speculators in the early decades of the century. Flint touted the ridges and valleys north of Glendale as "the new Pasadena" and made a fortune in real estate. The town of Flintridge was named for Frank Flint after he was appointed by the California legislature to fill a vacant U.S. Senate seat. Motley Flint lived at 811 Inverness Drive, La Canada/Flintridge. From the northbound Foothill Freeway (I-210) exit at Highland Drive. Go west to Corona Drive. Turn left to Inverness, then right to 811. The house is a lovely, rambling split-level Spanish Colonial with red tile roof and Moorish arches with a wonderful view of the valley below. The grounds are protected by ornate wrought iron; a pair of antique hitching posts greets visitors.

Marion Parker: Does her spirit still haunt the house she grew up in?
Photo: Courtesy of the Hearst Collection, USC Library.

13

THE KIDNAPPING AND MURDER OF MARION PARKER (1927)

Marion and Marjorie Parker were 12-year-old twins, the apples of their father Perry Parker's eye. Bright and happy children, they attended Mt. Vernon Jr. High School in Arlington, an affluent new suburb on the west side of young Los Angeles. On the morning of December 15, 1927, while getting ready for school, Marjorie said she felt sick. She stayed home for the day. Marion went off to school alone, off to unimaginable horror, off to a gruesome death and to the worst sort of fame.

Edward Hickman was a 19-year-old college student, a handsome fellow, short in stature. He was a psychopath. He was convinced that he had a brilliant mind, that he could succeed where an ordinary man would fail, that he was so superior a being that his own ambitions were of paramount importance to society. And he was convinced that he could raise the $1,500 he wanted for college tuition in ways ordinary men would never conceive.

Hickman had briefly held a menial job at the bank where Perry Parker worked. He knew the man, knew something about his family, knew that he had some money. And he knew that Perry Parker loved his children dearly. This made them ideal candidates for what Hickman had in mind: kidnapping for ransom.

So Hickman drove to Mt. Vernon Jr. High on the afternoon of December 15, and presented himself to the principal. He told a very convincing story: Parker, an officer of Los Angeles First National Trust and Savings Bank, had been hurt in an auto accident, said Hickman. He had been sent to bring the twins to the hospital. In that era before the highly publicized Lindbergh kidnapping, most people took children's safety for granted. Neither school officials nor Marion Parker had any obvious reason to fear the well-dressed, curly-headed young man who walked the little girl to a large sedan and courteously opened the passenger door for her. It was the last time anyone saw Marion alive.

An hour later a telegram was delivered to Perry Parker at his office:

> DO POSITIVELY NOTHING TILL YOU RECEIVE SPECIAL DELIVERY LETTER. MARION PARKER GEORGE FOX.

The wire had been sent from Pasadena. Parker wasn't sure what it meant, so he called the principal's office at Mt. Vernon Jr. High. He called his wife. He called the police.

A second telegram, originating from Alhambra, arrived in a few hours:

> MARION SECURE. INTERFERENCE WITH MY PLANS DANGEROUS. MARION PARKER GEORGE FOX.

The special delivery letter arrived on the morning of December 16. Hickman elaborately handwrote it, using several alternating printing and script styles and topping the page with a shaded triangle to represent "D" (for delta) followed by Greek-styled E A T H. Death. At the bottom he wrote "FATE" in oversize letters. In between were the details of extortion:

> P.M. Parker:
>
> Use good judgement. You are the loser. Do this. Secure 75-$20 gold certificates—U.S. Currency—1500 dollars—at once. Keep them on your person. Go about your business as usual. Leave out police and detectives. Make no public notice. Keep this affair private. Make no search.
>
> fullfilling (sic) these terms with the transfer of currency will secure the return of the girl.
>
> FAILURE TO COMPLY WITH THESE REQUESTS MEANS—NO ONE WILL EVER SEE THE GIRL AGAIN. Except the angels in HEAVEN. The affair must end one way or the other within 3 days. 72 hrs. YOU WILL RECEIVE FURTHER NOTICE, but the terms remain the same. If you want *Aid Against* Me ask GOD not Man.

And on the next day two more letters arrived, one from Marion:

> Dear Daddy and Mother,
>
> I wish I could come home. I think I'll die if I have to be like this much longer. Won't someone tell me why all this had to happen to me. Daddy

please do what the man tells your (sic) or he'll kill me if youdon't (sic)

Your loving daughter
Marion Parker

P.S. Please Daddy.
I want to come home tonight.

The other letter was from Hickman, still styling himself "the Fox." Through greed or simple stupidity—the issue has puzzled generations of crime writers—he either escalated or merely confused $20 bills with $100 notes:

Parker:

Fox is my name. Very sly you know. No traps. I'll watch for them. All the inside guys, even, (sic) your neighbor the B., know that when you play with fire there is a cause for burns. NOT W.J. Burns [a reference to a leading private detective] and his shadows either. Remember that. Get this straight. Your daughter's life hangs by a thread and I have a Gillette ready and able to handle the situation.

This is business. Do you want the girl or the 75—$100 gold certificates, U.S. currency? You can't have both and there's no other way out. Believe this and act accordingly. Before the day's over I'll find out how you stand. I'm doing a solo so figure on meeting the terms of Mr. Fox, or else FATE.

That night Perry Parker attempted to ransom his daughter. Following Hickman's telephoned instructions, he drove at 8:00 to the corner of 10th and Gramercy alone in his car, dimmed the headlights and waited. But police had surrounded the area, and Hickman knew it. He would not show himself. The next day another pair of notes arrived:

Dear Daddy and Mother:

Please don't bring anyone with you today. I cried all last night. If you don't meet us this morning you will never see me again.

Love to all,
Marion Parker

And from Hickman:

P. M. Parker:

Today is the last day. I mean Saturday, December 17, 1927. You are insane to ignore my terms, with death fast on its way. I cut the time to two days and only once more will I phone you. I will be two billion times as cautious, as clever, as deadly from now on.

If by 8 o'clock you have not heard from me, then hold a quiet funeral at your cemetery on Sunday, December 18 without the body. Only God knows where the body of Marion Parker will rest in that event. Not much effort for me to take her life. She may pass out before 8 p.m. so I could not afford to call you and ask $1500 for a lifeless mass of flesh.

Final chance terms. Have $1500, 75 $20 gold certificates U.S. currency. Come alone in car, license number 594,955. Stay in car.

If I call you, your girl will still be alive. When you go to the meeting you will have a chance to see her. Then without a second's hesitation you must hand over the money, any delay will cost her life.

Don't blunder. I have certainly done my part to warn and advise you.

But Hickman had already sealed both his own fate and Marion's. A few minutes after she wrote the second note, Hickman strangled her with a dish towel, then used a razor to sever both her legs, then started to cut her head off by slicing through her neck. But then he had a sudden inspiration and stopped.

Saturday night Hickman called Parker at 7:30. He told him to come to an address, a street in a wooded area near a main highway. Parker pleaded with the police not to interfere, and this time they agreed to stay away.

Parker sat in his car at the appointed time. Hickman drove up. Though a white handkerchief covered most of the young man's face, Parker recognized him. Hickman leveled a sawed-off shotgun at Parker, demanded the money. Parker asked to see his daughter. Hickman gently raised a blanketed bundle, and drew a corner of the blanket aside to show the child, wide-eyed but silent. Parker handed over a package of new $20 bills.

"Don't follow me, and be careful. I'll drive up there and put her out, and you can get her," said Hickman in a soft voice. His car moved slowly down the street, paused far ahead in the gloom, then drove off again at full speed.

Moments later Perry Parker came upon the blanketed bundle that Hickman had laid out on the sidewalk. The child's face had been powdered, her hair combed and brushed. Her eyelids were tied open with bits of black thread. She had neither legs nor arms.

In hours the population of the region was gripped by terror, exacerbated by sensational headlines in the tabloids and radio broadcasts. Frightened parents kept their children at home while the police mounted the largest manhunt the West had ever known, appealing to all citizens to arrest suspicious characters.

Officers had one important clue—that was not publicized—a bloodstained towel marked "Bellevue Arms Apartments" found early Sunday morning in a suitcase on the street where the ransom was paid. The towel was one of several used to wrap the limbs severed from Marion Parker's body. In minutes police surrounded the Bellevue Arms, while inside detectives interviewed its occupants.

One of them was Edward Hickman, who had registered under an alias. Police officers came into his room where the ransom money lay in plain sight on an ironing board. The bathroom floor was stained with blood. Two handguns were in the oven, and a sawed-off shotgun hidden in the space between a window screen and the sash. Police spoke with Hickman for a few minutes, then left.

That night, Hickman slipped away. Several policemen saw and recognized him, but did nothing to arrest him. He stole a series of cars and headed north, evading capture by thousands of peace officers and deputized citizens. By December 22 he had made it to Seattle, where he stole a green Hudson before doubling back to Arlington, Oregon, 86 miles west of Pendleton.

In Arlington, Hickman bought groceries with a $20 bill from the ransom. His face had been printed on the front pages of newspapers from coast to coast, and serial numbers of the ransom bills were published with it. Rewards totalling $60,000 were posted for his capture. The Arlington grocer took the $20 bill to the city editor of *The East Oregonian*. The newsman telephoned the Pendleton police.

Pendleton's chief of police and an Oregon state trooper set out in pursuit. Hickman was captured after a frenetic car chase along the Columbia River Highway. "I am the Lone Wolf," he said, as he was put in handcuffs. "Do you think I'll be as famous as Leopold and Loeb?"

Hickman was taken by train to Los Angeles. Along the way he made two unconvincing suicide attempts. His trial became a circus when the judge, Carlos Hardy—a friend of evangelist Aimee Semple McPherson—numbered the courtroom's seats and issued reserved seat tickets to political cronies and patrons. Hickman was found guilty and hanged at San Quentin in front of a standing-room-only crowd of 400 witnesses. Thousands more were turned away. He had to go through the awful procedure twice. The first time the rope broke. Prison officials replaced it, carried him back atop the gallows, and sprang the trap a second time.

Years later it was revealed that the detectives who came to Hickman's room at the Bellevue Arms knew perfectly well that they had the killer of Marion Parker in their grasp. But the body had been discovered only hours before and it was a Sunday. There had not yet been an opportunity for the First National Bank, the Los Angeles city council, or the county board of supervisors to meet and set a reward for Hickman's capture. The police, probably at the order of Chief James Edgar "Two Gun" Davis, decided to wait in hopes of collecting a cash reward. When Hickman escaped, the embarrassed cops harassed and defamed the Bellevue Arms manager and the building's tenants to cover their mistake.

LOCATIONS:

Thomas Brothers map reference: Page 44 at D1
Edward Hickman strangled and dismembered Marion Parker in his room at the Bellevue Arms, 1170 Bellevue Ave. From the Hollywood Freeway (U.S. 101) just north of downtown Los Angeles, exit at Echo Park. Immediately turn right onto Bellevue, which parallels the freeway for a time, then turns sharply left. At the corner of Boylston is the Brownstone Apartment Hotel. Though the address is 1168 Bellevue, this building occupies the same site as its predecessor, the Bellevue Arms.

Thomas Brothers map reference: Page 43 at C4
Marion Parker was abducted from Mt. Vernon Jr. High School. From Venice Boulevard, turn south on 12th Avenue to the school grounds.

Thomas Brothers map reference: Page 43 at D4
The Parkers lived at 1631 S. Wilton Place. From Venice Boulevard, turn south on Wilton Place to the sixth house on the right, a two-story shingled home with flagstone siding.

A Personal and Paranormal Footnote
For most of this book, Mader researched and Wolf wrote. However, Wolf has a good friend who now lives in the same neighborhood where the Parker kidnapping occurred, and he called her to get an address for another case. During the phone conversation, Wolf remarked that the friend happened to live very near the Parker residence. The friend said she was casually acquainted with the current owners of the house, who had bought it only a year earlier. Perhaps, she suggested, they might have some relevant information or old photos.

So Wolf telephoned Michelle Pelland, a 33-year-old graduate student and one of the owner/occupants of the house at 1631 S. Wilton Place. Pelland had never heard of Marion Parker, nor of Los Angeles' most famous kidnapping. She listened with interest to part of Wolf's brief account of the kidnap/murder.

"Oh, that accounts for our ghost," she interrupted.

"Ghost?" asked Wolf.

"Yes," said Pelland, "I call it a ghost, but it's not at all frightening." She said one of the primary reasons that she, graduate student Steve Daley, 33, and accountant Ed Harris, 42, bought the old house was that they had experienced good feelings when they entered it. "It felt like there had been quite a lot of love in this house," she said.

About nine months after they moved in, Daley began to notice . . . something. "I'm a skeptic," said Steve Daley. "I'm very reluctant to say it's some kind of physical manifestation of a spirit. But there is definitely something here. I've always had the feeling in this house that we've been sharing space with something. But it's not intrusive. I first noticed it after we got a kitten. Many cats are prowlers. They're all over the house. But not mine. This is a lap cat. Always stays very close. I'm often home alone, working on a school paper, or catnapping, or just quietly reading. And I hear footsteps. Sometimes I hear somebody on the stairs. At first I thought it was the cat, but it was always right there next to me in plain sight. Then I started to listen a bit more carefully. It's not just the sounds of an old house settling. There's definitely another presence in this house. But I never notice it when there's anybody else home.

"There's a softness, a distance to it," continued Daley. "It feels somewhat like a small child. It's never in your way. One afternoon as I went down the stairs I felt—I saw something out of the corner of my eye. I turned my head and there was nothing. Maybe it was only a flash of light from across the street—but I know I *felt* something get out of my way.

"Until I learned about the kidnapping, the spirit, or whatever it is, didn't have a name. It wasn't a persona to me. Now I'm inclined to call it Marion," said Daley. "I feel it's most often in my study. But never when I'm there. It's not invasive."

The ghost, if there is one, manifests itself in several ways. The household once had an Irish setter named Max, a skittish dog that bolted at sudden noises—and sometimes at things no one else heard. One day he reacted to some unknown thing, ran out the mysteriously opened front door, and never returned.

There are unexplained displacements of objects left in the kitchen. "Sometimes things get moved from the center of the table, but I'm the only one in the house," said Daley. "I'm sort of absent-minded, sometimes, but there have been several times when I'm very sure I put a dish or a cup in a certain place. I've been home all alone, but it's been moved somewhere else when I see it next."

Michelle Pelland said she "feels something" when entering an upstairs bedroom that she has always inexplicably referred to as "the kid's bedroom." "It's a benevolent spirit," said Pelland. "It knows when somebody is afraid. Then it stays out. My son, Nathan, hears it a lot. He's had the feeling that something was there. But it wasn't a threatening presence." Nathan is 12 years old, the same age as Marion when she was murdered.

When Pelland and Wolf spoke by phone, it was a dark and uncharacteristically stormy mid-December night in Los Angeles. And, purely by chance, it was the 47th anniversary of the week that Marion Parker was kidnapped and murdered. When Wolf described Marion's eventual fate, an eerie thing happened. "I thought you'd like to know that all the lights in this house are going on and off," Pelland gasped over the phone. Daley, sitting nearby, confirmed this.

Pelland and Daley are enrolled in a UCLA program leading to a Ph.D. in special education. "Exactly what is special education?" asked Wolf. There was a long and pregnant pause while Wolf heard Pelland rapidly exhaling. After several seconds she answered.

"It's teaching severely handicapped kids," said Pelland. "And I just made another mental connection. Because you told me that Marion Parker's legs and arms were cut off . . . Oh, my God, the lights are going on and off again," she whispered. "My hair is standing on end."

So was Wolf's.

Alexander Pantages: A well-deserved reputation as a womanizer became the weak link in his chain of theaters. Photo: Courtesy of the Hearst Collection, USC Library.

14

THE RAPE TRIALS OF ALEXANDER PANTAGES (1929)

Few men of wealth have been more fascinated by and less successful at breaking into Hollywood's inner circle than Joseph Kennedy. During the silent film era, the Boston bootlegger turned shipbuilder and banker began investing in a studio—FBO Pictures—and in a theater chain. He remained friends with several movie moguls during most of the Prohibition era by keeping them supplied with scotch and Canadian whiskey, but he wanted more than friendship. He wanted power. By 1929 his holdings, the Orpheum Circuit Theaters, were a distant second to the Pantages empire. If Kennedy could get Pantages, he'd be the most powerful theater owner in the country. That would give him clout with the studio owners, something he craved almost desperately. Kennedy had enough money—or could get it—to buy Pantages. There was only one thing stopping him: Alexander the Great.

Alexander the Great was Alexander Pantages. Born in Athens, he had emigrated as a penniless young man, worked as a shoeshine boy, hawked newspapers, and worked in penny arcades and nickelodeons. In 1902 he struck it moderately rich in the Alaska Gold Rush. Pantages parlayed his pile of nuggets into ownership of a weary and disheveled Seattle theater.

He turned it into a gold mine, for Alex, who could neither read nor write, had a natural flair for showmanship; he knew what people wanted to see. In the beginning, that was vaudeville, but as Edison's motion picture projector became more popular, Pantages added movies to his marquees. By 1929 he had 60 money-making theaters between Mexico and Canada, and the vaudeville players of the Eastern theater circuits knew that the road to stardom lay through bookings at Pantages' theaters. Alex was personally worth more than $30 million, the equivalent, in an era without inflation and income taxes, of more than $600 million in 1980's money. So there was no reason for Alex Pantages to contemplate selling Joe Kennedy anything but a ticket.

By 1929 Pantages was in his late middle years. A man of small stature and feeble physique, he was widely and snidely referred to as the "Great God Pan," not only for his showbiz omniscience but also for his goatlike appetite for an endless stream of oh-so-available stagestruck young women. Alex could have almost any woman he chose; he chose quite a number. Which might have given Joe Kennedy an idea.

Just before four o'clock in the sultry afternoon of August 9, 1929, a *zaftig* young woman ran screaming from the mezzanine of the Pantages theater at 7th and Hill Streets in downtown Los Angeles, ran screaming down the stairs, her red dress in immodest disarray. Screaming loud enough to disturb those in the full house watching a matinee titled *Why Be Good?* She emerged from the theater into the busy street, in full cry: "The Great God Pan! Don't let him get at me!"

Returning from 7th Street with a traffic cop, Eunice Pringle, a well-muscled, limber and athletic 17-year-old Garden Grove high school dropout and desperately aspiring novelty dance act vaudevillian, theatrically pointed at a rumpled and disheveled Pantages as he emerged from his mezzanine office. "There he is, the beast!"

Pantages grasped the situation immediately. "She's trying to frame me," he shouted.

Pringle tearfully asserted that she'd come to see Pantages about booking her dance act, and, taking advantage of the situation, he had torn off her clothes and raped her. She insisted on pressing charges.

Pantages was worried, but not *that* worried. His version of the story was that Pringle had bought a ticket to the matinee, went up to his office unannounced and uninvited, then flung herself upon him, pulling off his suspenders, yanking up his shirt and down his trousers and messing up her own clothing, all the while screaming. She was young and lithe and quite strong; he was a puny, scrawny old man. He tried to get her out of the office, but she clung to the doorknob as though it were a life preserver in a maelstrom. When she finally left the room, she screamed all the way out to the sidewalk. Pantages wasn't sure why Pringle was doing this, but her sharpy agent, Nick Dunaev, had more than once been known to tiptoe the fine line between slick and sleaze.

The newspapers loved the story. The Great God Pan! His Foreign Goatedness Caught Out! Lechery Exposed! An Innocent Defiled! According to the newspapers, Pringle was "the sweetest 17 since Clara Bow," or "a full-blown beauty," depending on whether you chose to believe William Randolph Hearst or Harry Chandler. Either way, Pringle would have her day in court.

Pantages retained the stodgily distinguished firm of Gilbert & Ford to represent him at the preliminary hearing on August 14. The district attorney, Buron Fitts, took personal charge of the prosecution. It was an ill omen for Pantages.

Pringle appeared in court wearing a long pigtail with a bow at the back, a blue dress with a Dutch collar and cuffs, black stockings, black flat "Mary Jane" shoes, black gloves and carrying a little black purse. She could have satisfied a Central Casting call for a convent novitiate. Looking at her, no one could see the lithe and lush woman's body concealed by her clothing. She looked as though she were barely 12 or 13.

Then, said Pringle, Pantages put his arm around her, told her she was wonderful, that he wanted her for his sweetheart, that he hated his wife and would give Pringle anything if she would be his sweetheart. But, insisted the demure young woman on the witness stand—all the while sobbing into an already dripping handkerchief—she told him she had no interest in being his sweetheart, that all she wanted was business, that she wanted Pantages to book her act. And then "He seemed to go crazy," said Pringle. "He seized me very tightly, drawing me to my feet . . . he said again he was crazy about me, and he started trying to kiss me . . . And I said, 'Please be a gentleman.'"

Under oath she told a tale of innocence and lechery. She had been trying to get Pantages to book her dance act, she said, since about the first week in May. Pantages kept putting her off, kept telling her to come back in another week or two. When she returned on the afternoon of August 9, Pantages invited her to his private office. It was a warm day; she took off her jacket and he took off his. Then he held her hand, told her it was beautiful, that he had admired her dancing and singing very much, that he intended to book her act.

But, said Pringle, Pantages was no gentleman. He kissed her chin, he kissed her throat. She started to scream. He clapped his right hand over her mouth, still holding her tightly by the waist with his left arm. He kissed her "madly." He smothered her with kisses. He bit her breast. He bit her shoulder. He pulled her onto the floor. He held her down with his chest atop hers. His right hand still covering Pringle's mouth, he used his left to pull up her dress and then pull down her underclothes. He forced her legs apart, still using his left hand. Then he pulled his own trousers down.

"Then what happened?" asked District Attorney Fitts.

"I don't know, I fainted," gasped Pringle on the stand.

It was great theater. Jury and courtroom were spellbound.

On the stand in his own defense, Pantages told his story of a frameup. He had declined to book Pringle's act on previous occasions, he said, because it was "too suggestive." As for attacking an underage girl in his own office in the middle of a matinee performance in the heart of downtown, that was just silly. There was no shortage of willing young women and no less likely place for him to attempt seduction.

Gilbert & Ford had retained, expressly and solely for the purpose of cross-examination, a young but promising trial attorney who had served an impressive apprenticeship under the great Earl Rogers. The lawyer's name was Jerry Giesler.

It was obvious from the faces of the jury that they sympathized with Pringle. Pantages, on the other hand, spoke broken English with a thick accent and displayed European airs that many Americans found pretentious. Giesler could see the mountain he had to climb.

He started by establishing that Pringle could cry on cue. When she told her story to the district attorney, it was punctuated by sobs. She was dry-eyed in her replies to Giesler's questions covering the same ground, though her answers were virtually verbatim. Which led him to ask, "Did your studies include a course in memory training?" Pringle admitted that they had. "Were you taught to express your emotions dramatically?" Her answer was the same. Giesler hoped the jury would understand the wide range of roles Pringle was capable of playing.

Giesler's own performance was amazing. In an attempt to inject a little levity into the emotionally charged atmosphere of the courtroom, he asked the chief deputy district attorney to play the role of Pringle while he himself played Pantages, to demonstrate the way in which Pringle alleged Pantages held her at the onset of the assault. So the chief deputy allowed Giesler to clap his right hand over his mouth while the two men stood in front of the witness box. Maintaining this position, Giesler fired questions at Pringle. The deputy tried to object to his line of questioning, but his utterances came as muffled grunts and gurgles through Giesler's hand. Finally the judge intervened to point out that the deputy was trying to speak. Giesler removed his hand.

"I was merely trying to object," said the deputy prosecutor. "I *still* want to object."

The first major breakthrough came with Giesler's demand that Pringle come to court dressed as she had on the day of the alleged rape. The prosecution fought this, but the judge finally granted the request. Pringle was ordered to duplicate the clothing, makeup and hair style she had on the day she said Pantages had attacked her.

What a difference a day made. Pringle appeared in a clinging, lowcut, relentlessly provocative red dress with full makeup and an adult hairstyle. As she climbed to the witness stand, her backside moved in primal rhythm. She was no longer a virginal little girl, but a sexy young woman who looked old enough to vote—old enough for many mature activities. But it was a Pyrrhic victory. Now the jury could see why a rich old goat might have been so inflamed as to risk attacking her.

In an effort to show that Pringle was not only voluptuous but about as pure as day-old New York snow, Giesler attempted to introduce testimony suggesting she'd been living with her agent, the dancer Nick Dunaev, in what he described as "intimate" circumstances. He intended to show that since the charge was forcible rape, if Pringle had previously had sexual relations with other men—he called it "unchaste behavior"—her testimony that Pantages had used "force and violence" in his attempt to have sex with her could be discounted. But the judge would not allow such testimony. It was irrelevant to the case, he ruled.

The jury wasted little time in coming to a verdict: guilty of forcible rape. The judge gave Pantages 50 years in San Quentin.

Giesler refused to quit. While Pantages remained free on bond, he prepared an appeal. It ran to three volumes and 1,200 pages, the most comprehensive treatise on the subject of statutory rape ever compiled, with hundreds of citations and an index of 26 typeset pages. The Pantages appeal contained several novel and original elements that soon became precedents for rape cases throughout the United States, precedents that stood virtually unchallenged for nearly 50 years and are even now only partially modified.

Up until the time of the Pantages case, judges prohibited any information about the sexual history of minors; it was held that a minor's morals were irrelevant since she could not legally give sexual consent. The Pantages brief explored the notion that when the charge is forcible rape, defendants are entitled to introduce evidence about the alleged rape victim's prior sexual activity, even if she were younger than the legal age of consent. Giesler also asserted that if the woman *had* participated willingly in sexual activity, the jury could decide that this discredited her claim that the defendant used force, and if

Eunice Pringle: A willing tool for the film colony's bootlegger.
Photo: Courtesy UCLA Library Special Collections.

Giesler also asked for reversal because of prejudicial misconduct on the part of the prosecution. The prosecutor had told the jury that the defense had acted in bad faith "by not producing promised evidence that Miss Pringle was lacking in virtue." Giesler had repeatedly tried to introduce exactly that kind of evidence; each time, the prosecutor objected and the judge upheld the objection.

Finally, the brief summarized why Pringle's testimony should have been hard to believe:

> Here was a young woman who on that day weighed in the neighborhood of 112 to 115 lbs., being between 5'2 1/2" and 5'3" in height, who had since she was eleven years of age and up to the day in question . . . been studying and practicing the art of dancing . . . including . . . toe and full-split dancing, and . . . acrobatic dancing, involving back flips, turns, side and back bends, which . . . she practiced several times weekly . . . to keep herself in condition for her career—and whose story of what occurred in the little room indicated that during the greater portion of the time both her arms and legs were free, and who testified affirmatively that she was kicking all of the time to the best of her ability and doing everything she could with her hands, feet, and legs to prevent the accomplishment of the act; and still . . . the defendant did not have a mark or a scratch of any character or kind upon him after the act is alleged to have been consummated.

Pantages, as Giesler pointed out, was an elderly man who weighed 128 pounds and was only a few inches taller than Pringle. How could he have kept his right hand on the mouth of a young, agile and exceptionally strong woman almost his size, and, using only his left hand, removed her clothing and forced her to submit? And why would he have done so in his own building, in broad daylight, near one of the busiest streets in the city? The California Court of Appeals couldn't figure it out either. They granted Pantages a new trial, which began in April 1931.

In the new trial, Giesler's cross-examinations sought to show that Pringle had more than a platonic relationship with Nicholas Dunaev, the Russian-born, 40-year-old dancer-turned-agent. Giesler's associate, Jake Ehrlich, brought in as witness the elderly widow who managed Moonbeam Glen Bungalow Court, where Pringle and Dunaev lived for some months before the alleged rape.

The elderly landlady had initially been a reluctant witness, persuaded by the Hearst newspapers, her minister's guidance and her own evangelical faith in the Bible that Pantages was a demon and a depraved beast. But Ehrlich used his vast powers of recall to quote endless passages of scripture. Ultimately he convinced the old woman where her duty lay. On the witness stand she destroyed Pringle's credibility when she testified that for months Pringle and Dunaev had lived together as man and wife. Eunice Pringle was a sexual sophisticate, not a virginal child.

Pantages was acquitted. The question of why a 17-year-old dancer had sought to destroy him went unanswered until Pringle lay on her deathbed. Then she confessed: It had all been Joe Kennedy's idea. He wanted to destroy Pantages and he paid Nick and her to do it, promising that when he controlled the Pantages theaters, she would be his star performer.

Kennedy never got his hands on Pantages, never got the power he wanted in Hollywood. But he lived to see his second son, John, become President of the United States in 1960.

Jerry Giesler became the most famous attorney in Los Angeles, and for decades was known as "attorney to the stars." In his memoirs, *The Jerry Giesler Story*, he attributed his rise to prominence to winning the Pantages case.

LOCATIONS:

Thomas Brothers map reference: Page A at 4C
The Beaux-Arts building that once housed the flagship of Alexander Pantages' theater empire is at 607 South Hill, on the southwest corner of 7th and Hill. It's a magnificent structure, somewhat gone to seed as the Los Angeles Jewelry Mart, a collection of wholesale and retail jewelry establishments. Take the Harbor Freeway north to Sixth, and Sixth east to Hill. Turn right to 7th.

Thomas Brothers map reference: Page A at 3C
Jerry Giesler's offices were in the Chester Williams Building at 215 W. Fifth Street, between Broadway and Hill Street. From the Jewelry Mart, go north on Hill to Fifth. The structure remains much as it was in Giesler's era.

Thomas Brothers map reference: Page A at 2C
Giesler's home for many years was at 545 South Figueroa, near the northwest corner of Sixth Street. The residence was torn down in the early 1960s and is now an office building. From Fifth and Hill, go west on Fifth to Figueroa, then turn right to the end of the block.

Winnie Ruth Judd: A jealous rage, a double murder, and a long life spent escaping from jails. Photo: AP/Wide World.

15

WINNIE'S BLOODY TRUNKS (1931)

She was five-feet-two, with big heart-rending eyes of blue. Winnie Ruth Judd was 25. She had a slender but curvaceous figure, a disarming smile and hair the color of burnt copper. She grew up in an affluent Illinois family, then came to California to study nursing. She married Dr. William Judd, respected Santa Monica physician. The she came down with tuberculosis. She was sent to live in the dry air of Phoenix, where she found work in a medical clinic.

And on the night of October 16, 1931, she shot and killed her best friends, former roommates Helwig Samuelson, 23, and Agnes Ann LeRoi, 30, at their home. Shot them with her little black-handled revolver. She shot them because these two very attractive women seemed to care more about each other than they did about Winnie, and because they had been partying with men whom Winnie considered her own property. After shooting them, she shot herself in the left hand, so she could claim self-defense. It was a crazy thing to do, but entirely in character. Because it seemed that Winnie Ruth Judd was insane.

Crazy but not stupid. She was stuck with two dead bodies lying on the floor of a Phoenix bungalow. So she called the clinic where she and LeRoi worked, saying they were both indisposed. She rolled the bodies into a big trunk. She telephoned for a baggage transfer man to haul the trunk down to the Southern Pacific station. She was going back to Los Angeles, and she'd just take those bodies with her on the *Golden State Limited*.

The porter, a man named H.N. Grimm, told her that the trunk was much too heavy to go as personal baggage on the train. "What the Sam Hill" was in it, he demanded, "a body?" Winnie told him it held her husband's medical books. The porter Grimm suggested she repack the books into smaller trunks, and then they could go as personal baggage without additional charges.

Winnie agreed and hired Grimm to haul the big trunk to her own apartment. She left LeRoi in the big trunk, but Samuelson was a problem. There just wasn't room in the smaller trunk. So Winnie got a surgical saw and a butcher knife. She hacked Samuelson's body into pieces, stuffed the pieces into a steamer trunk and a large suitcase. She filled in the empty spaces with her victim's personal papers and photos, including letters she herself had written. Then she called Grimm again to haul all three down to the railhead. Winnie checked her baggage and headed home.

At Los Angeles' Union Station she checked her bags and took a taxi to the political science building at the University of Southern California. She waited outside for her brother, Burton J. McKinnell, 26, a law student. She needed his help with her trunks at the train station. "You must help me get them. We must take them to the beach and throw them in the ocean," said Winnie.

Burt was mystified, more so because of the bandage on Winnie's hand. But, being her big brother, he obligingly drove Winnie to the station in his roadster. He went arm-in-arm with her to the baggage counter to retrieve her trunks. Burton hadn't a clue what was in the trunks, of course, and there was nothing in Winnie's face to arouse suspicion, so it should have been a piece of cake. Except for the deer poachers.

The poachers shot deer in Arizona and smuggled the venison into California. Some boldly sent the carcasses in steamer trunks, like the one that Winnie had checked. The one that smelled a little ripe. The one from which seeped a dark and viscous fluid. So the baggage clerk, who had been warned to look out for smuggled venison, was on his guard. A pretty young woman and a red-headed collegian in cords and sweater turned up to claim that smelly trunk. But not so fast, said Andrew Anderson, the Southern Pacific clerk. He'd have to look inside that trunk before he could turn it over to them.

But Winnie wasn't prepared for that. She told Anderson that her husband had the keys. She'd just go and get them and she'd be right back. All Anderson's mental alarms were ringing. He followed the couple out to their car and made careful note of the license number. Then he called the police.

Detective Frank Ryan arrived and assured Anderson it was venison. You could tell by the smell. His partner, Paul Stevens, got a crowbar. Ryan broke the lock, opened the oozing trunk. A crowd had gathered and some of the people got sick when they saw what was in that trunk.

Police traced the license number to brother Burt. They went to his Beverly Glen home, but Burt wasn't around. They found him at the Santa Monica home of his brother-in-law, the perplexed Dr. Judd. The doctor was shocked to learn why the police were seeking his wife. Burt already knew, at least some of it. While driving away from the station Winnie admitted there were bodies in the trunks. Who? Why? asked Burt. "The less you know about it the better off you are," said Winnie. She got out of the car at Sixth and Broadway, begged a few dollars from Burt, and vanished into the crowd.

Police launched a search. The tabloids of old Los Angeles, in particular *The Express*, had a field day. Two-inch-high headlines screamed about the "Velvet Tigress" and "The Wolf Woman." But Winnie had dropped from sight. No one had seen her since she got out of the car at Sixth and Broadway. Police questioned cab drivers, trolleymen, train ticketers. None had seen Winnie Ruth Judd. She had vanished.

Vanished by *walking* 20 miles to a disused building on the hilly grounds of the La Vina Sanitarium in the foothills above Altadena. Winnie had once been a patient there. She hid in the building for three days, sneaking into the kitchen at night for food. She hid until the infected gunshot wound in her hand began to throb unmercifully. It was then that she saw an ad in the newspaper taken by her husband, begging to give herself up.

Winnie called her husband's attorney, Richard Cantillon. Cantillon told her to phone another attorney, Patrick Cooney, the following day. When she did, Cantillon and Dr. Judd were there as well. Judd argued and pleaded and finally he convinced Winnie to surrender.

Winnie met her husband in the lobby of the Biltmore Theater, and they walked to Alvarez & Moore, Undertakers, at Court and Olive Streets. Dr. Judd treated Winnie's hand. Downstairs there were coffins, candles and corpses. When police arrived to arrest her, Winnie was lying in a bed, looking ill and worn.

Winnie Ruth Judd was extradited to Arizona, tried for murder, and convicted. She was sentenced to hang. On death row her case was reviewed. Psychiatrists said she was insane. Insanely jealous. At her sanity trial her mother testified to a long streak of family insanity, stretching back for generations, and Winnie obligingly performed the role in court, rending her clothes, tearing at her hair, staring into space and muttering in response to unseen voices. Winnie was spared the gallows but sentenced to lifetime confinement in the Arizona State Mental Hospital.

Confinement, however, didn't suit her, and she managed to escape seven times, often walking incredible distances across wilderness. Recaptured after a 1952 jaunt, she testified before a grand jury on hospital conditions. Doctors searched her afterward and found a razor blade under her tongue and a hospital door key in her hair. Winnie's last escape was in 1962. She made her way back to California and started a new life as a live-in housekeeper for John and Ethel Blemer, in Concord, where she earned spare money by babysitting neighbors' children.

Arrested in 1969, she was held for extradition and defended by no less than Melvin "King of Torts" Belli, who offered to take her into his own home as a housekeeper. Governor Ronald Reagan sent her back to Arizona. She was paroled in 1971, with the condition that she must live in California. She returned to a position in the Blemer home.

In 1983, after the death of Ethel Blemer, Winnie sued for part of her estate on the grounds that since her parole she had been kept by the family "as an indentured servant." After Ethel's death she was "thrown out" of the house, along with her menagerie of dogs, cats and chickens. After a protracted legal struggle, she was awarded $225,000 in cash plus $1,250 a month for the rest of her life.

LOCATIONS:

Thomas Brothers map reference: Page 40 at F4

From Montana Avenue in Santa Monica, turn south onto 17th Street. The house in which Winnie Ruth Judd resided with her husband before leaving for Arizona was at 823 17th St. The lot is now the site of a condominium complex styled in natural wood and brick.

Thomas Brothers map reference: Page 44 at E2

Union Station is little changed from the day when Winnie Ruth Judd went to pick up her bloody trunks. Take the Hollywood Freeway (U.S. 101) south to downtown Los Angeles and exit at Spring or Broadway. Turn left across the freeway to Sunset, then right to Alameda. The station is on Alameda and Sunset.

David Clark: He shot the city's top crime boss—and got thousands of votes for judge while waiting to stand trial. Photo: Courtesy UCLA Library Special Collections.

16

JUSTIFIABLE HOMICIDE BY DAVID CLARK (1931)

For years, Charles Crawford had been linked in the newspapers with various politicians and organized crime figures. Now, all of a sudden, Crawford had found the Lord. In the dog days of the summer of 1930, the Los Angeles newspapers twittered about Crawford dropping his diamond ring, valued at about $3,500, into the collection plate at St. Paul's Presbyterian Church. A few weeks later, Crawford was publicly baptized at St. Paul's. This event made the front pages of every newspaper in the city. Crawford made page one again after the Reverend R.P. Shuler, one of the city's leading Presbyterian ministers, denounced Reverend Gustav Briegleb, pastor of St. Paul's, for accepting Crawford's donation of $25,000 for the construction of a new parish house.

All this consternation over a reformed sinner was news because for years it was widely assumed that Crawford brokered the biggest backroom deals between corrupt Los Angeles politicos, crooked police, and the high chieftains of organized crime. Before Prohibition he was a saloonkeeper and afterward his ostensible profession was realtor and insurance broker. But in reality for many years he was the unseen right arm of Mayor Cryer, and played covert kingmaker to his successors.

Crawford was careful; he had been arrested only twice. In 1927, he was accused of conspiracy to frame a councilman on a morals charge. Charged as a co-conspirator was Albert Marco, Southern California's reigning vice lord. Midway through the trial, the judge abruptly ruled that there was insufficient evidence, and all charges were dropped.

In 1929 Crawford was indicted on bribery charges in connection with the Julian Pete* oil stock swindle, along with S.C. Lewis, former president of Julian Pete, and Jack Friedlander, former state corporations commissioner. When the principal witnesses against all three men refused to testify unless

115

given immunity from other related charges pending against them, District Attorney Asa Keyes refused. After two trials and two hung juries, the case was dismissed.

Crawford had one other brush with the law, but on that occasion he was the witness who sent reporter Morris Lavine to jail on extortion charges.** Lavine, acting as collection agent for a trio of organized crime figures, was left holding the bag after he accepted $75,000 from Crawford. In court Crawford swore the money was paid in exchange for Lavine's silence about *alleged* Crawford improprieties in the Julian Pete affair. But whatever the mobsters *thought* they had on Crawford was never revealed.

On Wednesday, May 20, 1931, Crawford was shot to death in his Sunset Boulevard office by former Deputy District Attorney David Clark, now a candidate for municipal judge. The story dominated the front page for months.

Clark, 33, was a strapping six-footer with a neat mustache and the physique of a football player, a man whose erect carriage was a tipoff to his Naval Academy training. He dressed very well, in the style of the day, usually sporting an Oxford suit and a straw boater. Clark earned a law degree at USC, and for eight years worked in the district attorney's office.

Clark was zealous in his pursuit of certain kinds of criminals. When he became a deputy district attorney, he personally prosecuted Albert Marco, the city's "vice overlord," on assault and attempted murder charges. Marco, a pimp and extortionist, was Crawford's man. In the 1920s, Boss Crawford brought him down from Seattle to run his 65 bordellos, while Crawford paid police to protect them. But during a drunken brawl in the Ship Cafe, a Venice speakeasy, Marco shot and seriously wounded another patron, Dominic Conterno. Clark went after Marco with a vengeance. The first trial ended in a hung jury; in the second Marco was convicted, sentenced to a term in San Quentin, and later deported to his native Sicily.

Far from being lauded for his efforts, Clark was transferred to the district attorney's corporate securities staff, where he had little to do with organized crime, and little chance to disturb the cozy relationship between organized crime and city law enforcement. In 1931 Clark resigned, announcing his intentions to go into private practice. But his supporters, mostly businessmen in the growing reform movement, soon convinced him to run for municipal judge.

On the morning of Tuesday, May 19, Clark promised his wife he would be home for dinner, climbed into his white Model A Ford roadster and drove to a sporting goods store. There he wrote out a check for $27, and left the store with his purchase, a .38 caliber Colt revolver. The storekeeper had no inkling that the check Clark wrote would bring his account to a balance of minus $96.00. Dave Clark was broke.

When Clark failed to return home that evening, his wife Nancy called Chief of Police Roy Steckel, a good friend of the Clarks, to report that David had disappeared "under mysterious circumstances."

Dressed with his usual elegant style, Clark walked into the bungalow that housed Charles Crawford's Sunset Boulevard office at almost exactly 3:00 on the following afternoon. Crawford came out of his private office at almost exactly the same moment, to greet Clark with an effusive handshake. The two went into Crawford's inner sanctum and closed the door. At 4:00, they were joined by political gadfly Herbert Spencer, former city editor of the defunct *Los Angeles Herald Express* and present editor of a local magazine, the *Critic of Critics*. Behind the closed door, no sound of the meeting was audible to the four people—Crawford's private secretary, a man visiting the secretary, the female stenographer and a real estate agent—working in the office.

At about 4:28, Crawford came out of his office, apparently in a jovial mood, to ask his stenographer about some routine matter. He returned to the inner office after less than a minute.

Two minutes later the silence was shattered by a pair of gunshots sounding in quick succession. The door to Crawford's office opened and Spencer staggered out, clutching his chest and spouting fountains of blood. He made his way unsteadily into the front office and collapsed onto the floor. A few seconds later Clark emerged, buttoning his coat. He went out a side door.

In the rear of the bungalow was a portrait studio, and peering through its open window were the photographer, Roger Fowler, and his assistant, Mildred Rohrback. They had heard the shots and came running. Without pausing, Clark asked, "Where did that man go?" and walked around the corner onto Sunset heading west. Thinking Clark was in pursuit of whoever fired the shots, Fowler and Rohrback trailed him. Still buttoning his coat, Clark quickened his pace. By the time he reached the corner of La Palma he was running.

Inside, Spencer was gurgling his last breath, while Crawford lay on the carpet with a .38 slug in his guts. The secretary called police, who took Boss Crawford several blocks to an emergency room. The bullet had perforated his stomach, shattered both a kidney and his liver. Despite the efforts of surgeons and the prayers of Reverend Briegleb, who came to the hospital almost immediately, Crawford was failing fast. In his final moments, Briegleb asked Crawford, "Who did it?" "Dave . . . ," gasped Crawford with his final breath, and died.

An all-points bulletin was issued by teletype and to the LAPD's new, radio-equipped squad cars. Two police lieutenants staked out Clark's home. But Clark eluded the police until 10:30 the following evening, when he telephoned District Attorney Buron Fitts. He would turn himself in shortly, said Clark. Half an hour later, still nattily attired but looking very tired and careworn, Clark surrendered to police in the parking lot of the Hall of Justice in downtown Los Angeles.

With remarkable forethought, Spencer had run a special box in the issue of *Critic of Critics* that appeared just days before the shooting. "If any member of the staff of this publication is molested in any way, it will be the signal for the opening by the authorities—and a certain daily newspaper—of a well-filled safe deposit box now reposing in the vaults of a certain bank. In that bank, among other things, are described the names, addresses, haunts and habits of all those who would be interested in closing the mouth of the editor." But the contents of this box, if it ever existed, were never made public.

Despite intense questioning, Clark refused to say what had happened in Crawford's office, or to discuss his defense strategy. Nevertheless, while still in jail, he got more than 60,000 votes for judge in the June election. He was able to raise $100,000 in bail. So popular was Clark with the public that when his first trial—for killing Spencer—opened on August 3, his friends managed to arrange for Judge Stanley Murray of Madera County, a man presumably not beholden to anyone in Los Angeles, to serve as magistrate.

On the stand, Clark insisted that both killings were in self-defense. Spencer was angry at Clark, said the defendant, because in his campaign for municipal judge Clark had repeatedly hammered away at the power that those responsible for gambling and prostitution had over city government. Spencer wanted him to back off. On May 18, he telephoned Clark.

"Dave, one of these nights, if you don't stop this, you will drive home into your driveway, but you won't get out of your machine," said Spencer.

Clark refused to back off. Spencer conveyed more threats. Later that day, Crawford called Clark's office to offer his services as a peacemaker, and Clark agreed to a meeting at Clark's office.

But Clark knew that both Spencer and Crawford, at least by reputation, always went armed. Fearing a trap, he bought a pistol, even though his bank account was overdrawn. At the arranged meeting of the three men, instead of acting as a peacemaker, Boss Crawford made Clark an offer: help him to frame Chief of Police Steckel on a morals charge and his victory in the coming election would be assured.

"You dirty skunk," said Clark. "You've joined the church and put a diamond ring in the collection basket. Now you want to frame our friend."

Crawford was livid. "No S.O.B. can talk to me that way," he growled, reaching for his gun. But Clark was quicker. His first shot, at point-blank range, went into Crawford's stomach. "Get him, Herb," said Crawford, as he staggered backward.

Clark whirled around to find Spencer reaching beneath his coat for a gun. Clark shot him as well, then put the gun away and followed the dying Spencer out of the door.

The state's star witness was the photographer's assistant, Mildred Rohrback, who testified that upon entering Crawford's office after the shooting, she saw Crawford lying on the floor, clutching a cigar in his hand, which she later saw a policeman remove. If Crawford *had* a cigar in his hand, he couldn't have also held a gun, and so Clark had lied. But who was telling the truth?

Clark's attorneys dug up an interesting fact about Rohrback. After the shooting, she had secretly married Ed Dudley, an investigator in the district attorney's office. All but one of the jurors found Rohrback less credible than

Clark. The trial ended in a hung jury. After a second trial, Clark was acquitted of killing Spencer. The second charge, killing Crawford, was dropped.

LOCATIONS:

Thomas Brothers map reference: Page 34 at B3
Crawford and Spencer were shot to death at 6665 Sunset Boulevard. Exit the Hollywood Freeway (U.S. 101) at Highland, go south to Sunset, turn left and proceed just past the first street, La Palma. On the left, in the two-story adobe bungalow that once housed Boss Crawford's real estate office and a portrait studio, is Our Lady Gift Shop, which sells religious artifacts, chiefly of the Roman Catholic variety, to tourists and pilgrims visiting the huge Spanish Mission-style church next door, Crossroads of the World.

Thomas Brothers map reference: Page 34 at B6
David Clark lived at 162 South Detroit Street. From Sunset and Highland, go west on Sunset to La Brea, then south to Beverly Boulevard and west to the first street and south on Detroit to the middle of the second block. In Clark's time the building was a grand single-family residence; it remains an attractive apartment building of dun stucco with wrought iron balconies and a red tile roof.

Thomas Brothers map reference: Page 43 at D6
St. Paul's Presbyterian Church was at 2232 West Jefferson. It's long gone; the location is now a retail store. Exit the Santa Monica Freeway at Arlington, go south to Jefferson and east to 2232.

*See Chapter 12, *Motley Flint and the Julian Pete Scandal (1927)*.

** See Chapter 9, *On the Trail of the Tiger Woman: Clara Phillips (1922)*.

Paul Bern: Why did he send his wife home to mother?
Photo: Marc Wannamaker Bison Archives. (1932)

17

THE ENIGMATIC DEATH OF PAUL BERN (1932)

He was not without some experience at suicide. He'd tried it once before, after his infatuation for the darkly beautiful Barbara LaMarr had come to naught, when Barbara died before they could marry.

But this time Paul Bern—originally Paul Levy—would pull it off. He would disrobe, he would perfume his 43-year-old but boyish little body with Mitsuoko, the favorite fragrance of his 21-year-old sex-goddess bride. He would stand before a full-length mirror, put one of two .38 revolvers he had obtained to his head. And he would pull the trigger. The bullet passed through his renowned and much-admired brain and buried itself in the wall.

The note police read was addressed to his wife of two months, Jean Harlow:

> *Dearest dear: Unfortunately this is the only way to make good the frightful wrong I have done you, and to wipe out my abject humiliation. I love you.*

There was a postscript:

> *You understand that last night was only a comedy.*

That's the "official" version of Bern's death. Almost certainly not a complete account, it might well be as creative a scenario as any Hollywood scriptwriter has ever invented.

Paul Bern was one of Hollywood's authentic geniuses. Born in Germany in 1889, he emigrated with his family to New York when he was nine years old. Self-educated, he worked as an actor, became a stage manager, then a press agent. He came to Hollywood during the era of silent films, working as a film cutter and as a script editor before directing his first film. In 1926, the year before the first talkies appeared, he became an MGM supervisor. Bern was soon spotted by the legendary Irving Thalberg, who recognized his rare talent for knowing what would work on the screen. Moreover, Bern was a sensitive man, compassionate and intellectually superior to most of the Hollywood hierarchy. Thalberg made Bern his general assistant.

And Bern didn't let him down. It was he who persuaded Howard Hughes to sell MGM the contract of a rising star, Jean Harlow. It was Bern who pressed the studio bosses into giving her the starring role in *The Red Headed Woman*, though the moguls had originally created the film as a vehicle for Clara Bow.

Though he was one of Hollywood's important men in an era of supreme flamboyance—decadence, some might say—Bern stood mostly on the sidelines. He preferred a good book or a new script to a wild party. He chose to live in a house so remote that few could find it unaided.

So it must have been a surprise to gossip columnists when, in the spring of 1932, Bern was seen at a succession of the very best Hollywood restaurants and the most desirable social events. And a shock that his date was always Jean Harlow. The real stunner came when the couple was wed on July 2, 1932, the bride in a white, off-the-shelf dress and fringed shawl.

The couple delayed their honeymoon; both were busy with heavy shooting schedules. Rumors quickly blossomed. If Bern looked a bit haggard, gossips speculated that he'd been fighting with his wife. Bern shrugged off questions. Bern's body was discovered by his butler on Labor Day, September 5, 1932. A servant's first duty is to his master's interests. Even in death, the butler knew what those interests were and who to call first. In minutes Irving Thalberg and Louis B. Mayer, head of MGM, were separately on their way to the Bern house in Benedict Canyon. Mayer arrived first.

About two hours later, the police were called. What may have happened at the suicide scene in this interval will never be known. In one widely reported version Mayer pocketed the suicide note, but then MGM's head publicist persuaded him to turn it over to police.

But others suspect the "suicide" note was a total fabrication, the result of a scenario conference held over the dead body of Paul Bern. The handwriting wasn't Bern's, say those who suspected foul play, and the handwriting, most curiously, was never subjected to police graphanalysis. Ben Hecht wrote, in 1960, that studio heads forged the note to protect MGM's image, because Bern had been murdered by a mysterious "other woman," a woman he'd been seeing secretly, and that an assignation with this mystery woman was the reason Bern had sent his wife off to her mother's home the evening he died. As Hecht opined, the moguls sought to protect their investment in Jean Harlow. Her box-office appeal rested on her fabled sexuality. Perhaps her image might have been tarnished, were it disclosed that her husband of two months had been secretly carrying on with another woman.

In fact, there were hints of a mysterious female visitor at the Bern house the night he died. A woman who made some effort to stay out of sight when servants were near and who left behind a wet swimsuit, found beside the swimming pool. And there were other clues: Two empty glasses were found on a poolside table. A Bern servant reported hearing an unfamiliar woman's voice, a voice that was heard in a single scream later that night. Another servant reported seeing broken glass and what he insisted was a tiny puddle of blood next to a poolside chair Bern favored.

The police, though informed of these facts—all were disclosed at the coroner's inquest—evidently did nothing to learn what they might mean, or who they might lead to. Nor was Mrs. Paul Bern, the distraught and excitable Jean Harlow, ever called to testify, a glaring omission that was in violation of established policies. Many people speculated that someone high in the district attorney's office had been paid to sit on his hands and that the money had come from MGM.

The truth is there *was* another woman in Bern's life, another gorgeous blonde. And she died under equally mysterious circumstances at 4:45 a.m. the day after Bern's body was found. She was Dorothy Millette. For years she called herself "Mrs. Paul Bern" while living with Bern in his pre-Hollywood years. Less than 48 hours after his death, she folded her coat over the steel railing, stepped out of her shoes and jumped from the deck of the *Delta King*, a Sacramento River steamer. Her body was discovered by fishermen, two weeks later.

About the time Bern first came to Hollywood, he broke off his romance with Millette, who suffered from amnesia. She subsequently spent years confined to mental institutions. But Bern continued to support her financially until the day he died. His secretaries, most principal business associates and close friends—probably including Harlow—all knew of his attachment to Millette. And most Harlow biographers insist she and Millette met secretly a few weeks before she married Bern.

It is possible that Millette, last seen alive on the night of September 4, could have killed Bern though it would have been very difficult. It would have required her leaving the Bern house in remote Benedict Canyon then getting to Union Station in time to catch the late (10:00 p.m.) train to San Francisco, which arrived there about 10 hours later. She would then have had enough time to return to her hotel, pack a bag, then catch the steamer from which she leapt to her death.

But how could she have gotten to Union Station in time to catch the last train? She might have called a taxi to pick her up. But there is no record of any such call that night.

Could she have gone afoot, several miles over dark and twisting canyon roads to a place where she could have called a taxi? No taxi drivers reported remembering anything like that within walking distance of the Bern home. Or perhaps Millette hired a car. Some neighbors reported seeing a chauffeur-driven limousine on the street toward early evening. A heavily veiled woman was seen getting out of it. But no one at the Bern residence could—or would—recall hearing someone arrive, or depart.

Maybe Millette, if she was at Paul Bern's home, walked some distance to where she had parked such a car, then drove away. However, there is no record of such a suspicious car rental transaction on that night.

But neither is there any record that police ever tried to find any evidence of this sort.

It is difficult to come up with a plausible rational motive for Dorothy Millette killing Paul Bern and then taking her own life, especially in light of what she would have had to accomplish to escape undetected. Except that she had had a long love relationship with Bern, who had never married before. And Bern dead could not consort with any woman's ultimate rival, a sexy, 21-year-old film queen. But Bern alive was her only source of financial support. Perhaps looking for a rational motive is a mistake. People don't always behave rationally about emotional matters. And Dorothy Millette had a tortured history of irrational behavior.

LOCATION:
Thomas Brothers map reference: Page 32 at F2
Bern died at 9820 Easton Drive. From Sunset Boulevard, take Benedict Canyon north about three miles. Easton Drive is on the right side, about 100 yards past Westwanda. The house is on the right side of this very narrow street, about 2/10 of a mile up. It's a two-story building that sits against a wooded hillside and hides behind high fences and abundant foliage.

Thelma Todd: What caused the bruises inside her throat?
Photo: Marc Wannamaker Bison Archives.

18

MYSTERIOUS VOICES, UNEXAMINED CLUES: THELMA TODD'S DEATH (1935)

She was billed as "The Ice Cream Blonde." Thelma Todd played opposite the Marx Brothers in *Horsefeathers* and in 69 other films between 1926 and 1935—an amazing number for such a span of time, and an amazing tribute to her box-office appeal. But Thelma was amazingly talented. And amazingly beautiful. So beautiful that a jaded Hollywood film mogul offered her a movie job on the strength of a single photograph. She was hilariously funny, on the screen and off, but she was also capable of serious dramatic roles. On the screen, Thelma *looked* sexy; in person she was even more so. She didn't mind sharing her charms with the right partner for a night, for a few nights, for as long as she was amused. And Thelma Todd was often amused.

Her father was a leading Massachusetts politician, and Thelma grew up in an affluent and loving household in Lawrence, Massachusetts. She earned a degree in education, and began teaching sixth graders. She supplemented her modest teaching salary with a few modeling jobs after she entered a beauty pageant and was named Miss Massachusetts. A family friend sent her photo to Paramount producer Jesse Lasky. Lasky sent her to a studio acting school in Astoria, New York, where she studied for six months.

She made her screen debut in 1926 in a silent film with 15 classmates. *Fascinating Youth* launched her—and classmate Buddy Rogers—on an escalator to fame. She had a wonderfully throaty voice, which helped her make a swift transition to the new talkies that audiences demanded after the success of Al Jolson's 1927 hit, *The Jazz Singer*.

By 1935 she was one of filmdom's favorites, starring with Buster Keaton, Laurel and Hardy, ZaSu Pitts, Gary Cooper, Joe E. Brown and the brothers Marx. But looking down the road she saw it couldn't last forever. She put her money into bonds and real estate and in 1933 she took top billing and a half interest in a swank new Palisades roadhouse, "Thelma Todd's Roadside Rest," which soon became popular with the rich and with the beachgoing film colony.

Her business partner, director and producer Roland West, 51, was married to actress Jewel Carmen. But West was soon sleeping with Thelma, on and off. Thelma had more than one lover both before and after her 1934 divorce from her only husband, talent agent Pasquale "Pat" DiCiccio. While both Todd and West had other homes, they usually preferred to share a spacious apartment above the roadhouse and parked their cars in a large garage with a loft above it. This was attached to a bungalow, and the whole complex was owned by West. The only access *from the coast road* to the garage and bungalow atop the Palisades was a flight of 270 stairs cut into the steep cliff behind the restaurant.

The evening of Saturday, December 14, 1935, was special for Thelma. She was guest of honor at the Trocadero, one of Hollywood's most celebrated nightspots. Her host was the distinguished British comedian, Stanley Lupino, who had earlier worked with Todd in London. With Lupino were his wife and his actress daughter, Ida. Sid Grauman was also present.

It was a small dinner by Hollywood standards, about a dozen people, but it was not without drama. At the last minute another guest had been added: Pat DiCiccio, who wangled an invitation after a chance meeting with Ida Lupino. He said he was still friendly with Todd, so Ida invited him to the party and set a place for him next to Todd.

Thelma arrived alone. DiCiccio did not. He had *two* companions, the lovely actress Margaret Lindsay and one of her equally attractive starlet friends. Todd dined next to a vacant seat while DiCiccio enjoyed himself at another table. This did not sit well with Todd. She approached DiCiccio's table, told him quite emphatically that she didn't find his stunt amusing. Some guests recalled the ensuing discussion as a "terrific argument."

Several hours later, Thelma's friends escorted her to a chauffeur-driven limousine she had rented for the evening. Before leaving in it, she turned back to her entourage and with a theatrically grand flourish said "Goodbye!" In the limo she told driver Ernest Peters to take her to the Roadside Rest. Very soon afterward she urged Peters to go faster. They were being followed, she said, by gangsters. She was afraid of being kidnapped or murdered. Peters got moving. At speeds up to 70 mph the big car careened westward around the curves of Sunset Boulevard, until the sea and Thelma Todd's restaurant appeared ahead.

It was 2:00 Sunday morning when they pulled up before the roadhouse. Normally, Peters escorted his employer right up to her front door. But this time, despite her earlier worries about gangsters, Thelma told Peters, "That won't be necessary. Go home, Ernest." Peters drove off.

Monday morning, December 16, Todd's maid reported for work, but Thelma was nowhere to be found. She wasn't in her apartment above the Roadside Rest, she wasn't downstairs in the restaurant. The maid looked around for Thelma's new Packard convertible. She thought perhaps she could see it through the partially opened doors of the garage atop the cliff, where it was usually parked. An elderly man named Smith, who kept the books for Roadside Rest, lived in the loft above the garage. The maid thought that Todd might be visiting with the bookkeeper.

At about 10:30 that morning the maid climbed the 270 stairs, entered the garage, turned on the light. There was the new Packard. There was a key in its ignition. And there was Thelma Todd, slumped sideways on the seat, wearing the same outfit she had worn when she left the Trocadero party more than a day earlier. The same mink coat, the same sheer mauve and silver evening gown. The same diamond necklace adorned her throat, the same jeweled rings were on her fingers. But there was blood on her dress, her coat, the car, the garage floor, and on her head and face. Thelma Todd was dead at age 30.

Her demise launched one of the strangest death probes in the history of Los Angeles. Strange because of contradictory clues, because of leads that were never followed up, suspects never questioned, or never questioned seriously. Stranger still because the coroner's jury insisted Thelma Todd died by her own hand, perhaps intentionally. The official cause of death was carbon monoxide poisoning. The official version was that Todd, finding herself locked out of her apartment, had climbed the 270 steps from the street to the garage and had huddled for warmth in the front seat of her Packard, started the engine, and was asphyxiated by the exhaust.

This was a neat and tidy solution to a potentially big problem. Thelma Todd was dead and nothing would bring her back. An official finding of death by her own hand, accidental or otherwise, put an end to speculation about murder. It got Thelma Todd, her studio and the whole film industry off the front pages with a minimum of fuss. The fact was that if Thelma Todd had been murdered, the most obvious suspects were her ex-husband, a film industry talent agent with an Italian name; her lover, a film industry producer and director; her lover's wife, a film actress; or some unidentified mafioso. The studio bosses didn't want to know.

The studio bosses were worried that many of the Americans who paid to see movies wouldn't tolerate yet another Hollywood scandal. They might quit going to the movies for a while. And in the Los Angeles of December 1935, this would be a catastrophe for both the lords of the film industry and for the police and the city's political leaders, who had a long history of accommodating the film industry to the profit of both. Pre-World War II Los Angeles had only one big business, the movies, and just at the time Todd's body was found, noted choreographer and director Busby Berkeley was being tried for the drunk driving murder of three innocent people who were killed very close to Todd's cafe.

Another murder scandal might imperil the profits of the whole industry. A neat and tidy solution was needed. And found.

But if it was neat and tidy, the official version simply could not have been true. If Todd had wanted warmth, why did she use an open car instead of sitting in the unlocked sedan parked right next to it? The Packard's engine had been shut off, but there were over two gallons of gasoline left in the tank. How could that have happened? If Todd was suicidal, as studio publicists leaked to the Hollywood gossip mill, why hadn't she used the closed interior of the sedan, which would have been faster and surer? Why had she personally wrapped about 100 Christmas presents just days earlier? And why had she recently started work on a new film? Why had she confided to Ida Lupino at the Trocadero party that she was in love with a businessman from San Francisco?

And there are more obvious holes in the coroner's theory. If Todd climbed 270 steps, why were her feet unmarked and why didn't her new, delicate dress slippers show scuff marks or other signs of wear from the narrow wooden stairs? Todd's mother insisted that Thelma had a heart condition and would never have attempted to climb those steps. But even if Thelma *had* climbed the stairs, opening the garage doors and starting the Packard's cold engine between 2:00 and 3:00 a.m. would have caused quite a noise. Why didn't old Mr. Smith, the bookkeeper who lived in the loft above, hear anything? Smith read a book until 2:30 a.m., he testified. The garage was being redecorated, and the ceiling plaster had been removed; he was sure he would have heard the engine turning over. But he had heard nothing at all.

The way the police investigation was handled yielded more questions than answers. The coroner fixed the time of death as the small hours of Sunday morning, and insisted the last person to see Thelma Todd alive was her chauffeur, Ernest Peters. But no less than four other people came forward to say that they'd heard or spoken to Thelma in the interval between 2:00 a.m. Sunday and 10:30 a.m. Monday.

There was Jewel Carmen, separated from but still married to Roland West. She knew Thelma Todd very well and told police she saw Todd on Sunday morning, in her highly distinctive Packard convertible at the corner of Hollywood and Vine. A handsome, swarthy, well-dressed man sat beside her. Carmen said she had never seen him before.

Mrs. Wallace Ford heard from Thelma about 4:00 Sunday afternoon. Todd called from a pay phone to say she would indeed be attending Ford's cocktail party that evening. Attending it with a surprise escort. "When you see who's coming with me, you'll drop dead," said Todd to Ford. A pharmacist swore that Todd had made the call from the payphone in his establishment.

And there was a report from a man named Person, a liquor store owner on Figueroa, who told police that Todd had come into his store Sunday evening about 11:00. She was wearing the same gown she'd worn at the Trocadero, but without a hat or coat. Seemingly dazed, she asked him to dial a telephone number on the payphone. Person couldn't remember the prefix, but the last four digits were 7771. Person said she left the shop, joined a handsome man who appeared out of the alley holding her fur coat. She walked across the street with this man. She sat on the steps of a church and talked with him for several minutes, perhaps half an hour, then got up and left.

Not only were there people who saw Thelma Todd alive long after the coroner had her dead, there was also physical evidence that was ignored. An autopsy revealed food in Todd's stomach that had been eaten only a few hours before her body was found. The same autopsy revealed more alcohol in her system—.13 percent—than would have been possible from the four drinks she had consumed at the Trocadero, two before eating dinner and two after. But it wasn't nearly enough to have caused her death or incapacity. Neither did the coroner have an explanation for the blood on Todd's clothing and on the floor, nor for the abrasion on her lip. Note was made of the state of Thelma's clothing, which was in such disarray that it suggested a struggle, but the coroner took no account of this. And while he noted the very odd bruises *inside* Thelma Todd's throat, no attempt was made to explain what might have caused them. One veteran police reporter opined that they were caused by someone shoving a bottle down her throat.

The coroner's attempt to fix the time of death at early Sunday morning was further undermined by the weather on Sunday night. It had been unseasonably cold, and a strong sea breeze blew throughout the night, a breeze which might—or might not—have retarded the decomposition of Todd's body.

The actions of Roland West on the night of December 15 are also mysterious. Sid Grauman called him at the restaurant about "2:00 or 2:30" in the morning. He told West that Todd was leaving soon, would be home in under an hour. West closed up shop, sent the help home, went upstairs to bed. And he bolted from inside the heavy door between the stairwell and the apartment, bolted it so that Todd could not possibly have come in using her own key. If he was expecting her within the hour, why did he lock the door against her? West never answered that question. If she had pounded on the door, wouldn't he have heard her pounding? No, said West, probably not. The wind and surf made so much noise that he couldn't have heard.

West told police that he was awakened by a barking dog at about 3:30, after he had fallen asleep. He said he heard the sound of running water and assumed Todd had entered her room in the apartment. But he must have known that she couldn't have entered with the only door bolted. West said that after the noise stopped he went back to sleep.

The following morning he arose and noted that Todd hadn't arrived. Did he worry? Did he call the police? He did not. He said later he assumed she had gone to sleep at her mother's house. Nor did he take alarm after several phone calls for Thelma came on Sunday and none of her friends could locate her.

But on the morning of Sunday, December 16, neighbors said they heard West in a bitter quarrel with Thelma at his house on the cliff above the restaurant. Questioned about it, West downplayed this disagreement. It hadn't been such a big deal, he implied. But neighbors said they heard West throw Thelma out the front door, and for 10 minutes she had beat on the door with her fists, screaming curses and obscenities.

The police never pressed the matter with West. But Todd's friends recalled that West, as a film director, had an affinity for convoluted murder mysteries. He had directed *Alibi, The Monster* and *The Bat Whispers.* These friends whispered that West had an obsessive interest in "the perfect crime." That he had hired another actress friend to play the role of Thelma Todd in their heard-but-not-seen clifftop shouting match on Sunday morning. That all the while Thelma lay dead in the garage and that West had killed her. And that West's motive was his jealous anger at being thrown over for a new lover, the mysterious businessman from San Francisco.

And West may have had another motive: greed. After Thelma's death, West asserted that her only investment in the restaurant was her name, for which she received half the profits. None of her heirs ever contested this. The space occupied by the restaurant and the quarters above were leased from the building's owner—Jewel Carmen, West's estranged wife. For some time after Todd's death, West continued to operate Thelma Todd's Roadside Rest. He was never arrested for Todd's death and died in obscurity in 1952.

Several months before her death, someone sent Todd two crude notes demanding she pay $10,000 to bandleader Abe Lyman. If not, the notes promised, "our San Francisco boys will lay you out." As she and Lyman had once been lovers, Todd did not take the matter lightly. She hired bodyguards for several months. Lyman was questioned by police, but insisted he had nothing to do with it. He said it was merely someone's queer idea of a joke. There is nothing to link her death with this attempted extortion, for which two men in New York were eventually arrested.

Another possible reason for Thelma's death was the growing presence of Eastern mafia gambling operations in Southern California. Above Thelma's Roadside Rest apartment was a third floor, a spacious tower. Filmland insiders, among them friends of Todd who pressed for a second inquest, claimed that gangsters had pressured her to allow an illicit gambling casino in the tower, a casino sure to be favored, because of its location and affiliation with Todd, by the same sort of monied folk that made her dinner club a success. When Todd refused, claimed these insiders, the mafioso had her killed. There is little to substantiate this. But by an odd coincidence, the community where she died was and is called "Castellammare." That is the name of the region in Sicily where the Mafia originated. Despite much public clamor, the police refused to expand their superficial investigation. There was never a second inquest. But, as subsequent events were to show, police corruption and ties to organized crime in Los Angeles were at or near an all-time high. It is well within the realm of possibility that organized crime did away with Thelma Todd and paid the police to look the other way.

Thelma Todd died leaving a will that paid one dollar to her ex-husband Pat DiCiccio and the rest to her mother. Soon after the will was read, her mother changed her story about Thelma's heart condition and publicly accepted the coroner's official version of Thelma's death. The official Hollywood version. The official scenario that none of the great movie moguls would ever have dared bring to the screen. The scenario for which no audience could have suspended its disbelief beyond the first reel.

But Thelma Todd is gone and no one knows why.

LOCATION:
Thomas Brothers map reference: Page 40 at A4
Thelma Todd died in Roland West's garage at 17531 Posetano Road. The house behind it was built after Todd's death and is visible from the highway, easily the most imposing structure in this part of the palisades. From the junction of Pacific Coast Highway and Sunset Boulevard, take Castellammare Road, the first street north of the junction. Follow this street to Seretto Way, then turn right. The road ends in a tiny cul-de-sac before a majestic white Mediterranean-style villa that climbs the hillside in several steps. The blue doors of the garage are studded with black iron bolts. The body of Thelma Todd was found inside.

Raymond James: A barber who used life insurance policies to finance his kinky extramarital affairs. Photo: Courtesy UCLA Library Special Collections.

19

THE RATTLESNAKE MURDERER: ROBERT JAMES (1936)

Tall and beefy, with jug-handle ears and skin somewhere between pale brown and sickly yellow, he wasn't handsome in the conventional sense. But his dark red hair was well oiled and perpetually curled into an undulating landscape. More importantly, he dressed well, as befitting a slickly suave, free-spending fellow, a courtly Southern gent with that special note of pleading in his voice that few women could long resist. In fact, barber Bob James was a lady's man, a dandy, a genuine lady-killer who always seemed to have one too many women in his life.

He called himself Robert S. James, but his real name was Major Raymond Lisenba. Born in 1895 to a sharecropper father who had a large family and a small Alabama cottonpatch, Major went to work in a cotton mill at age eight. He was rescued by the husband of an older sister, a kindly master barber who sent him to a Birmingham barber "college," then hired him as an apprentice. He proved an able barber. He took an early interest in women. He married Maud Duncan of Birmingham in 1921 but couldn't confine his attentions to her alone. Soon he was involved with others. He began to develop an acutely kinky boudoir manner; when Maud filed for divorce, she cited numerous occasions when he had become aroused by shoving hot curling irons under her fingernails. After their divorce, a few of his pregnant paramours—there were several—began to press him for marriage. Or at least some financial support. Major skipped town. It was shortly afterward that he decided to invent a new name for himself.

He turned up as Robert James in Emporia, Kansas, and opened a small barber shop. The publisher of the Emporia *Gazette*, the noted writer, author and editor William Allen White, came to prefer Robert James' close shaves to any other available.

James married a movie cashier, Vera Vermillion, but their union didn't last long. One morning a local farmer made a scene in the James tonsorial establishment, claiming that his daughter was pregnant and that James was the cause. After dark that night James hit the road in his Model A Ford.

He stopped for gas in Fargo, North Dakota, and discovered there were few barbers in town. He joined them, opening his own place. Soon he met willowy Winona Wallace. She was blonde and beautiful, as open, trusting and unwary as any small-town girl. The James charm flowed. It gushed. In August 1932 they were married.

While James was an excellent barber, he never seemed willing to work very hard. Barbering took time—time he preferred to spend filling his life with new women. But then he also needed quite a lot of money to enjoy life and women the way they were meant to be enjoyed. It was a dilemma that was temporarily resolved by his mother's death.

She had a small insurance policy and he was the sole beneficiary. It wasn't a lot of money—a few hundred dollars—but it was unexpected and hadn't cost him any time. A few months later, one of his nephews was killed in an auto accident, after a steering mechanism failed and the car went over a cliff. But Robert James had, providentially, purchased a life policy for his nephew only a few weeks earlier. He had also loaned the nephew his own car, after he had personally repaired the steering gear. When James found himself so quickly enriched, life insurance suddenly seemed a bargain to James. Or maybe much more than a bargain. Maybe it could be the road to easy street.

His third wife, Winona, also knew about life insurance. She'd taken out a $1,000 policy while still in her teens, naming her mother as heir. After she married James, he convinced her to make him sole beneficiary. And he paid the first quarter's premiums on two new policies, both offering double-indemnity payments in case of accidental death. Dead accidentally, Winona would be worth upward of $14,000 to husband Bob.

He set out to make it happen on their Colorado honeymoon in September. Late one night, well-scrubbed and nattily attired, as usual, he walked into the office of the Pike's Peak Toll Road. To an increasingly skeptical company superintendent he told an incredible story. Winona had been driving. She lost control and the car went over the side of a deep chasm. He had jumped at the last moment. The superintendent eyed James' spotless suit in disbelief, but dispatched a rescue team.

Winona was lucky. The car had been snagged by a huge boulder only 150 feet down the slope. Winona had been tossed out by the collision, and lay next to the car. The super noted the ground was soft but there were no footprints leading up the cliffside from the spot where James had supposedly leaped. And one of the rescuers noticed a blood-drenched hammer behind the seat.

A Colorado Springs surgeon saved her life. But the doctor was puzzled by the terrible wounds at the back of her head; he couldn't recall ever seeing such injuries from a car accident. Winona seemed not to recall how it occurred, and the surgeon didn't share his suspicions with anyone at the time. There was no police investigation.

Winona went to recuperate with her husband in a remote cabin near Manitou. She was young and healthy, and rapidly began to mend. Then she suddenly died. James returned home one day with a grocery clerk who was helping him carry supplies up to the cabin, and they found Winona naked and dead, with her head and shoulders in the cabin's bathtub. Apparently, she had fallen in and drowned.

Despite these peculiar circumstances, there was no police investigation. James collected the insurance company's $14,000. He'd never seen that much money at one time in his whole life. Some of it went to a new car, a Pierce-Arrow convertible coupe. More went for fancy clothes and a fine set of luggage. And then the widower Robert James headed home to Birmingham to show it all off.

He really enjoyed Birmingham. He treated his family to new clothes, he bought groceries and restaurant meals. He enjoyed throwing his insurance money around. But most of all he enjoyed comely, 18-year-old Lois. His older sister's daughter. His niece. James promptly seduced her, and when he drove to Los Angeles, Lois left with him. He introduced her to motel clerks and others along the way as his wife.

In 1934 he opened a five-chair shop at Eighth and Olive, a prime location in the midst of the Los Angeles business district. He sent Lois to school to learn manicuring, and soon she was working in his shop.

The shop was well situated and busy. Considering it was the middle of the Great Depression, and that 25 percent of American workers were jobless, James was making a good living.

But not good enough to pay for his endless affairs. Bob James liked to overwhelm female conquests with visits to expensive restaurants, costly gifts, and ostentatious spending. Soon he was facing a cash crunch. He tried to remedy that when he married Helen Smith in 1934. But Helen objected to visiting a doctor to satisfy the requirements for a life insurance policy. "I don't believe in insurance. People who have it always die of something strange," she told James. He insisted on an immediate annulment.

While the annulment was pending he began to court a sexy, 25-year-old strawberry blonde, Mary Busch. He hired her as a manicurist. Soon she agreed to marry him. But there was one small problem: the annulment from his marriage to Helen Smith hadn't yet been confirmed.

So James found a wino named Joe Riegel, who for $50 played the role of minister. He stole a Gideon Bible from a skid-row flophouse, rented appropriate attire, and conducted a credible ceremony. Mary applied for a $10,000 life insurance policy, and James paid the first premium. Several weeks later, when the annulment was granted, James told Mary a fanciful tale and marched her before a real minister for a legal wedding.

Robert and the last Mrs. James rented a secluded bungalow in La Canada, a cozy place with a small fishpond screened behind thick hedges. While he never gave up all his other women, James found in Mary a kindred sex partner. He loved to inflict pain in the bedroom—and also loved receiving it. According to accounts obtained later from curious neighbors attracted by the nocturnal screams, by mid-1935 Robert James required a sound thrashing with a leather whip before he could achieve sexual arousal. Mary, appropriately attired in leather, cooperated by beating him regularly. She soon became pregnant.

By July 1935, James was getting desperate for a new infusion of cash. But he had a plan. On the evening of August 5, 1935, James invited two friends over for dinner. His house was a little hard to find, he explained, so he'd just pick them up on his way home from work downtown. He'd be bringing the steaks. Mary would have prepared everything else by the time they all arrived.

But Mary wasn't in the kitchen. Nor in the bedroom, the bath or the living room. James found some flashlights and his guests went looking for her in the garden. Mary was face down in the fishpond, dead. Drowned in six inches of water. Strangely, her left leg was a hideous purple and swollen to twice normal size.

An insect bite, decided the coroner. Some weird bug. Poor Mary had probably become dizzy from her pregnancy, had fallen while watering the garden, hit her head and drowned. Accidentally.

James filed for the insurance money. The insurance company, with no thought of foul play, conducted its usual routine records check. They discovered Robert and Mary James were not legally husband and wife at the time he paid the first (and only) premium. An insurance investigator tracked down Joe Riegel, who for $50 was glad to tell about his short career as a minister in the service of Bob James.

But Mary was dead. The coroner had ruled it accidental and the insurance company decided to see how little of the $20,000 Bob would settle for. He agreed to $3,500.

These peculiar events did not entirely escape the attention of the police and prosecutors. Detective Captain Jack Southard, the district attorney's chief investigator, was tipped by an insurance investigator: something smelled. But it was not until March 1936 that the district attorney's office was able to turn its full attention to the mysterious death of Mary James.

They started with copies of James' insurance records. The mysterious death of Winona was ample reason to send a man to Colorado. Interviews with the doctor and Pike's Peak Toll Road officials made it clear that Winona hadn't died accidentally.

Chief Deputy District Attorney Eugene Williams ordered 24-hour surveillance on Bob James. Detectives rented the house next door, and surreptitiously installed listening devices in the James house. After a month they had learned nothing whatever about Mary's death. But they did discover that Bob was regularly having sex with several women, including, most often, his niece Lois. Sexual intercourse between uncle and niece was incest. The district attorney had no case against James for murder, but he could arrest him for the crime of incest.

Williams was certain Mary had been murdered. He decided to shake the tree and see what might fall out. He ordered his men to carefully loosen screens and jimmy windows in James' bedroom. And on April 19, they broke in to arrest Bob James in the midst of a sex act with his niece. He was charged with incest. Williams gave reporters not only the juicy details of James' kinky sex life, but also the sensational story of the many curious parallels between the deaths of Winona in 1932 and Mary in 1935.

And when it hit the front pages, the fruit that Williams had hoped for came tumbling down. A liquor store owner told a *Herald-Express* reporter a curious tale about a sometime customer who had come into his store in August, sorely in need of a drink and babbling about buying and testing rattlesnakes. About a pregnant woman who had been bitten by these snakes. A woman who hadn't died of snakebite but instead had been drowned in a bathtub and her body put in a fish pond.

But who was the customer? The shopkeeper knew him only by his last name: Hope. And one thing more: He owned a rather distinctive car. The reporter took the tip to Williams.

The California Motor Vehicle Department performed a laborious manual check of car registrations. There was only one Hope who owned that particular car in Los Angeles County: Charles Hope, a short-order cook at a Hermosa Beach hamburger stand. The police brought him in for questioning.

At first Hope seemed unwilling to talk. Investigators took him for a visit to the James residence. That shook him up. When he regained his composure, he seemed almost relieved to tell his tale.

In June 1935 Hope had chanced into the James barber shop and asked for a haircut on credit. James agreed. While he was cutting, he asked Hope if he knew anything about rattlesnakes. Why? asked Hope. James told a tall tale about a friend who wanted to bump off his wife by having her bit by a rattlesnake. If Hope could find him a couple of mean and deadly snakes, there was $100 in it for him.

After some difficulty, Hope got hold of two Colorado vipers named Lethal and Lightning. They belonged to an Ocean Park herpetologist named Snake Joe Houtenbrink who sold them for seventy-nine cents a pound, venom guaranteed. James put chickens into their cage. They were promptly bitten and soon died. James was satisfied and paid Hope his $100.

But James had another mission for Hope. He had pursuaded the pregnant Mary that she should have an abortion. It would take place in their kitchen. Hope was to play the role of the doctor.

On August 4, a Sunday, Mary, clad only in a slip, lay strapped to the kitchen table. Her eyes and mouth were taped shut. James had convinced her that since abortions were illegal, the doctor demanded protection from her as a possible witness. After James gave her several ounces of whiskey to drink for "anesthesia," Hope came into the kitchen carrying a box with a sliding glass door. He opened it. James thrust Mary's leg inside. The snake promptly bit her. Hope left. He threw the boxes away in a vacant lot and sold Lethal and Lightning back to Snake Joe for half price.

Meanwhile, Mary went through increasing agonies. Her leg swelled to twice normal size and an ugly purple arrow of dying cells inched its way upward from her leg to her vital organs. It passed her knee, her thigh, her hip. James kept her strapped to the table while he tidied up the house, getting rid of incriminating evidence. Toward evening Hope returned and both men sat around drinking whiskey in the garage while Mary writhed in agony on the kitchen table.

James grew impatient. Mary was taking too long to die. "The snakes were no damned good," he said. Hope suggested calling a doctor. James said he thought they'd both be strung up if they did. After more whiskey he decided to end Mary's agonies. He went into the kitchen, carried her limp but living body to the bathtub, and drowned her as he had drowned Winona. At about six in the morning of August 5, he got Hope to help carry her out to the fish pond. They put her body in, head first, to look as though she had tripped on the path and fallen in.

Hope was to dispose of the tape, towels, blankets and rope. He incinerated all but the blankets. They were almost new. He took them to a dry cleaner's shop.

Arrested on incest charges, James at first laughed when police accused him of murdering Mary. "There's no such crime," he protested. He refused to even talk about Mary's death. "It was an accident," he said. After 11 days in jail, James was shown Hope's statement. That shook him and he agreed to talk. It had all been Hope's idea. Hope had offered to kill Mary in return for half the insurance money. He, James, had tried to back out at the last minute. "I couldn't kill her. She'd been too good to me," he told prosecutors. He denied any knowledge of the details of Mary's death, claiming he had left Hope to perform an abortion and returned to find his wife dead.

James and Hope told their stories in a packed courtroom with a nervous jury eyeing Lethal and Lightning, in attendance as evidence. Though it was a brief trial, it attracted national press interest. Walter Winchell came from New York to report on the proceedings. Actor Peter Lorre spent half a day watching James testify, hoping to find something in his manner that he could use in his characterization of a psychotic killer in an upcoming movie. Hope was the state's star witness. One of James' lovers testified that he had offered her $2,000 to swear he'd been at his barber shop the day Mary died.

The jury's deliberations were short. Both men were convicted of first degree murder. Hope got a life sentence. James, whom the state now referred to by his legal name, Major Lisenba, was sentenced to hang. During the six years his appeals wound their way through state and federal courts, he became known to San Quentin inmates as "Rattlesnake Lisenba." In 1942 California eliminated the gallows in favor of the gas chamber. On May 1, 1942, Robert James was hanged, the last person so executed in California.

LOCATION:
Thomas Brothers map reference: Page 19 at B3
Take the Glendale Freeway (State 2) and exit at Verdugo Boulevard, La Canada/ Flintridge. Follow Verdugo east to the 1300 block. There is no longer a house at 1329, the former site of the James bungalow. The whole block has been redeveloped into a secluded residential area behind large old trees and a low stone wall, parts of which date back to the mid-30s, to the era when Robert James brought rattlesnakes home to kill his pregnant wife.

Paul Wright: He caught his wife and his best friend making love.
Photo: Courtesy of Hearst Collection, USC Library.

20

PAUL WRIGHT: WHITE FLAME OF TEMPORARY INSANITY (1937)

Paul Wright was crazy about his gorgeous young wife, Evelyn. He worshipped her. Evelyn, much less infatuated, accepted this tribute as her due, and in fact used Paul's adoration as a way of getting whatever she could from his limited resources.

She wanted a big house in a good Glendale neighborhood. Buying it was out of the question. Even renting was really beyond his modest junior executive's salary—but he came through anyway. She wanted a new convertible. Sick with the thought of possibly losing Evelyn, he went further into debt and bought one. He was desperate to please her. She wanted expensive new clothes—constantly—and he stuffed her closets with them, though his own wardrobe consisted of three mail-order suits. After the birth of their daughter a doctor advised Evelyn not to have more children. Paul found a surgeon to sterilize him, in an era when such surgery was risky and expensive. But Paul was crazy with love for Evelyn.

So imagine how he felt in the small hours of the morning of November 9, 1937, when, roused from sleep in his own bed by a single note, repeated over and over on the piano in his living room, he walked half asleep into the hallway and found his darling wife and his best friend facing each other on the piano bench.

Imagine the white flame of unreasoning passion that exploded in his brain as he saw his wife fondling his best friend's penis. Imagine Paul Wright, filled with uncontrollable rage, returning to his bedroom. Imagine him removing an

143

automatic pistol from a nightstand drawer, returning to the living room, and firing all nine rounds at his much adored and blatantly unfaithful wife and at his treacherous best friend.

Evelyn Wright and John Kimmel lay bleeding on the floor, their bodies entwined. Kimmel's left foot was on the piano keyboard. Paul began to return to his senses. He saw the smoking gun in his hand. He saw life ebbing from his victims. He pulled himself together and called the police. "I have just murdered my wife and my best friend, John Kimmel," he told them on the phone. "You'll find me waiting for you in my home when you get here."

He was waiting on the sidewalk when the police came. A long and repetitive interrogation began. Evidence was collected. Crime-scene photographers snapped flash photos of the living room. At about daylight, just as the bodies were carried out, the family maid appeared. Wright, once again in possession of reason, wrote out a check. "I have not much money, but I will give you $70.00. That will take care of you and the baby until I get things straightened out," he told her. Police allowed him to call his father in Milwaukee. "There has been a terrible tragedy in my home—I've shot Evelyn. I caught her cheating. It's just as you said it would be. You will stick by me, won't you, Father?" he begged.

Later that morning Wright engaged Jerry Giesler as his attorney. Wright had limited means, but the usually expensive Giesler thought the case was so challenging that he agreed to a fraction of his usual fee.

Giesler faced many difficult challenges in trying to get Paul Wright off and the way he met those challenges became a source of inspiration that generations of screenwriters would draw on in devising courtroom dramas. Nearly 40 years after the fact, Giesler's tactics seem at best merely familiar variations of Perry Mason reruns. At the time they were very daring and immensely innovative.

Aside from Wright's unbidden confessions that he had murdered his wife and his best friend, the physical evidence showed that he had indeed fired the shots that killed them. The district attorney's theory was that Wright had long known of the affair between John Kimmel and Evelyn Wright, and had lured Kimmel to his house in hopes they would do something that would justify his shooting them. Wright, said prosecutors, only pretended to be asleep. According to their charges, Wright had lurked outside the living room, gun in hand, waiting for an appropriate moment to kill them both. He was charged with first degree murder.

Giesler's approach was to attempt to convince the jury that his client was temporarily insane at the moment he pulled the trigger. If Wright were insane at the time, he was not responsible for his actions. And if he were now sane, he could not be confined in a mental hospital. But proving Wright's temporary insanity would almost drive Giesler crazy.

With painstaking research, Giesler established the events preceding the shooting: Wright and best pal Kimmel had dined together at the Hollywood Athletic Club at an all-male social gathering of the Quiet Birdmen, an aviator's club. Afterward Paul invited John to his home for a drink. Evelyn joined them.

About three in the morning, a weary Paul went off to bed, expecting John to leave momentarily. When he was awakened by the piano, the lights were still on but his wife wasn't in the room. He went toward the living room and saw his wife and best friend making love on the piano bench. John's finger was repeatedly striking the piano key; apparently he thought this would reassure Paul that nothing but piano was being played.

"A white flame exploded in my brain," said Wright. Unthinking, uncaring, he went back to the bedroom for his gun. He started shooting even before he was in the living room. He fired two shots from the doorway. One of them went wide, into a French window (a latticework of many panes). He moved closer and fired the rest of the shots into the couple.

Giesler had to convince the jury that what Wright saw when he entered the room was so graphic that he lost control of his mind. And that required demonstrating two points: depicting what had been going on between the couple on the piano bench and proving that Paul had first fired two shots from the doorway before advancing into the room to shoot them again. The prosecution contended that he had coolly fired all nine shots at pointblank range.

Giesler consulted police photographs of the death scene, then spent hours on the actual bench and piano, with his wife playing the role of Evelyn, trying to discover how John Kimmel could have ended up dead on the floor with his left foot on the keyboard. To prove how it happened, he brought the piano and

Jerry Giesler became the City of Angels' leading trial lawyer by combining meticulous research with a sense of courtroom drama. Photo: Courtesy UCLA Library Special Collections.

bench into court. Kimmel's foot had been on the piano when the shooting started. His fly was open. A fully-clothed Evelyn sat very close, facing John, making love to him. She was hit in the back by the first shots and toppled over onto the floor. He was hit in the front and fell over partly atop her body. Demonstrating this to the jury, Giesler started in the same position Kimmel had been in, fell over onto the floor and continued his speech to the jury from that unlikely position.

Wright testified about the "white flame" that had "exploded in his brain." The prosecution, seeking to undermine this account, brought in Wright's nearest neighbor to testify about the gunfire she heard. The crucial part of her statement related to Wright's insistence he had fired two shots from the doorway and the rest some seconds later from close range. The witness, a kindly-looking elderly spinster who lived across the street, testified she'd heard five shots fired "in rapid succession, without a break."

Giesler was stymied. Her testimony directly contradicted Wright's. If there had been no interruption in the shots, then Wright had lied. Worse, the witness was a sympathetic figure, a sweet old lady of obviously sincere manner. The best he could do was minimize things by not reacting to her testimony at all, and getting her off the witness stand as quickly as possible.

And then Wright got a break, one of those incredibly lucky things that could never have been planned. Before the witness was excused, an all-but-gloating prosecutor held a whispered conference with his junior associate. Then he returned to the witness stand with a pencil. He asked her to use the pencil to demonstrate the manner in which the shots were fired. She was to tap out the sequence with the pencil.

After thinking about it for what seemed like an eternity, she picked up the pencil and started tapping. *Tap tap.* A pregnant pause. *Tap tap tap.*

This tiny pause bought Wright a jury verdict of not guilty of murder in the first degree. He was found guilty only of manslaughter.

In the second phase of the trial, Giesler sought to prove that his client had been insane at the moment he pulled the trigger. Giesler reached deep into his bag of tricks. He told the judge that as always, in the first phase of the trial, the defendant had the presumption of innocence and the prosecution bore the burden of proof of murder. Accordingly, custom dictated that the prosecution make the first opening argument and the last closing argument.

But now, the defendant bore the burden of proof of his insanity, said Giesler. He was presumed to be sane and must prove he wasn't. Accordingly, argued Giesler, *he* should be allowed the same privilege of first opening and last closing statements.

The prosecutors were speechless, then angry. Giesler's audacious motion was without precedent. The judge recessed the court and invited both sets of attorneys into his chambers. After a heated discussion, Giesler won his point.

Allowed to rebut the prosecution's statements at the very end of the trial, Giesler once again pressed home how the sight of his wife and best friend betraying him in his own living room had ignited the "white flame" that seared Wright's consciousness.

After nearly two days of deliberations, the jury filed back into the courtroom. As the first juror flashed a smile directly at Paul Wright, Giesler knew he'd won. Wright was found not guilty by reason of temporary insanity and, after psychiatric examination revealed he was no longer insane, he was set free. Though this was not California's first successful example of the insanity defense in a murder trial, it remains one of the most imaginative.

LOCATION:
Thomas Brothers map reference: Page 25 at F1
Take the Glendale Avenue/Verdugo Boulevard exit from the Ventura Freeway (Route 134) in Glendale. Go north on Verdugo until it joins with Canada Boulevard; take the right fork to the third street on the right, then right on Verdugo Vista. Though very close to a busy thoroughfare, Verdugo Vista is, as it was in 1937, a leafy glade of old trees and fairytale houses. The Wrights lived at 1830, a red-tile-roofed, dun stucco structure with brown trim. A unique home whose architect might have been inspired by a Norman castle, it sits atop its own hill, surrounded by a miniature forest of palms, ferns and Scotch pine.

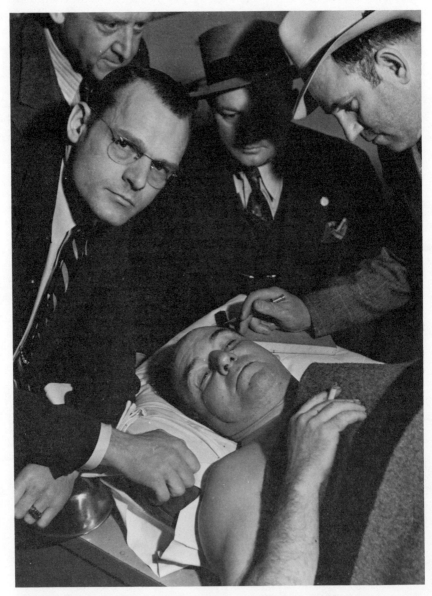

Clifford Clinton (left, glasses) with Harry Raymond: Not afraid of bombs or lawsuits, they fought City Hall—and won. Photo: Courtesy UCLA Library Special Collections.

21

EXPLOSIVELY INCORRUPTIBLE: HARRY RAYMOND AND CLIFFORD CLINTON (1938)

Between the twenties and thirties, Los Angeles was a wide-open town. Sex by the hour, day, or month; brown bottles of bootleg hootch or widemouth jars of clear moonshine; cocaine, marijuana, morphine—the whole illegal, addictive and expensive pharmacopeia; elegant roulette rooms, smoky underground poker palaces, backroom betting parlors, back alley crapgames and numbers runners patrolling protected territories; loan sharks, torpedoes, gunsels, button men. Los Angeles was everything your vice desired. A tough and ruthless syndicate of career criminals reaped the wages of sin from more than a thousand brothels, bookie joints and gambling dens. Though it maintained loose links with mobsters in Chicago and New York, the L.A. syndicate fiercely defended its turf against outside interests and invited freelance crooks to join their organization or risk sudden death. It was an offer that few refused. Those that did became even fewer.

The government authorities who were elected to protect public interests made all of this not merely possible but cozily convenient. By 1936, corruption among elected city officials was epidemic and almost open; the police department acted more like syndicate enforcers than protectors of the public weal.

Genuine attempts at reform were feeble and infrequent. Even most of the city's newspapers sided with the syndicate, supporting the crooks in city hall against their detractors.

In 1933, Councilman Frank Shaw ran for mayor on a platform of honest government, "free from graft and private exploitation." He announced plans to appoint a chief of police "who will run the gangsters and racketeers out of town and put a stop to commercialized vice."

Despite loud and predictable opposition from the racketeers, Shaw was elected. He immediately appointed his brother Joseph, a former naval officer, as his private secretary. And he appointed James E. Davis, who had headed the police force during much of the 1920s, as his new chief of police.

The syndicate leaders immediately understood: A *new* era of corruption was beginning. It was not quite business as usual; prices for bribes and payoffs were higher. Organized crime would have to do business at the executive level. So brother Joe became the mayor's bagman. Crooks needed the eyewash of campaign contributions—and suitcases full of small bills—to buy the cops, judges and politicians. But buy them they did. By 1937 the syndicate bosses' biggest worry was where to stash the millions of dollars overflowing their coffers.

Into this rotten state of affairs came Clifford Clinton. The son of Salvation Army missionaries, a straitlaced but kindly, compassionate man, Clinton opened Cafeteria of the Golden Rule, the city's first cafeteria, which offered generous portions of wholesome food at rock-bottom prices. During the depths of the Great Depression he became the city's most admired citizen after announcing that patrons "in financial distress" would be served even if they couldn't pay. He also saved thousands of indigents from malnutrition or even starvation with "five-course dinners" (bread, soup, salad, jello and coffee) for a nickel.

Clinton and Shaw were destined to collide head-on. For appearance' sake, Mayor Shaw was obliged to make a cosmetic effort at ending corruption. When he was reelected in 1937, he empaneled a new grand jury, stuffed with his cronies and stooges. To back his claim of honesty and rectitude, however, Shaw also appointed Clinton and three other genuine reformers. It was a mistake.

Clinton and a few courageous followers tried to investigate corruption, but when they targeted the hoods under Shaw's protection, the district attorney's office denied them funds to pay for an investigation. Clifford Clinton dug into his own pocket for the money and formed his own strike force, Citizens Independent Vice Investigating Committee (CIVIC). He recruited some 500 church, community and business leaders. And to get indictable evidence on corrupt police and politicians, he hired Harry Raymond.

Raymond was a paradox. A fearless investigator, imaginative and incorruptible—crooked money couldn't buy him—he was also a hot-headed brawler who, while he was himself a cop, once knocked out another officer and sometimes arrested suspects without proper evidence. In the years after World War I, when Venice by the Sea was a separate city, Raymond was its police chief. He was fired amid unsubstantiated charges of extortion and false arrest after taking important syndicate men into custody. In 1920, Raymond was hired—and then fired—by Los Angeles Police Chief George Home. Home was himself dismissed a few months later. Raymond became San Diego's police chief, serving several years before resigning to become a private investigator.

In 1937 Clinton directed Raymond to document the web of police corruption that he believed led all the way to Mayor Shaw's office. His investigation disclosed a lurid picture of corruption: Through Mayor Shaw's brother, the racketeer kingpins of gambling and prostitution paid huge sums to Shaw. In return, Shaw appointed their handpicked strawmen to the police commission. Commissioners appointed as chief of police a man the vice lords controlled, James Davis. Davis put his loyal followers into key positions on the vice and police intelligence squads. The money flowed, the rackets flourished, and any cop trying to do an honest job was bribed, transferred, dismissed or buried.

Clinton issued a "grand jury minority report" also signed by three other jurors, detailing the LAPD situation and similar corruption in the district attorney and Los Angeles County sheriff's offices.

Syndicate leaders were furious. Mayor Shaw pulled a few strings and the county assessor slapped Clinton's dining establishment with an additional $6,700 in property taxes. A license to open another cafeteria was refused without explanation. Several people inexplicably "fell down" the steps of his establishment and promptly sued Clinton for damages. Other "customers" complained of food poisoning; they too filed lawsuits. A cannister spewing foul and malodorous smoke was set off in the cafeteria, stampeding panicked patrons. A few days later, another stink bomb went off in the kitchen. Clinton's family got threatening letters and phone calls. When he brought witnesses before the grand jury the police arrested them. Some were beaten while in police custody. One was held incommunicado five days after being arrested on a trumped up vagrancy charge. Clinton himself was cited for contempt before the grand jury. He was undeterred.

Then on October 27, 1937, a powerful dynamite bomb destroyed the basement and first floor of the Clinton home. Clinton and his family, though sleeping upstairs, were unhurt by the blast. Nor was he intimidated. "I'll never stop now," he said.

Raymond was investigating corrupt connections between the LAPD intelligence squad and the mayor's office. Arrayed against him were all the powers of the city. Assigned to discredit or destroy Raymond was Police Captain Earl Kynette, head of the intelligence squad. Kynette promptly put a tap on Clinton's phone.

Kynette's men swarmed over Raymond's Boyle Heights neighborhood. They rented the house across the street and ostentatiously tailed him as part of round-the-clock surveillance. The cops did nothing to keep their activities secret. Practically everyone in the neighborhood knew the police were leaning on the grand jury's investigator. Raymond knew it too.

Raymond was scheduled to give public testimony about sources of Shaw's campaign funds in late January 1938. He had by then unraveled the whole sordid story. Shaw and Davis could not let him testify. Kynette was given his orders: Stop Raymond.

Early on the morning of January 14, Raymond stepped out of his modest home and sauntered down the sloping driveway to the neat little garage at the rear of his property. A curious quietude gripped the neighborhood. The cop cars that had been parked down the street for weeks were gone. In the house across the street, no detectives were seen staring around curtains at Raymond's house. Not a cop was in sight, anywhere. Raymond opened the garage door. He climbed into the front seat of his car. He fumbled for the key, then slipped it into the ignition. His right foot pumped the gas once, twice. His left foot depressed the clutch pedal. Raymond turned the key.

And was blown into the air by the force of a tremendous explosion. He saw the car's engine sailing by. He saw clouds of splintered boards, pieces of the roof, sailing up, then settling back on top of him. He was deafened. He was a mass of broken bones. What wasn't broken was bruised. But, battered and bloody, bleeding from more than 100 wounds, he was alive. A neighbor ran up to help, and dragged Raymond from the wreckage. "This is a rotten way to try to get a man," mumbled indestructible Harry Raymond.

Raymond's salvation was that the massive bomb wired to his ignition was made of black powder. Unlike such superfast-action explosives as dynamite—or more recent inventions—black powder explodes comparatively slowly. The force pressing upward and outward was more like an irresistible giant hand pushing everywhere at once than it was like a sudden cutting force.

More than anything else, the bomb blew the lid off the cesspool in city hall. The public might tolerate booze, bimbos and bookmakers, but they drew the line at bombs. Raymond was wheelchaired into court to testify about payoffs and black bags. A special prosecutor, Joseph Fainer, was appointed. The Mob immediately threatened his family. Fainer put them on a cruise ship for Hawaii and promised to find the men who tried to kill Raymond.

Chief of Police Davis ordered his cops to be silent. Undaunted, Fainer got a court order to confiscate Kynette's files. In them was direct evidence linking Kynette and a subordinate to the bombing. Kynette may even have installed the bomb himself. After a sensational trial, the police captain and his accomplice were sentenced to 10 years in prison.

Every newspaper in Los Angeles except the *Times* attacked the Shaw administration. The *Times*, whose publisher, Norman Chandler, owned vast real estate holdings and had a vested interest in continued population growth predicated on an image of clean government, stuck with the doomed Shaw until his rapid exit from politics.

Clinton put together a broad coalition of community leaders and launched a petition to recall Frank Shaw from office. Less than a year after his reelection, Shaw became the first big city mayor in the country to be thrown out of office.

His brother Joe was convicted of 66 counts of corruption in connection with the sale of patronage positions and bribes. He got 10 years in prison. Also implicated was LAPD Lieutenant Pete DelGado, who fled to Mexico and was never again seen in Los Angeles.

Elected in Shaw's stead was Judge Fletcher Bowron, who though sometimes ineffectual would not tolerate corruption. Bowron appointed Arthur Hohmann, a lantern-jawed ex-Marine, as his new police chief. In a two-day period in 1939, Hohmann replaced the vice squad with an 18-man task force dedicated to arresting gamblers; reorganized the LAPD's 14 patrol divisions into six; abolished 398 temporary department positions and promoted, fired, demoted or transferred 500 men. He was denied permission to fingerprint and photograph every citizen in Los Angeles, which he wanted to do to cut the time in booking arrested citizens. Later Hohmann replaced the city's 14 precinct captains with three handpicked officers, two of whom had been his close rivals for the chief's job. He set up a plan of 90-day rotations for all sworn officers, a scheme designed to eliminate graft. Hohmann lasted only two years before he was removed by political foes. Later he was reinstated as deputy chief in charge of technical services. Until his retirement in 1960 he was the department's forgotten man.

The departure of Shaw was not the end of vice in Los Angeles. It was merely the beginning of the end of highly centralized operations protected by police corruption. While the pimps, gamblers, loan sharks and mobsters were looking around for some new place to do business, World War II began. When it was over, they found a new location from which to serve their old markets. It was a small, dusty desert town called Las Vegas.

LOCATIONS:
Thomas Brothers map reference: Page 45 at A5
Harry Raymond's garage was at 955 South Orme, Boyle Heights. Just before the northbound Santa Ana Freeway (I-5) becomes the Golden State Freeway, exit at Soto. Turn right to 7th Street, then go right (east) to Orme, the fourth street on the left. Turn left to 955, about halfway up the street on the left. The original house still stands, completely renovated in 1985. The garage, a shedlike affair, was in the left rear corner of the lot. The present garage replaced the one that was blown to bits in 1938.

Thomas Brothers map reference: Page A at C4
Clinton's original cafeteria was at 618 S. Olive. It's now a parking lot. But in 1935, just before Clifford Clinton launched his fight against corrupt city officials, he opened a second cafeteria at 648 S. Broadway, which is still operated by Don Clinton, Clifford's son. They still offer simple wholesome food at low prices, with discounts for senior citizens. On the walls are historic photos of the era when Clinton stood almost alone against the power of Los Angeles vice lords.

Thomas Brothers map reference: Page 34 at E2
The Clinton home, bombed in October 1937, was rebuilt and still stands at 5470 Los Feliz Boulevard. From the Hollywood Freeway (U.S. 101) exit at Western and go north 2.5 miles to the southeast corner of Los Feliz and Western, across the street from Immaculate Heart College.

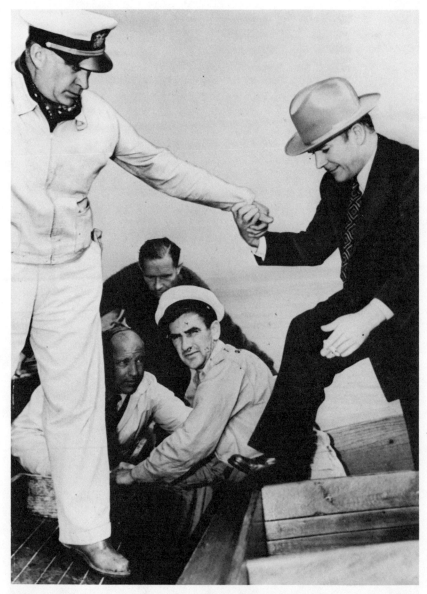

"Admiral" Cornero: His fleet of gambling ships was a thorn in the side of law enforcement. Photo: Courtesy of Hearst Collection, USC Library.

22

"ADMIRAL" TONY CORNERO AND THE BATTLE OF SANTA MONICA BAY (1939)

Lured by full-page ads in Los Angeles dailies and in Hollywood trade papers, on May 5, 1938, thousands queued for water taxis on Santa Monica pier. They were housewives and hipsters; gagmen, gangsters and gardeners; businessmen, busboys and bartenders; touts, wags and waitresses; grips, gaffers, carpenters and film editors; actors, foley engineers, fraternity men, flunkies. Men and women from every calling, every social stratum, from every part of the city. And gamblers all. At dusk, "Captain" Tony Cornero flipped a switch on *Rex*, anchored just over three miles away—outside California's jurisdiction—and the light of a million candles twinkled across the waters of Santa Monica Bay. Leading city, county, state and federal law enforcement officials gnashed their teeth in impotent rage. But on the pier a cheer went up from the crowd as their first boats departed for the *Rex*, the biggest, most luxurious floating casino California had ever seen.

Tony Cornero was no vicious hood. While sometimes involved in thuggery, in his mature years he usually took great care to be at some distance from scenes of violence. Tony only involved himself with such distasteful incidents at all because, in his chosen line of business, it was sometimes necessary to fight fire with fire. Tony Cornero was not into hurting people for pleasure.

On the contrary; Cornero, an immigrant, saw himself as a grateful, loyal American citizen playing an important role in providing outlets for his fellow citizens' constitutionally protected pursuits of happiness. Tony provided goods and services to serve their most ardent needs. That these commodities were usually illegal was not so much Tony's concern as was his profit margin; if what his customers wanted—booze and gambling—had been legal, there was no way Tony could have turned much of a profit. And profit, as Tony saw it, was the American way.

And profit he did. He was worth $1 million before he was 30. A million, untaxed. A million, unreported to the IRS. A million, starting out with nothing but moxie. And a shotgun. The former San Francisco taxi driver would display this shotgun in the dark night to bootleggers landing cargoes of illicit liquor on Malibu beaches. He used it to convince these noble businessmen of his noble purposes and to inspire in them the good sense not to resist while he hijacked their hootch.

Tony was born Antonio Cornero Stralla, in 1895, on a farm near the Swiss border in northern Italy's Piedmont region. When he was five, his father lost at cards. Lost every last *lira* of the money paid for his annual harvest. Meanwhile little Tony, playing with matches in a field, accidentally set a fire that destroyed all the grain. Soon afterward, the Stralla family sold their land and booked passage for San Francisco.

In 1922 Tony walked away from his San Francisco taxi driver's job and started a hijacking business in the secluded coves of Southern California. By 1924 Cornero was king of the California rumrunners. In 1926 he became the major source of smuggled booze in Los Angeles, serving wholesale customers from a 4,000-case stock on the S.S. *Lily,* anchored 150 miles west of the city. Nocturnal deliveries were made with a fleet of fast launches.

In 1926 he became the object of a huge manhunt. Federal agents tried to arrest him on a train from Los Angeles to Seattle. Pursued by agents with drawn guns, he leaped from a moving coach into the wilds of Northern California. He found his way to a remote airfield and chartered a small plane to fly to a town near Portland, Oregon. There he reboarded the same train, only to find Feds still waiting. Again he jumped from the train, near Seattle, and escaped pursuit. He went on to Vancouver, British Columbia, his original destination, by other means.

The States were a little too warm, so Cornero went to Europe and South America, where rumors of his big bootleg deals wafted back to California. But exile didn't agree with Cornero. In 1929, he returned to California and surrendered himself to federal agents on smuggling charges. Sentenced to serve two years in the federal prison at McNeil Island in Puget Sound, Tony told a reporter that he became a bootlegger out of patriotic motives: "I had to keep 120 million Americans from poisoning themselves with bathtub gin and moonshine," he said.

While serving time, Cornero made a major career decision. He'd always liked gambling, even if he'd never forgotten the humiliation of his father's fleecing in the Piedmont. Even if in his first adolescent gambling experience he'd lost all his money in a dice game and had to walk miles home in ignominious dejection. Tony liked gambling and he had a pet theory about game-playing people. They were not suckers. They were, rather, squirrels. "There will always be a full crop of squirrels in the world," he once confided to Los Angeles reporter Florabel Muir. "California probably has more of them per square inch than any place in the world." Cornero had his own definition of a "sucker," a word he found distasteful. "There is only one kind of sucker in the world. That is the sucker who is looking for another sucker. A squirrel is different. He is looking for fun, entertainment," chirped Cornero.

So, with faith in an unending supply of squirrels, Tony became a gambler. If gambling was illegal in most of the United States, it flourished, scarcely concealed and often protected by corrupt police,* throughout Los Angeles and especially in Hollywood. Dozens of drugstores boasted backroom slot machines. Backstreet bingo parlors sucked quarters out of bored housewives. Card rooms were all about. The Clover Club, a mecca for Hollywood highrollers, was well known for its luxurious "private" casino. Cornero, with some of his erstwhile colleagues from the bootlegging industry, invested in the *Tango*, a converted steamship, and anchored it off Santa Monica.

The *Tango* was outfitted with card and dice tables and with roulette wheels; gamblers were brought out from the mainland on small boats. It was such an obviously good idea that competition soon sprang up. Between 1929 and 1935, Cornero, his associates and their rivals operated a dozen gambling boats off the California coast. By Cornero's estimate, *Tango* and his other gaming ships attracted about 13 million visitors in some 10 years of operation.

But something was gnawing at Cornero. He did not care for the standards his partners applied to their gaming. He did not care for the way the take was split. He did not think his three partners were carrying their shares of the management. So, in 1935 he offered to buy them out, or to sell his share to them. After exhaustive bargaining, a deal was carefully stitched together. Cornero would buy his partners' shares.

At the last minute, Bill Blazer backed out. The others wavered. Cornero was disgusted. Forgetting his farmer father's fleecing, forgetting his own early experiences with the dice, he offered to settle the matter in the manner of a squirrel. "The hell with it," he told Blazer. "One roll of the dice for the boat." Blazer agreed.

"I lost the *Tango* but I won my peace of mind, which is more important," he said years later.

After losing his share of the *Tango*, Tony immediately set out to bring gambling afloat up to a new standard. The Cornero standard.

He found the S.S. *Star of Scotland*. She was something out of a Jack London or Joseph Conrad novel. Launched in 1887 as the *Kenilworth*, a four-masted wooden barkentine, she plied the Pacific carrying grain. Rechristened *Star of Scotland* in 1903, she joined the Alaska floating cannery fleet. In 1930 she became a sailing barge, hauling well-heeled passengers between Catalina and Santa Monica in luxury and style. Cornero found her a splintering, water-logged hulk, still serving the public as a live-bait barge for groups of bay fishermen. He bought her on the cheap but invested $300,000 to create the *Rex*.

Cornero's *Rex* became the toniest gambling ship of its era, a huge floating pleasure palace anchored 3.1 miles off the Santa Monica beach. In 1938, six months after it opened, Los Angeles Mayor Frank Shaw was recalled from office by reformers. * The Clover Club went dark, as did most of the city's bingo rooms, card parlors and bookie joints. The *Rex* and its competitors, *Tango* (anchored off Venice), *Show Boat* (off Long Beach) and *Texas* (off San Diego), became the only open action in Southern California. Soon the reformers focused their attentions on "Cornero's Navy."

But so did legions of "squirrels." *Rex* offered in one floating location more gaming than any other West Coast gambling establishment. There were 150 slot machines, most purchased in exchange for 25 percent of the take from those who formerly operated them in Los Angeles drugstores. There were 400 seats for bingo and there was chuck-a-luck and a "Chinese lottery." There was roulette, tango, bridge, craps, faro, blackjack, high spade, stud poker and 21. There was a betting room for West Coast racetracks, with race results beamed to the *Rex* via shortwave radio.

And *Rex* offered style. There was always a good orchestra and a tidy little dance floor. A chef hired away from Hollywood's Trocadero produced tasty meals and Tony kept prices low. Prohibition had been repealed in 1933, so Tony served only the best liquor, each bottle conspicuously bearing both California and U.S. tax stamps, though Cornero's attorney often told reporters that since the ship was in federal waters there was no requirement for state liquor seals and that Tony paid the taxes out of a feeling of generosity toward the state. His patrons never publicly quarreled with this assertion. There was room on the *Rex* for almost 2,000 squirrels and staff.

To keep *Rex* operating safely and at maximum efficiency required a staff of 325 and a daily payroll of $3,000. To meet maritime licensing laws, a licensed captain was aboard at all times. Since maritime law decreed that the home port of a ship was the domicile of its master, the "skipper" kept a Santa Monica address. The purser doubled as a pit boss; dealers, stickmen and lookouts carried papers as assistant pursers and stewards. The attractive young women who worked as shills for five dollars a day were listed as stewardesses and the crew list always included a ship's doctor and a nurse.

Mindful of the potential for piracy, Cornero put two machine-gun nests on the topmost deck, manned in shifts around the clock. He also stationed flint-eyed "checkers" at the water taxi landing and near the entrance gangplank. These armed men, looking for known hoods, quickly and efficiently patted down anyone who seemed suspicious. Visitors' handguns were unloaded and kept in the check room.

These precautions were not without foundation. At dawn on July 9, 1935, under cover of a dense fog, a gang of 11 pirates had boarded *Show Boat* off Venice. They took $40,000 in cash and jewelry, and left everyone except one woman—she'd hidden in a restroom—chained up. A couple of years later other pirates had kidnapped Zeke Caress, a well-known gambler, and held him for ransom.

Cornero, perhaps aware of the growing reform movement, pushed *Rex* for all it was worth. He continued his full-page newspaper ads. He hired skywriting airplanes to etch mile-long letters of smoke spelling REX in the skies above Los Angeles. He publicized big winners with news releases, in a manner imitated decades later by Las Vegas and Atlantic City casinos. Tony made himself very accessible to the press. They rewarded him by recognizing his original contribution to Southern California gaming. Since he had invented the notion of the gambling ship and since he had for a time owned an interest in several, Tony Cornero became admiral of the gambling fleet, thereafter known to everyone as Admiral Cornero.

All this adulation enraged Los Angeles County Prosecutor Buron Fitts and California's tough, law-and-order attorney general, Earl Warren.

So on May 13, only eight days after the *Rex* went into all-too-conspicuous operation, Fitts and a coterie of sheriff's police commandeered water taxis at the Santa Monica pier, then went aboard the *Rex* to arrest Cornero and 50 of his employees on gambling charges. All were immediately freed on bond, but Fitts used the excuse of their indictments to choke off water taxi service. Cornero responded by having the *Rex* towed—its engines served only to provide power for light and refrigeration—to a point off Redondo Beach and continued taxi service from the Redondo pier. Customers didn't seem to mind the change.

An uneasy truce prevailed until September 7. Once again water taxis brought Fitts and his raiders, who carried off as much gaming equipment as the little boats could hold. In October, Cornero moved *Rex* farther south, into the Catalina Channel, and anchored 12 miles out. But many "squirrels" got seasick en route to *Rex* on the choppy channel, and business slacked off.

So in early 1939 the *Rex* returned to its old spot, miles off the beach at Santa Monica. Earl Warren was outraged. Cornero was defying him. Warren huddled with Buron Fitts, who had struck an unlikely alliance with the owners of Southern California racetracks, the legal gamblers who felt that *Rex* was taking money from their purses. Together they sought a new strategy to sink Cornero's navy. By July they had a plan.

Warren served abatement orders on all California gambling ships, ordering them to cease and desist. The orders were simply ignored. So state and county sheriff's police once again set out in water taxis. They boarded *Show Boat* and *Tango* and *Texas*. They smashed tables and other furnishings with axes and carried off slot machines and roulette wheels.

And then they came after *Rex*. But Admiral Cornero and his 27 junior partners were netting $100,000 a month. They would not give up without a fight. For nine hours lawmen in water taxis circled the *Rex*, repeatedly attempting to board her. And for nine hours *Rex* crewmen kept them off with high-pressure hoses. And all the while the press, in their own rented boats, circled the scene, periodically cruising close to *Rex* to accept bottles of brandy to bolster their spirits. Finally the law weighed anchor and retreated in defeat. The naval action called the Battle of Santa Monica Bay was over.

But the campaign on dry land would continue. When Cornero attempted to land at Santa Monica pier the next day, he found a squad of lawmen waiting. Investigator Tom Cavett, a little too zealous, tried to leap into Cornero's boat. But Cornero decided he'd leave the area and Cavett suddenly found himself in the drink. Tony's men pulled him aboard. When the boat was beached some miles south, Cavett was put ashore with the other passengers. District Attorney Fitts threatened to indict Cornero on kidnapping charges but never did.

The forces of law and order had the last laugh. On November 20, 1939, California's Supreme Court held that the three mile limit, as it related to Santa Monica Bay, was to be measured, not from the beach in Santa Monica, as Cornero argued, but from the headlands marking the mouth of the bay. So *Rex* was in California waters after all. Cornero struck his colors and surrendered the following day.

Cornero moved on to Las Vegas, where for a time he managed a casino. The *Rex* was drafted into the U.S. Navy and spent World War II as a motorized cargo barge. The Navy sold her for $10 to a San Francisco man who planned to turn her into a nightclub but could never raise the money.

No sooner was World War II over than Admiral Cornero returned to the high seas. He bought a retired Navy minelayer, outfitted it with a 100-foot bar and dance floor, added slot machines, card tables and betting parlors. He christened it *Lux* and on August 7, 1946, sailed it to a point six miles off Long Beach. Angelenos, starved for a little action, swarmed aboard to test the tables.

California Governor Earl Warren was aghast. "Cornero has absolutely defied us," he fulminated. "No human being in the country is big enough for that." Warren ordered the Long Beach Port Authority to shut off water taxi service and that was the end of Admiral Cornero's adventures afloat. He was arrested on gambling and conspiracy charges, and the *Lux* was seized for violating a number of Coast Guard regulations.

But it was not quite the end of Cornero. He went into legitimate maritime shipping, operating a small fleet of cargo ships. But one of his vessels sank and Tony went heavily into debt. He survived for a time teaching wealthy men the hard lessons of table stakes poker in quiet little games, but made enemies playing "squirrels" for pigeons. In the early 1950s, after surviving an attempt on his life at his Beverly Hills home, Cornero moved to Las Vegas.

There he began to put together what would be his biggest deal, a 1502-room hotel-casino, the Stardust. But Tony got in over his head trying to raise his share of $6 million for start-up money. Since gambling was what he knew best, he set out to win his hotel with dice. In July 1955, with only his name as collateral, he borrowed a casino's money to play on their craps table. Down nearly $10,000, he suffered a heart attack and died on the table. There was only $800 in his pocket. His friends insisted on a fitting funeral and chipped in $3,500 for one of the best Las Vegas had ever seen.

LOCATIONS:

Thomas Brothers map reference: Page 41 at A1

The Santa Monica pier is at the end of Colorado Boulevard in the city of Santa Monica. Take the Santa Monica Freeway (I-10) and exit at Lincoln. Go north to Colorado, then west to the pier. The water taxi service used to depart from the ocean end.

Thomas Brothers map reference: Page 67 at C3

Redondo Beach pier is at the north end of Harbor Drive in the city of Redondo Beach. From the San Diego Freeway (I-405), exit at Torrance Boulevard, and go west to Catalina. Turn south to the Esplanade, then follow the signs to the municipal pier. Water taxi service ran from the seaward leg of the pier.

* See Chapter 21, *Explosively Incorruptible: Harry Raymond & Clifford Clinton (1938)* for a full treatment of Los Angeles corruption in the 1930s and the rise and fall of Mayor Frank Shaw.

Louise Peete: All of her husbands were suicides.
Photo: Courtesy of Hearst Collection, USC Library.

23

LOUISE PEETE AND HER DEADLY LIES (1944)

She wasn't beautiful, not really, but she radiated a most compelling aura, a highly refined sexiness. Men were fatally attracted. All four of her husbands committed suicide. She shot and killed at least two other men and abused a third to a bitter end. But then she murdered a woman and was strangled by the law in a noose fashioned from the skeins of her own silken lies.

Lofie Louise Preslar was born in Bienville, Louisiana, in 1883. She was given the best New Orleans education her newspaper publisher father could buy. Louise was a classic Southern belle, cultured and refined. And Louise was unscrupulous, voluptuous and promiscuous. The combination caused her expulsion from an elite finishing school and brought about a marriage at age 20 to a traveling salesman, Henry Bosley.

Bosley soon found her in bed with a New Orleans oilman. Less than 48 hours later he took his own life. Louise sold or pawned Bosley's meager possessions and moved to Shreveport. She excelled at her new profession: call girl. "I'm expensive, but 'guaranteed,'" she confided to a friend.

After acquiring some working capital, Louise moved to Boston, appropriated a wealthy and respected name—Gould—and practiced her amorous trade among the scions of Beacon Hill. And among the *péres* and *grands-péres* or anyone else who could pay the price. She took to visiting the mansions of the rich—in Madam's absence. And she took any of Madam's small valuables that might be lying about. One day she very suddenly and very prudently took a train to Waco, Texas.

There she made the acquaintance of free-spending, diamond-bedecked wildcatter Joe Appel. She shot him in the back of the head and his diamonds mysteriously vanished. Louise was arrested, and appeared before a grand jury.

In her best Louisiana accent she told an eloquent and moving tale of attempted rape. She was an innocent, a well-bred Southern lady of quality, and Appel, a horrid Yankee carpetbagger, had attempted to force himself upon her protesting self. So she took his gun and shot him. In self-defense. The grand jury ordered her released. They applauded her as she grandly left the jail.

In 1913, she turned up in Dallas, broke. She quickly married Harry Faurote, a hotel clerk, and went back to whoring, the work she knew best. She went at it, with her usual gusto, in Harry's own hotel. He soon hanged himself in the basement.

She went to Denver in 1915 and married Richard Peete. They bought a small house. Louise bore a daughter in 1916. But Peete, a door-to-door salesman, would never make the money that Louise wanted. In May 1920 she picked a fight with him, packed a bag, took a train. She headed for the bright lights, for the quick score. She headed for Los Angeles.

There she found Jacob Denton, a millionaire businessman, a worldly widower. He owned an English Tudor mansion near the Ambassador Hotel on booming Wilshire Boulevard. He was preparing to take an extended trip east; he wished to rent out his house. Peete moved in on him, moved into his house and into his bed. Soon she proposed marriage. Denton was enraged—but not for long.

Sometime around the end of May, Denton disappeared. Peete told the caretaker that Denton wished to have a ton of topsoil removed from the garden and placed in the basement. He was fond of mushrooms, said Peete, and she would show him how to grow them.

Denton's absence was soon noted. Peete had explanations, many different ones. She was incredibly inventive, never at a loss for an answer. Though many of her tales were plainly incredible, her elegant, cultured manner, her unflappable composure and the tightly-woven fiction of her background deceived nearly all. An attractively plump, mature woman, she was at all times utterly charming and utterly believable, an utterly sympathetic figure.

A business associate complained that Denton had missed an appointment. Louise said Denton had received an urgent telegram and left immediately for San Francisco. An insurance agent arrived for an appointment with Denton. Denton had gone to the beach, Louise explained, but had asked her to handle this matter. Would the agent be kind enough to add her to his auto policy, since she would be driving his car while he was absent? The agent assented. Denton had another appointment with Hudson salesman Hal Haydon. Denton had ordered a new car, which he would pick up in Michigan, and he wished to trade in the old. When he failed to bring it in, Haydon came to Denton's house.

Denton, Louise told Haydon, had gone to Arizona, had returned, and then left for San Francisco. And he had somehow been wounded in the right arm. The wound had become infected. "Mr. Denton is ashamed of the wound," Louise told Haydon. "He doesn't want people to know about it." By the middle of June, said Louise, the arm had to be amputated. There would be no trip East. So he had left instructions for the new car to be delivered to his home. Louise returned the old one to the dealership.

Now her story became more ambitious, more inventive, more convoluted. And less believable. Louise said Denton had given her power of attorney to sell his house, and to take a $3,000 commission on the asking price of $27,500. Louise was inventive, she was creative, she had vast, perhaps unlimited, stores of moxie. She sometimes even convinced herself that her inventions were truth. But Louise wasn't nearly as smart as she had believed. Had she bothered to inquire, she would have learned that most reputable realtors would have charged only about half that much.

On June 5 she went to the Farmer's & Merchant's Bank. She had the key to Denton's safety deposit box and a check made out to her for $300 on his account. Another check to her for $450 had been cashed elsewhere. Neither of the signatures matched Denton's signature card. What was going on? Louise told her new, improved story to a bank official. Denton was in Seattle. He had gone to Missouri, but would return. His arm had been amputated above the elbow. Out of the goodness of her heart, she was helping the poor man with his affairs. She was helping him by writing checks and by signing his name. He held on to the end of his pen with his other hand, she said, so it was legal, wasn't it? The banker appeared puzzled. He couldn't honor Denton's checks, but neither could he bring himself to call the police about this dear, sweet woman.

And then Louise added a dramatic flourish. The Spanish Woman. The Spanish Woman was a mysterious figure who first turned up with Denton in May, or perhaps it was early June. She and Denton were an item, said Louise, but they quarreled, often violently. The Spanish Woman was in some way connected with the loss of poor Denton's arm, Louise hinted.

The charade continued through the hot days of summer. Louise rented out rooms and collected rents. Denton was in and out of town, but was so ashamed of his disfigurement that he would see no one except Louise. He telephoned from time to time but spoke only with Louise. Louise continued to act as though Denton had charged her with keeping his affairs in order. Small checks came by mail. Endorsing them with his name, she cashed them. She forged a lease agreement giving her the right to occupy the property. She charged a few dresses to Denton's account at Bullocks. She had a few of his silk shirts altered into blouses for her own use. Louise gave away a few of Denton's clothes, pawned one of his rings. But the big score eluded her.

In mid-August she leased the mansion to a couple named Miller, and made a show of her return home to Denver. But she continued to write to Los Angeles realtors and auto dealers, making minor ripples in Denton's financial affairs. Denton was still nowhere to be found.

On September 23, Denton's family hired an attorney, Rush Blodgett. He hired a private detective, A.J. Cody. Cody and Blodgett came calling with spades. They found Jacob Denton at home. His body lay on the floor of the basement. Some of the dirt Louise had ordered had been loosely shoveled on top of him. The coroner used an X-ray photo—at the time, a new and daring forensic innovation—to reveal the cause of death: a .32 caliber bullet fired at close range into the back of his neck. The bullet came from Denton's own gun, which now lay in an upstairs drawer with one spent cartridge still in its chamber.

Los Angeles Chief Deputy District Attorney William Doran was fairly certain Louise Peete had killed Jacob Denton. But he also knew that Peete was in Colorado and that she was extremely persuasive. Extradition in that era was far from foolproof. Doran thought it likely that Louise could convince Colorado authorities not to turn her over to California. Or she might simply flee.

So Doran decided to turn Louise Peete's own method against her. He concocted a fiction, a story designed to lure Louise back to California. He sent a man to Denver to ask her to help Doran find Jacob Denton's killer. Louise, as everyone knew, was Denton's good friend. No one knew as much about his final days as she. Wouldn't she come to Los Angeles and help her good friend and strong supporter, the assistant district attorney, solve this mystery?

Louise took the bait. With her husband in tow, she boarded a train for Los Angeles on October 2. But Doran had an arrangement with the Santa Fe Railroad and the train made an unscheduled stop at the summit of Cajon Pass, in the San Bernardino Mountains. Doran persuaded Louise and an increasingly reluctant husband to leave the train for a car he had provided. They drove to a remote resort hotel, Glenn Ranch. Doran kept Louise comfortable and well-fed, but isolated from her friends—and most especially from the press—and he began his game of cat and mouse.

Doran's probing produced one incredible story after another. Louise claimed that if the man in the basement was Denton, then the man who lost an arm, the man who slipped back into town only to see Louise, the man who took up with the Spanish Lady—this man must have been an impostor. Find him and you'll have the killer, she told Doran. And find the Spanish Lady and you'll find him. As the questions continued, Louise spun new stories, often contradicting her earlier tales. She invented unlikely new characters, odd reasons for past actions, convoluted justifications for her illegal actions. She was a novelist, always quick to invent a new twist to a plot she had never quite thought through to its conclusion. But despite Peete's inventiveness and wondrously sincere delivery, Doran became firmly convinced that she had killed Denton. And Louise, caught up in the glow of an appreciative audience, was equally convinced that no jury would ever convict her.

Then she arrived in Los Angeles to learn from the newspapers that it was Doran who had ordered the X-rays used to determine the cause of Denton's death. Doran had outwitted her, had earned her confidence under a pretense and deceived her about his real intentions. Doran played her own game, but he played it better. Losing her composure, Louise refused to face the grand jury and was indicted for Denton's murder.

But she quickly regained her old self-assurance. In custody she provided eager newspaper readers with new and elaborate variations on her basic story. She told police that one day, while she was in her room at Denton's, she heard a shot. Racing to the kitchen, she found Denton at a table. The Spanish Woman bled from a wound in her shoulder—or maybe her chest. And a bullet was "spinning around in the sink."

Her trial convened January 21, 1921. A parade of witnesses poked gaping holes in her elaborate lies. One testified that on the night Denton was murdered, Louise had sung and danced and put flowers all around the house. Her public defender asked the jury how such an obviously refined woman as Louise could have behaved in this way with the knowledge that Denton's still-warm body lay in the cellar below. This convinced some of the spectators, and many who read the newspapers, that Louise could not possibly be the killer. It failed to convince the jury.

After deliberating four hours and casting six ballots, they found Peete guilty of murder in the first degree and sentenced her to life imprisonment. Following her suggestion, husband Richard divorced her, but remained her most loyal supporter, promising to "wait forever" for her release. In 1924, she stopped replying to his letters, refused to see him, broke all contact. He went to Tucson on business and there put a bullet through his head. Three husbands, three suicides.

During the trial, her friends Margaret and Arthur Logan looked after Betty, Louise's five-year-old daughter. And during Peete's 18 years in prison, first at San Quentin and then at the woman's prison at Tehachapi, the Logans remained convinced of her innocence. They wrote, they visited, they bestowed small gifts.

In April 1943, Louise won parole. She was somewhat heavier than she'd been in her call-girl days, but her health was good, her face unlined. She appeared far younger than her 60 years. Her probation officer, Mrs. Latham of the Parole Board, had supported her innocence during the Denton trial. Latham invited Louise to move in with her. Louise agreed. Soon the elderly Latham had a stroke. She went to a hospital where she soon died. Louise, who had taken a new name—Anna B. Lee—stole the late Latham's .32 caliber Smith & Wesson revolver. Then she inveigled an invitation to move into the Logans' comfortable Pacific Palisades home.

Arthur Logan was 74, and thought to be perhaps a little senile, though harmless. He took long daily walks, went to the post office, conversed with his neighbors at length on subjects that held his interest. Margaret Logan held a real-estate license. But this was the middle of World War II. She worked at

Douglas Aircraft as her contribution to the war effort. Louise was paid $75 a month plus room and board to look after Arthur Logan while his wife was at work.

Louise began to spin yet another web. Almost at once she began to tell people that old Arthur was crazy, dangerously crazy. He had kicked Margaret in the face, she told family members. And Louise said she herself had been so assaulted. Using this as ammunition, Louise, five weeks after she moved in, persuaded Margaret to file a court petition asserting Arthur was "mentally ill, dangerous, and insane." Arthur was committed to Patton State Hospital. He remained there for 19 days, before doctors released him to Margaret's custody. Early in 1944 Mrs. Logan left Douglas and returned to real estate.

Louise soon told Margaret Logan about the $100,000 trust fund in Denver she was about to inherit. Then Louise told her she was interested in buying a certain Santa Monica house for $50,000. Margaret would handle the sale. There was to be a 70-day escrow, and Logan was to be co-purchaser. Logan stood to make $2,500 in commission, but had promised half to Louise. Louise announced she intended to resell the property for a profit. But first there was the matter of the $2,000 down payment.

The Bank of America turned down her application, trust fund story notwithstanding. That put the entire burden on Margaret, who had believed in Louise for nearly 20 years. She borrowed $2,000 against her own savings account, put it in the escrow account. Louise planned a trip to Denver to "collect her trust fund." Margaret bought two train tickets. Later Louise persuaded Margaret it was better if she went alone. From Denver she telephoned Margaret to ask for a loan of $300. The money was promptly wired. A few days later she returned by train.

In early May Louise met and married 65-year-old Lee Judson, a semi-retired Glendale bank messenger who had no idea "Anna B. Lee" was really the convicted murderess Louise Peete. She told Judson about her impending inheritance, but added that it might be jeopardized were it known she had married. Though it was flimsy, this fiction got Judson to keep their marriage a secret from the Logans.

And all the while Louise artfully continued to spread her lies about Arthur Logan's growing insanity. He was violent, she said. He was dangerous. He could not remember afterward the frightening things he had done. And probably Arthur's strange behavior also accounted for the small items of jewelry that Margaret noticed were missing.

In mid-May Louise got Margaret to buy two more train tickets for a June 14 Denver trip. A few days later, on May 19, Louise forged a check to herself on Margaret's account. When the Logans' bank noted the phony signature, Margaret told them Louise would repay the funds. But what had become of the Denver trust fund? There was some unexpected delay, explained Louise. Soon all would be in order. But Margaret Logan now stood to lose the $2,000 she had put in escrow. This may well have been when she began to doubt her faith in

Louise. If she could forge a check, if there was no trust fund, if the stories about her husband's mental condition were lies—then Louise Peete was surely capable of other deceptions.

On May 29, 1944, almost 24 years to the day Jacob Denton was murdered, Mrs. Logan was in the act of telephoning—possibly the parole board—when Louise put a .32 caliber revolver to the back of Margaret's neck and pulled the trigger. Perhaps Louise twitched at the last moment or Logan may have moved her head, because the shot did not kill her. She died from loss of blood from the gunshot wound and from myriad wounds inflicted by repeated blows to the back of her head with the steel butt of the little gun that Louise had stolen from the late Mrs. Latham.

Louise dragged Margaret's body into the back yard, buried it in a shallow grave beneath the avocado tree, then cleaned the blood and evidence of violence from the floors and walls. And then she sang gaily, danced a happy little dance, and put bright flowers throughout the house.

On May 31 Louise cashed in the Denver train tickets and used the money to repay Margaret's bank for the forged check. She hoped this would also stop the police from investigating. Later that day Louise told Arthur Logan that Margaret had been injured in an auto accident. She was in the hospital. And that same day Louise got Arthur to help her pack Judson's bags. He helped Lee Judson move in to the Logans' home.

On June 1, Louise used the accident story to get Arthur to come along to the hospital. At the psychiatric ward of Los Angeles General Hospital, Louise said she was Arthur's nurse and his foster sister-in-law. She asserted that Arthur had become so violent she could no longer care for him, and that he had beaten and bitten his wife's face. Arthur said he couldn't remember any of that. Louise exchanged a knowing look with the doctors, told her tales, signed the papers. She left Arthur at the hospital, and four days later he was recommitted to Patton. He died there, lonely and bewildered, on December 6, 1944. Louise generously donated his body to medical science, thereby saving herself the cost of his burial. And a neighbor noted the gay flowers she put out that day; noted the chic new clothing she put on; noted the spring in her step that day, and wondered.

There remained the matter of Margaret Logan's disappearance. To the questions of Margaret's friends, neighbors and relatives, Louise had wonderfully imaginative answers. Mrs. Logan had to have plastic surgery because of Arthur's violence to her face. She was in a hospital close to the one where Arthur was staying. She had breast cancer and had gone away to Oregon. She was in a rest home, humiliated by her husband's attack and her facial disfigurement. She wasn't seeing friends or relatives until she felt well enough. It was all very believable. It was said with great conviction.

From June to December, Louise filled her days with taking over the Logan's possessions. She flim-flammed the seller of the Santa Monica house into refunding half the $2,000 Margaret had put up as earnest money. She sweet-talked the bank into taking her "X" for the "crippled" Margaret's mark on the refund check. She sold or gave away valuable items from the household: an electric mixmaster, a laundry mangle, sterling flatware, fine china, linens. She had some of Margaret's clothing altered to fit her. She took the Logan car for her own use. She appropriated the Logans' ration cards and food stamps, documents that all civilians required to get food during World War II. And on December 20, 1943, she and Judson broke open the Logans' home safe. They were going through its contents when the policeman rang the doorbell.

The cop at the door was Captain Thaddeus Brown, head of LAPD homicide. Louise Peete was no stranger to him. He took her and her husband downtown to the district attorney. There Judson was shocked to learn that Anna B. Lee was the murderess Louise Peete and shocked to realize how he had been duped.

Judson was held as a material witness until January 12, when police were satisfied that the highly respected messenger was just one more innocent victim of the Louise Peete charm. The next day Judson took an elevator to the 13th floor of the Spring Arcade Building and dove headfirst into the stairwell. His battered, lifeless body came to rest on the landing between floors four and five.

In April 1944, another jury listened to Louise's latest string of lies. She had not killed Margaret Logan. It was Arthur who shot her. Crazy Arthur. Louise tried to stop him but he was just too crazed. After the shooting, Arthur beat Margaret's head with a steak hammer. When she died, Louise was afraid to call the police. Surely they would not have believed *her*, a convicted murderess. So instead she cleaned up the mess, buried poor Margaret, had crazy Arthur committed, and went on about her life. That was the substance of her story. The details were involved and presented at length, with enormous verisimilitude.

But physical evidence from the Logan home contradicted all of Louise Peete's wonderful inventions. The jury was allowed to hear some of the similarities between the deaths of Denton and Margaret Logan. "Mrs. Peete, who was a Dr. Jekyll and a Mrs. Hyde, must have sat in her prison cell figuring what went wrong the first time and plotting this new crime," said Deputy District Attorney John Barnes, in his jury summation. The jury deliberated three hours, returning a verdict of guilty of murder in the first degree, without recommending mercy. Louise Peete died in the San Quentin gas chamber on April 11, 1947. Charming to the end, she spoke her last words to the warden: "Thank you for all your many kindnesses."

LOCATIONS:
Thomas Brothers map reference: Page 43 at F3
The house where Peete killed Jacob Denton was at 675 South Catalina Street. The site is now a multistory garage for the Texaco Building, three blocks west of Vermont Avenue and a few steps south of Wilshire Boulevard.

Thomas Brothers map reference: Page 40 at D4
The Logans lived at 713 Hampden Place, Pacific Palisades. From Sunset Boulevard turn south onto Swarthmore, then left on the fourth street, Hampden Place. The house is near the middle of the block, one of very few pre-WWII homes left in the community.

Thomas Brothers map reference: Page 35 at C3
The Spring Arcade Building where Lee Judson became Peete's final victim is at 541 S. Spring. From the Hollywood Freeway (U.S. 101) exit at Spring, a one-way street running south. The Spring Arcade Building is between Fifth and Sixth Streets, on the right side. Once an office building housing elite attorneys and physicians, it's now a unique bazaar with a strongly Mexican accent. The interior is a hollow square, surrounded by tiers of balconies. Judson leaped to his death from the top floor.

Elizabeth Short: Her fiendish killer has never been found.
Photo: Security Pacific National Bank Photographic Collection/Los Angeles
Public Library.

24

FAMOUS IN DEATH: ELIZABETH SHORT (1947)

Few people remember her name and fewer still would know her face. Nevertheless Elizabeth Short found the fame she so desperately sought, fame that lasted long after many of the Hollywood hustlers she admired quietly faded away. Short found fame only in death. In death—an agonizing, hideously cruel, demented, and still unsolved death—she became known as the Black Dahlia, the victim of perhaps the most famous of Los Angeles' unsolved murders.

She was a slender but curvy 22, with sharply striking features, blue eyes, flawless white skin, long hair carefully died jet black—and a red rose tattooed high on one creamy thigh. Born in Medford, Massachusetts, she ran away from an uncertain, sometimes dreadful homelife at age 17. She came to Los Angeles, mecca for the star-struck and an irresistible lure to someone as physically attractive and utterly defenseless as Beth Short.

She didn't stay long, that first time in 1943, just long enough to get hooked on the excitement, the sense that maybe, probably, something big was coming her way, maybe not today, but soon! And maybe she'd be discovered! When she was in the movies, she'd be rich and famous and loved. Especially loved.

She went up to Camp Cooke (now Vandenburg AFB), north of Los Angeles, landed a straight job in the PX, stayed long enough to get voted "Cutie of the Week," but cleared out after taking a few bruises from an angry G.I. Then she turned up in a Santa Barbara dive, drinking with a girlfriend and a couple of soldiers and was busted for being underage. Her fingerprints were taken and mug shots made and the police made sure she was more than sorry before they let her go.

She went back to Boston and tried the straight life again, slinging hash in a restaurant and running the register. She took off for Miami the second winter but returned. She took up with a Harvard man, fell utterly in love with him—but he had a different agenda, and marriage to Beth Short wasn't on it.

She headed west, pausing first in Indianapolis and then Chicago, living in downtown hotels. She met an Air Corps flier and again fell in love. He went west, to Long Beach, California, and wired her to join him. They spent some time together, most of it in a Hollywood hotel room. And then one day he left.

She moved in with a fast 15-year-old, a blonde who was wise beyond her years, and was introduced to the frenetic society of postwar Hollywood, with its phony producers, pious pornographers, schemers, opportunists, petty chiselers, hustlers, crooked cops, and endless one-night stands. It was a town that promised beautiful Beth more than it could ever deliver. She moved in with a middle-aged theater owner, then with six young women in a small flat on Cherokee, then with a butch blonde of uncertain age. She became known around town as the Black Dahlia, because of her dyed jet-black hair and the perpetually black clothing she affected.

She hung around radio stations, went on casting calls—and soon descended into the netherworld of the street hustler where scoring a meal, a drink, a new dress, or a little folding money was as easy as finding a willing guy on Sixth Street. For a few months in 1946 she was a fixture of the Hollywood street scene, a pretty girl not too mindful about where or with whom she slept, a girl pretty and desperate enough to pose nude for sleazy pornographers, a pretty girl descending into a private hell.

By December 1946 she was nearing bottom. She lost her clothes to a landlady after she couldn't come up with the rent. She owed money to all her friends. She spent a drunken night in a Hollywood hotel with a traveling salesman in return for a bus ticket to San Diego and pocket change. In a San Diego all-night movie theater she found a sympathetic, motherly cashier who listened to her tale of woe, took her home for the night and kept her off the streets for almost a month.

Then she found herself another traveling salesman, this one with a car, and accepted a ride to the Los Angeles Biltmore Hotel on January 10, 1947. The salesman offered dinner—and perhaps wanted something more—but Beth Short had a story ready about a cousin from Berkeley. She checked her bag at the bus depot then hung around the hotel. Hung around for three hours near the lobby phones, changing a dollar at the cigar stand and making one or two phone calls, apparently waiting for a call that never came.

When she left at about 10:00 p.m. the doorman saluted her with a tip of his cap and watched her walk down the sidewalk in her red shoes, confidently swinging south on Olive toward Sixth, marching toward her horrid fate.

On January 15 at 10:30 a.m., a woman walking south on Norton Avenue with her five-year-old daughter found Beth Short's body a few inches from the sidewalk in the weeds of a vacant lot between 39th and Coliseum Streets. Medical examiners later placed the time of death at about midnight the night before.

Whoever killed her acted out a macabre and brutal fantasy. The killer tortured her for two or three days as she lay spread-eagled, loosely bound at the wrists and ankles by ropes. He—or she—stabbed her with a small blade, over and over, thrusts that were agonizingly painful but which couldn't kill, then repeatedly applied a lighted cigarette to her breasts. The killer widened her mouth at the corners with his blade, finally ending her agony with an ear-to-ear throat slash. Elizabeth Short choked to death on her own blood.

The killer was far from finished. The rose tattooed on her left thigh was gouged out. The initials "B.D." were carved on the other thigh. Her body was cut in half at the waist like a department store manikin. Every drop of blood was drained from each half, and the mutilated pieces scrubbed clean. Her hair, including her eyebrows, was shampooed, hennaed to a deep red and carefully set, perhaps a message from her killer about Short's lifestyle.

Ten days after her body was discovered, a mail truck driver, emptying a box near the Biltmore, found a cardboard carton wrapped in plain brown paper. Affixed to the wrapper was a message carefully assembled from letters clipped from newspapers: "Los Angeles Examiner and other papers, HERE! is 'Dahlia's belongings...Letter to follow." Inside the carton were Short's purse, Social Security card, birth certificate, a bunch of her personal papers, letters, cards, and scraps of paper with numbers or names on them. Her address book was there as well, with about 100 pages ripped out. And everything had been dunked in gasoline then carefully dried. A long and careful analysis turned up no fingerprints, nor any clue to where the papers and documents had been. The promised letter never came.

The killer of Elizabeth Short was never found, though Los Angeles police put 250 men on the street, though they interviewed thousands of possible witnesses, though they remained obsessed with the case for years, though over the decades more than 50 people offered false confessions, though several books and movies have offered neat and tidy fictional solutions.

Over the years public interest in the case has periodically reawakened, and the personal circumstances of Elizabeth Short have acquired a patina of sentiment. Those who delight in dwelling on the macabre often embellish her history, elevating her to budding movie starlet or making oblique reference to her bit-part roles. There were, however, no bit parts, for the Black Dahlia was never a starlet. Like many thousands of young women who have haunted the streets of Hollywood before and since, she was never more than a pathetic shadowy player at the fringes of a culture frantically fluttering around Hollywood's glowing lamp like a painted colony of doomed moths.

LOCATION: Thomas Brothers map reference: **Page 51 at C1**
Exit the Santa Monica Freeway (I-10) at Crenshaw and go south to 39th Street,

go east two blocks to Norton, then north to the middle of the block. The body was found on the west side of the street about halfway between 39th and Coliseum Streets. Nearly all the homes on this quiet residential street were built after the crime.

Bugsy Siegel: The most dangerous man in America.
Photo: Courtesy of the Hearst Collection, USC Library.

25

BUGSY SIEGEL'S CONTRACT IS A BIG HIT (1947)

Only individuals with a death wish called Benjamin Siegel "Bugsy" to his face. "My friends call me Ben, strangers call me Mr. Siegel. And guys I don't like call me Bugsy," he once told a reporter. "Guys he didn't like" had a habit of waking up dead, a fact that didn't escape his criminal colleagues. He was "the most dangerous man in America," according to Joe "Joey A." Adonis, himself a contract killer in his youth and later a top syndicate boss.

Nevertheless, almost everybody in Hollywood seemed to like Bugsy. In the years just before and after World War II, he was the focus of much social attention from Hollywood's glitterati. He was best friends since childhood with actor George Raft. He was often seen in the company of movie stars, leading sports figures and motion picture industry executives.

In 1940 Siegel spent several weeks in one of the cells of the Los Angeles County Jail. He was being held for the murder of "Big Greeny" Greenburg. But Bugsy still had his connections. While waiting trial he was allowed a few special privileges. Prison food didn't agree with him, it was widely known, so the authorities allowed him his own chef. A man of his stature must entertain, even in such unpleasant surroundings, so he was permitted to bring bonded whiskey to his cell. Lest he get lonely, he was given the privilege of entertaining female guests in his cell. Even so, he found prison inconvenient and disruptive of his social and business life.

So when screen actress Wendy Barrie asked for the pleasure of his company at lunch, he was temporarily released. Just for a few hours. Not long after this, the two main witnesses against Siegel for Big Greeny's murder suddenly died. It was all very abrupt. One day they were in perfect health and the next they were dead. The district attorney no longer had a case against Bugsy. He was released from jail. There was no trial.

Bugsy's girl, Virginia Hill, threw fabulous parties for Hollywood's elite. She studied acting, had a contract with Columbia, picked up thousand-dollar tabs run up by her friends night after night at the swank Mocambo Club. She tipped waiters with hundred dollar bills. She always presented a stunning figure, dressed in the very best outfits. Everybody in Hollywood loved Virginia.

She claimed to be an heiress, claimed the vast sums of money she showered on Hollywood's realtors, decorators, clothiers, jewelers, caterers, restaurants and night clubs, came from the considerable fortune of her late husband, George Rogers. But Rogers was a myth. The money came from the Mob. From drugs, prostitution and gambling. Virginia's ostentatious life of luxury was subsidized by human misery.

And Virginia had tasted that misery. She was one of 10 children born to an itinerant and alchoholic handyman in rural Alabama, and she fled from this privation at age 17. She took with her all she possessed—her long chestnut hair, her quick mind and street smarts, her disarming southern drawl, her elegant features and her voluptuous body. In Chicago, she got a job slinging hash in a greasy spoon, where she was shortly discovered by the scrawny, balding, hawk-faced Joseph Epstein. The very rich Mr. Joseph Epstein. He fell in love with Virginia and showered her with more money than she had ever dreamed existed.

He was Epstein the brain. Epstein the mathematical genius. Epstein the man in charge of Al Capone's Chicago bookmaking operation. He became Virginia's finishing school. A man with endless money and boundless love of his own peculiar sort, he gave Virginia a nickname, the Flamingo, for her long legs and her reddish hair, and introduced her to the lords of crime: Lucky Luciano, Frank Costello, Tony Accardo, Frank Nitti, the brothers Fischetti. And Joe Adonis.

Hill became the mistress of Joey A., who had worked his way up from being Ben Siegel's associate in Murder, Inc., to a more lucrative position. He was involved with Mob heroin and cocaine smuggling and with lending and laundering Mob money. Soon the Flamingo, with her cool head and her fabulous looks, parted company with Joey A. to become the Mob's most trusted bag lady. She took long train and steamer trips with stacks of suitcases filled with bundles of cash.

More and more of this cash went to Mob drug deals, mostly in Mexico. Virginia graduated from bag lady to deal maker. The Mob sent one of its most powerful and trusted lieutenants to establish a West Coast headquarters. He was to take charge, convert Virginia's Mexican drug contacts, couriers and smuggling routes into a big operation. The Mob's choice for the man to head up this operation was one of Meyer Lansky's protégés—Bugsy Siegel. And when

Virginia Hill met Bugsy, she met "the love of my life." They became lovers, friends, confidantes, partners in crime.

After World War II, Bugsy helped convince the Mob's top bosses that the path to power lay through acquiring a legal front for their illegal activities. He talked the *capos* into investing Mob money to build Las Vegas' first modern casino and hotel. Bugsy was in charge of the whole project. The hotel had 280 rooms, and Bugsy named it after his girlfriend. He named it the Flamingo Club.

Bugsy's big problems began with the Flamingo. Even before it opened he lost control. His gaming organization was riddled with double dealers, skimmers, fast-buck artists and con men. Dealers skimmed house winnings from the table and dealt winning hands to friends or confederates. Supervisors rigged the daily count and pocketed vast sums. The casino lost so much money that Bugsy's checks for construction expenses bounced, including two for a total of $150,000 to construction magnate Del Webb for final payment on construction costs. The Dons were very worried about their investment. They were even more worried about their image.

They demanded that Bugsy return the syndicate's money. Bugsy flew into one of his famous rages, the kind that earned him his nickname. He told the Mob bosses to go to hell. He would repay them when he pleased. And he threatened the life of Lucky Luciano, along with some of his confederates.

For this reason, and for others, Bugsy became one of the country's most sought-after men. Chicago police planned to arrest him for his drug-smuggling operation. The Federal Bureau of Narcotics was also getting ready to pounce. And on Capitol Hill the Kefauver Committee added his name to a long list of people they intended to subpoena.

In early June 1947, events began to close in on Bugsy. Virginia went to see him in Las Vegas. She tried to persuade him to apologize to Luciano. To return the money. To give up his vision of creating a glittering gambling metropolis out of the seedy sands of Las Vegas. When he refused, she announced plans for a trip to Paris on business and pleasure. She should have known this would bother Bugsy. He told her not to go. "You don't own me, Ben Siegel," she said. And then she raised the subject of Marie "The Body" MacDonald, a flamboyant actress who was spending a lot of time in Siegel's company. Virginia left for Paris on June 10.

Siegel went to Beverly Hills, to the splendid home at 810 Linden, one of several mansions Virginia leased from Juan Romero, an "admirer." And on July 7, 1947, nine rifle shots were fired through the picture window of the living room. Siegel was hit three times in the head. He died sitting upright on a sofa.

In Paris, Virginia fainted at learning this news. For the rest of her life she never publicly spoke a bad word about Bugsy Siegel. In Beverly Hills, police professed to be baffled by his murder. With the aid of helpful press agents and the newspapers, they advanced several more-or-less credible theories about the reasons for his death. Siegel had died because of a gangland war for control of a news service to bookies. Or perhaps he had been slain in a fight over stolen jewelry. Maybe he was hit because of a gangland connection to a West Coast shipping strike. Or it was part of a Mob war over the distribution of Scotch whiskey. Possibly it was all just a love triangle involving Virginia Hill and one of her scores of admirers.

Historically, the Mob has always dealt with its own problems the way they dealt with Bugsy. And Benjamin Siegel was definitely a problem. Aside from the money difficulties, Bugsy's very public attitude toward Mob bosses was a major embarrassment to an organization that relies on fear to enforce discipline. And it was embarrassing for such an organization to be preyed upon by the petty chiselers Bugsy hired to run the Flamingo.

But at the time there was little public speculation that Bugsy had been hit because of his huge losses at the Flamingo. One reason for this silence was that a great many legitimate investors had their money in it, and some of them had excellent connections with Los Angeles newspapers.

Officially, the murder of Bugsy Siegel was never solved. But it seems a good bet that Virginia Hill, close friend and valued associate of the crime lords, was sent to Paris for her health. Staying too close to Bugsy might have proved fatal.

Virginia died in 1966, after writing a note saying she was "fed up with life." She took a handful of sleeping tablets then walked into a Salzburg, Austria, snowbank. She was 49 and had nothing left of the millions of dollars she had casually dispensed as homage to the good life. On the day she died, Virginia was residing in a hotel room shared with her 15-year-old son. For months, both of them had subsisted on his earnings as an apprentice waiter.

LOCATION:
Thomas Brothers map reference: Page 33 at A6
Take Santa Monica Boulevard west from center city or east from San Diego Freeway. Turn north on Linden Drive. The house where Bugsy Siegel was shot is at 810 Linden Drive, on the east side of the street, just before the junction with Whittier Drive. The exterior of the house is much as it was the day Bugsy died.

Caryl Chessman: Thug, jailhouse lawyer, best-selling author—but not a killer. Photo: Courtesy of the Hearst Collection, USC Library.

26

THE RED LIGHT BANDIT: CARYL CHESSMAN (1948)

He was a ruthless hoodlum who robbed and raped at gunpoint and a brilliant, self-educated scholar who won worldwide repute by setting a standard for jailhouse "lawyering" never before equaled. He was arrogant, crude and overbearing, hated by prison guards and fellow inmates, but he won the admiration of reporters, attorneys and others who worked hard for his freedom. He was a best-selling author who used his royalties to finance a 12-year fight against death in the gas chamber. He became a media star and center of a worldwide movement to end the death penalty, and numbered among his staunchest supporters the leading luminaries of the global liberal intelligentsia. Not ashamed to admit he was a violence-prone robber, he denied to his last breath that he was the "Red Light Bandit." In the end, Caryl Chessman lost his case, and with it he lost his life.

Chessman was paroled from Folsom Prison in December 1947, after serving time for a prison escape and armed robbery. Though only 26, he'd already completed other prison sentences before Folsom and served two terms in a "youth camp" for violent juvenile offenders. Make no mistake: Caryl Chessman was a habitual criminal.

On Tuesday, January 13, 1948, just weeks after his parole, Chessman stole a white 1946 Ford club coupe from Mrs. Rose Howells of South Pasadena. The car had a small spotlight affixed near the driver's window.

At about 4:30 a.m. on Sunday, January 18, a Pasadena dentist, Dr. Thomas Bartle, was returning from a night out with Ann Plaskwitz. Driving south on Pacific Coast Highway from Malibu, their car was overtaken by a light colored

Ford coupe, which flashed a red light. Bartle pulled over to the side of the road. The man who got out of the Ford, Bartle thought, might be a cop. He was "about 30, 5'6" tall," with crooked front teeth. He wore khaki trousers, an olive-drab jacket and a gray felt hat. The man demanded Bartle's identification. A little suspicious, the dentist countered with a request to see *his* I.D. The man reached into his hip pocket and came out with a gun. The bandit took all his money—$15—and drove off. Bartle drove to the nearest police station and reported the robbery.

Later that same day, Floyd Ballew, a car salesman visiting Los Angeles from Custer, Oklahoma, went on a beach date with Elaine Bushaw, younger sister of a woman he'd known for years. After an afternoon sunning and talking, they stopped to eat at a drive-in. At dusk they drove over to see the Rose Bowl in Pasadena. They parked on a deserted road overlooking the stadium. A little before 8:00 p.m., a car drove up beside them. The driver turned on a red spotlight, then stopped a few feet away in the darkness. This couple also assumed their visitor was a policeman. He climbed out of the car and approached Bushaw's side of the car. In one hand he clutched a penlight. He played its narrow beam onto the back seat of Ballew's car, then shined it into Bushaw's face. He displayed a .45 caliber automatic pistol.

"This is a stickup," he said. "If you don't give me your money, I'll kill both of you." Ballew took out his wallet. It had a lot of valuable papers in it, said Ballew. The bandit said he'd settle for the money, and the salesman gave him $20. Then he asked to see what was in Bushaw's purse, which was in plain sight on the back seat. She boldly declared she didn't have a purse—and made an obvious effort to study the bandit's face. Later she would say he was about 35 years old, with a pointed chin and a ruddy complexion, weighed about 150 pounds and stood five feet seven inches tall. "Turn your face, sister," he ordered her. Then he stood around for a few minutes doing nothing, apparently thinking, before returning to his Ford and leaving. Ballew gave chase but lost him after several miles when a city bus cut them off in an intersection. The couple found a telephone and called the police.

Two armed robberies by a bandit in a white Ford with a red spotlight were enough to qualify the Red Light Bandit for a county bulletin, which went out over Sheriff Eugene Biscailuz's signature. On the next day, sheriff's deputies began a series of stakeouts, some using smaller male officers dressed in women's clothing as bait.

The police were mightily peeved. What they told newspaper reporters later was that it had been more than 20 years since "lover's lane" stickups had been committed in this manner in Los Angeles. But the truth was that lover's lanes were routinely patrolled; sometimes errant cops found lone couples vulnerable to a shakedown, or got thrills from catching semi-naked couples. Because most lover's lane victims were embarrassed, most incidents were unreported. But now the Red Light Bandit threatened to expose these police diversions.

The Red Light Bandit may have known that he'd become the object of a manhunt, but he'd found an almost foolproof *modus operandi* and he wasn't ready to quit. Later the next day, he found Jarnigan Lea and Mrs. Regina Johnson.

Lea and Johnson were in Lea's prewar Chevy, parked near the Academy of The Sacred Heart in what is now Altadena. From their spot in the Flintridge foothills above Devil's Gate Dam, they could see Los Angeles spread out before them like a vast, softly glowing galaxy of twinkling lights beneath a twilight sky. Jarnigan and Regina were not really a couple. Lea was 34, a bachelor who lived with his parents in La Canada. Johnson, the mother of a 13-year-old, was a neighbor. Her husband, a retiree 25 years her senior, had declined Lea's offer of a sightseeing ride after dinner. He was home watching TV.

A light-colored Ford rolled up, its tires crunching gravel, and stopped 22 feet away. A red spotlight was turned on. A dark figure swung his legs out from behind the wheel and leisurely strolled over, clutching the inevitable flashlight. "I'll have to see some identification," said a tough voice.

Lea wasn't alarmed. "We were just looking at the lights," he said. The shadowy man insisted. Lea took out his I.D. cards: a driver's license and membership cards for the Elk's Club and for a Masonic order. As the flashlight descended, light was reflected from the cards. Lea saw that the man questioning him wore a white handkerchief over most of his face.

"This is a holdup," said the voice through the handkerchief. He pushed his .45 through the window and grabbed Lea's wallet, which contained "between $35 and $50," while demanding Johnson's purse. She was frightened but not panicked. Coolly she let her diamond-encrusted watch and her expensive rings slip to the floor. "Give me your purse," said the masked man. Johnson turned to hand it to him, but stopped when he ordered the couple to keep their heads turned away. To reinforce his orders, the bandit cocked his pistol. The audible click sent a chill of fear through Lea.

Lea told the bandit he could have their money, but he must leave Johnson alone. "This lady has only been out of the hospital a short time with infantile paralysis," he said. The masked man paused.

He told her to give him the purse—and abruptly changed his mind. "Oh just keep it, because I'm taking you with me," he said.

Regina protested. She couldn't walk as far as the other car, she said. But the bandit left her no choice. She painfully made her way toward the bandit's Ford while he reached in and plucked the keys from the Chevy's ignition. He told Lea that he was to face away from the Ford. "Don't make a move, or I'll let both of you have it. I'm not kidding."

The bandit settled Regina Johnson into the passenger's seat of his Ford. He shoved the gun into her side. He told her to take off her clothes, and she hesitantly removed her outer clothing. He insisted she remove her underwear, pressing the gun hard into her ribs. She took off her underwear. Since she was shivering, the bandit allowed her to pull her coat around her shoulders. As he began to unbutton his fly, Regina told the bandit she was having her period. "I don't want it that way," he said.

Instead the masked man commanded his frightened victim to use her mouth to give him sexual release. Terrified, she complied. A few minutes later the bandit gave her a handkerchief with which to wipe away his seminal fluid. He bade her open her purse, and ordered her to give him $5.00. And he told her that if she told police about his attack, he'd come back and kill her. And then he asked for her address.

She made up a phony number on an imaginary street. And then both victim and rapist heard the sound of an approaching car. Johnson suggested that it might be the police, that the bandit should drop his mask so as not to attract undue attention. He removed his handkerchief and she got a good look at his face in the glow of the approaching headlights. He was a "tough-looking egg," with "real dark eyes." He was of average height—about five feet eight inches or a little taller—and wore kid-leather gloves, a light-colored felt hat, dark trousers and a herringbone sports jacket.

When the car passed without incident, the bandit told his victim she could go back to the other car. After she'd gone slowly a short way into the dark, he called her back. Now she was sure he would kill her. Instead the rapist put the keys to the Chevy in her hand before starting his own car and disappearing into the blackness.

Lea took the sobbing woman to a gas station. In the harsh light of the lady's room she saw the stain of the bandit's semen drying on her coat and started to cry again. Lea drove directly to the Montrose sheriff's substation. "I couldn't do a thing to help her...I never felt so helpless in my life...he'd have killed us both," he told officers. They launched an immediate search of the area, but the Red Light Bandit was long gone.

Gone, in fact, over to Hollywood, to another lover's lane area along Mulholland Drive. About midnight on the 19th of January he pulled up behind a car parked on the shoulder. Pulled up so close that the bumpers of the two cars touched. The red spotlight glowed nearly as bright as the moon shining on Laurel Canyon below. In the car Gerald Stone, a truck salesman, was enjoying the considerable charms of Esther Panasuk, a PanAm stewardess. Once again the penlight, the mask, the gun, the demands. All Stone had in his wallet was a single dollar bill, which he obediently surrendered. Panasuk also had only a dollar, and the robber took that, too. Before leaving he made Stone promise he'd stay there one hour, but as soon as the light-colored coupe was out of sight Stone cranked the engine.

He told Hollywood police that the robber was about six feet tall, weighed perhaps 180 pounds, had black hair and "looked Italian." He said he thought he could identify the man again. Though this was the fourth robbery with the same pattern in less than two days, though virtually every cop in Los Angeles was looking for the Red Light Bandit, the powerful men who ran the LAPD and the sheriff's office sat on the story. There was no release to newspapers, no public warning to avoid lover's lane areas.

The Red Light Bandit laid low for a couple of days. Until about two on the morning of January 22. Then he came upon a Plymouth. In it was 22-year-old Frank Hurlburt, a Loyola College student, and a beautiful 17-year-old whom he knew only as "Mary Alice." Frank had met her at a church dance earlier in the evening and now he was taking her home. With a small detour back into the Hollywood Hills, and up Mulholland to Woodrow Wilson Drive, where they had an excellent view of the city lights.

The routine was familiar by now. The red light, the flashlight, the gun. "Give me your money," said the bandit. Hurlburt said he was broke. "Okay, I'll take the girl," said the masked man. He pulled Mary Alice into his car. Then he ordered Hurlburt to drive down the road and park. But when young Frank tried to do so, the bandit gave chase. He tried to run him off the road, but Hurlburt, who had often driven the canyons at night, put his foot to the floor and after a dizzy chase got away. He drove straight to the police.

Which left the bandit with Mary Alice. They drove around for a couple of hours. The masked man stopped in a remote location and tried to rape Mary Alice. She said later she didn't know if she'd been raped or not. She, too, was menstruating. The bandit was unable to complete the act. Brandishing his gun he forced the terrified young woman to perform the same act that he had forced upon Regina Johnson two nights earlier.

It took police a couple of hours before someone thought of searching Hurlburt's car for some clue to Mary Alice's last name. They found her purse wedged between the seats. In it were her name and address. Sometime after 5:00 a.m. police hurried over to the Meza home to tell her parents their daughter had been abducted. They already knew. Mary Alice had returned home at 5:00 a.m., a few minutes earlier. The Red Light Bandit had let her out of his car at 4:05, and she had walked two or three miles back to her home, sobbing and wondering if he would come back and kill her.

Hurlburt gave the police a description. The bandit's car had been a dark-colored Ford sedan. He was about 35 years old, he told police, and might be Italian. He had a slight accent, a dark complexion, was about five feet ten inches tall and weighed 175 pounds.

But Mary Alice, who had spent hours in the bandit's car, said he was younger, maybe only 23 or 25. He was shorter, perhaps only five feet six inches tall—but then again he might have been as tall as five feet 10 inches. He had a thin or medium build, wavy dark brown hair, dark eyes, crooked teeth, a small hump on the bridge of his nose, a sharp chin, and what looked like a scar over his right eyebrow. The car was either beige or light gray. It had split front seats, so that it was easier to climb into the back seat, and she described the dashboard in detail.

About 6:00 on the evening of January 23 the police radio broadcast an All Points Bulletin (APB) on the Red Light Bandit, including a composite description of his clothing, appearance and his car. They also included a guess that the suspect removed his license plate before each crime and put it in the trunk, replacing it sometime later. At 7:37 p.m. the APB was sent a second time, by police teletype, to all law enforcement officials in the state. Newspapers also got the bulletin.

While the Red Light Bandit's method of operation was being beamed around the state, the bandit was busy shopping for new clothes. More specifically, he and a pal were holding up Town Clothiers in Redondo Beach. They came into the store at about 6:40 p.m., and after listening to salesclerk Joe Lescher pitch his wares, pulled their pistols. They took his wallet and that of owner Melvin Waisler, then forced both into a storeroom at the rear. One man trained his .45 automatic on the clothiers while the other picked out about $300 worth of clothing, items Lescher had assured them were the epitome of style. The man with the .45 took the opportunity to bash Waisler's forehead with his gun, opening a deep cut over his eye. Having gotten his point across, he made the merchant open his cash register, which held $227.

The bandits sped off in their car. Waisler gave chase in a taxi, though he soon lost the fleeing gunmen. He called the police, and identified the bandit's car as "a gray Ford or Mercury." Then he went to a hospital emergency room for six stitches to close his head wound.

At almost exactly 8:00 that evening LAPD officers Robert May and John Reardon were on their regular patrol in eastern Hollywood. Heading north on Vermont near the intersection of Hollywood Boulevard, they saw a car matching the APB description broadcast a couple of hours earlier. Reardon spun the police car through a U-turn while May called in their location. They followed the light-colored Ford, staying several cars back. But they were soon spotted. The Ford pulled into a gas station, continued slowly through the station and exited onto a side street. Reardon used flashing lights and siren to signal the car to stop.

Instead it screeched off down the side street. Reardon gave chase, while May called for assistance. He also stuck his .38 service revolver out the window and took several aimed shots at the fleeing car. For the next several minutes the Ford led the police on a merry chase. It ended at Sixth and Shatto. The bandits tried a wide turn from Sixth, and Reardon gunned the police unit, ramming the Ford. As radio cars converged to block off the area, the two men inside the Ford jumped out. One stuck his hands in the air and surrendered. The other was Caryl Chessman. He was not going to give up without a fight. He fled down an alley, May in pursuit. May stopped for an instant to snap off two shots, and the fugitive stumbled, fell, picked himself up and kept going.

Now May was joined by other officers. Emerging from the alley, Chessman gambled on which way to turn. He ducked into a backyard from which there was no escape. He was still not ready to quit. It took a blow from May's revolver, delivered to his head, and the arrival of four more cops, before he was subdued and handcuffed.

By the time Chessman was dragged to a waiting squad car, Reardon had found the .45 that Chessman had dropped in the street near the car. The man with him was David Knowles, a 32-year-old who stood five feet eight inches and weighed 160 pounds. Chessman was described at the moment of his arrest as five feet 11 inches, 190 pounds. He had dark-brown wavy hair, a long narrow nose with a small hump on its bridge and brown eyes. Among items police found in the car was a functioning penlight. The car also contained an assortment of new clothing. It matched the list that Waisler had provided police after his shop was robbed. Under the rear seat were a pair of license plates. Between them, the police report said, the bandits carried $157 in cash.

The Hollywood cop shop was bedlam. Reporters and photographers jostled each other to see the *two* "Red Light Bandits." While the newsies accumulated, Chessman and Knowles went through what Chessman would later describe in detail as a brutal interrogation. What actually happened is the subject of considerable controversy and became the basis for many of Chessman's appeals. In his version, police handcuffed his wrists behind his back, shoved him against a row of lockers in a back room on the second floor, and proceeded to beat hell out of him. Chessman said a sergeant named Donald Grant called him "a rapist son of a bitch," beat him with his fists, and kicked him in the groin and in the shins.

Then according to Chessman, they turned their attention to Knowles. After Knowles was battered and bruised, Grant beat Chessman some more. And kept beating him until he agreed to sign a confession. Chessman said Grant beat him so badly that there was blood in his urine for days. He also took, said Chessman, a roll of bills hidden in his clothing, a roll worth "about $500" that had somehow been missed during the first search of his person immediately after his arrest. Grant never responded to that particular allegation, but he vehemently denied beating a confession out of Chessman.

According to the police, during Chessman's career as the "Red Light Bandit"—between January 3 and 23 of 1948—he committed no less than 18 offenses: robbery and attempted robbery, grand theft auto, rape and attempted rape, sexual perversion and kidnapping. He was convicted of 17 counts in a trial presided over by the stern and uncompromising Judge Charles Fricke. Considering the circumstances, the trial came to an end rather quickly, on May 18, 1948.

Despite conflicting physical descriptions by several witnesses, Caryl Chessman was convicted on three counts of "kidnapping with great bodily harm." The first was the "abduction" of Regina Johnson from Jarnigan Lea's car to his own, followed by "forcible sexual perversion." The second kidnapping was the abduction of Mary Alice Meza, during which she was forced to commit "an act of sexual perversion." Crucial to conviction was Chessman's confession, which he later repudiated, claiming it was obtained under coercion. A third kidnapping conviction was for forcing clothier Melvin Waisler into the storeroom of his own Redondo Beach store. Though Chessman had neither demanded ransom nor killed any of his victims, the jury's verdict—guilty of "kidnapping with great bodily harm"—carried the death penalty. Fricke sentenced him to die in the gas chamber at San Quentin.

Even prosecutor J. Miller Leavy was surprised at this sentence. Regina Johnson was unhurt and Mary Alice Meza was physically unharmed though hospitalized with schizophrenia. "Chessman took a mind, not a life," said Leavy. But the court psychiatrist believed she had been schizophrenic since suffering thyroid disease at age 12.

David Knowles was also convicted of "kidnapping with great bodily harm" in the Redondo Beach robbery. He was also sentenced to die in the gas chamber.

The sentences were much harsher than those given to men who had actually killed their victims or had demanded ransom. It set off a furor over the death penalty, the echoes of which continue to reverberate even now, nearly 40 years later. The Chessman case became an international cause célèbre, the focus of a decade-long movement to end the death penalty. Leading American intellectuals, famous entertainment figures—and soon their European and South American counterparts—became involved in a 12-year battle to save Chessman's life. Millions of people worldwide signed petitions urging clemency.

Chessman, initially representing himself in appeals, won a reputation as a formidable jailhouse lawyer—and as a best-selling author, after penning *Cell 2445 Death Row*, the first of four prison books. His publishers paid Chessman his book royalties much more quickly than most authors are privileged to receive them, and he used most of this money to hire some of the best legal talent in the country to aid in his defense. There was even a movie made about his struggle, but Chessman was never paid for that.

For more than a decade he cheated his fate with a blizzard of appeals, requests for stays of execution, requests for a new trial, charges of prison-official malfeasance, and a hundred other ploys. In time he began to see his own struggle as a punishment more cruel than the gasping death of the gas chamber itself. In his first book he wrote:

> While I have waited to die, one woman and 69 men have been executed in that Green Room below. Others have gone mad. A demented few have cheated the executioner by violently taking their own forfeited lives. I myself have been within hours of having my life snuffed out before desperate legal action abruptly halted the execution. I am not disturbed by outraged assurances that I am headed straight for the hottest and most horrible part of Hell the moment I inhale those lethal cyanide fumes. Whenever and however it comes, my physical death will mean only a total

cessation of consciousness. And if this Christian hell, by some one-in-ten-billion chance, turns out to be an afterlife reality, I am convinced that the Prince of Darkness will be taxed to devise a torture I would regard as merely an annoyance after my conditioning by the sovereign State of California. . . .

David Knowles eventually won a California Supreme Court appeal, which changed his death sentence to life in prison. Later, the California legislature used his case as a reason to change the sentencing laws in some kinds of kidnapping cases, and repealed the "no parole" provision of his sentence. Knowles was paroled in 1959. In 1960 the legislature changed the kidnapping law so that prosecutors can no longer tack on kidnapping charges in robbery, rape or assault cases unless more "movement" occurs.

But despite the public outcry and repeated appeals, Chessman was executed at San Quentin on May 5, 1960. A last-minute reprieve by U.S. Justice Louis E. Goodman was delayed when his secretary misdialed a single digit while trying to call the warden. The call arrived seconds after the cyanide pellets were dropped into the acid.

Just before he lost consciousness, Chessman signaled *San Francisco Examiner* reporter Will Stevens by a prearranged code. Stevens wanted to know if the inhalation of lethal gas was in fact the humane method of execution the state insisted it was. Chessman had agreed that if he felt great pain, he was to move his head up and down. As the gas filled his lungs, Chessman stared at Stevens and bobbed his head vigorously.

LOCATIONS:

Thomas Brothers map reference: Page 43 at F2
Chessman was apprehended at the corner of Sixth and Shatto, a block east of Vermont. Exit the Hollywood Freeway at Vermont, go south to Sixth, then turn left one block to Shatto.

Thomas Brothers map reference: Page 35 at C1
At the time of his arrest, Chessman lived at 3280 Larga. Exit the Golden State Freeway (I-5) at Glendale Boulevard, go north to Larga, then turn right. The house is near the end of the second block, on the right.

Thomas Brothers map reference: Page 42 at F3
Mary Alice Meza, the 17-year-old girl abducted and raped by Chessman, lived at 1568 S. Sierra Bonita. Go east on Venice from Fairfax; turn north on Sierra Bonita. The house is near the beginning of the second block, on the right.

Thomas Brothers map reference: Page 34 at A1
From the Hollywood Freeway (U.S. 101) exit at Cahuenga. Go north to the Mulholland Drive/Woodrow Wilson Drive overpass. Turn left, and follow

Mulholland (Woodrow Wilson dead-ends about 1/2 mile up, and resumes further into the hills) about one mile to the junction of Woodrow Wilson. There is an area on the shoulder from which much of Hollywood and downtown Los Angeles may be viewed. This is where Frank Hurlburt and Mary Alice Meza were parked at the time Chessman abducted Mary Alice.

Thomas Brothers map reference: Page 26 at E2
From downtown Los Angeles, take Figueroa Street north to the Ventura Freeway (State 134) and go east to the North San Rafael exit. Turn left and cross the freeway then proceed uphill to Glen Oaks Boulevard. Turn right on Glen Oaks. Topping the crest, the Rose Bowl appears ahead. Along this road is where Chessman robbed Floyd Ballew.

Thomas Brothers map reference: Page 26 at E2
From the Rose Bowl go north on Arroyo Boulevard and continue, passing under the Foothill Freeway, to Woodbury. Turn right to Lincoln, then north (left) until just before the road ends at La Vina Sanitarium. The Academy of The Sacred Heart is no longer in this area, but near the road's end are places to observe the foothills above Flintridge. It was along here that Chessman raped Regina Johnson.

Thomas Brothers map reference: Page 67 at C2
Town Clothiers in Redondo Beach was part of the city's older section. When the harbor was redeveloped in the 1960s, the street vanished. The approximate location is 200 yards east of Yacht Basin Number Two.

Mickey Cohen: A gambler and a dandified clotheshorse, his closets were stuffed with fine garments, but his haberdashery was merely a front.
Photo: Courtesy UCLA Library Special Collections.

27

SKATING THROUGH THE VICECAPADES WITH MICKEY COHEN (1948-50)

Mickey was the answer to every Los Angeles newspaper's circulation problem: He was quotable, personable and fashionable. If he was sometimes inscrutable, even that made good copy. And Mickey liked reporters. Small wonder, then, that his name appeared regularly on page one and that practically everyone in the city knew the Mob's West Coast gambling czar better than any Los Angeles crook.

He was a scrapper, a local boy from the Jewish ghetto of Boyle Heights, son of a widowed Russian immigrant who ran a small grocery. Meyer Harris Cohen was a graduate of the university of the meaner streets. At six he was hawking newspapers on downtown corners. At nine he was making small deliveries for bootleggers—for which he was arrested in 1922. His employer "fixed" things with police, and Mickey learned a lesson he would emulate throughout his career.

Mickey went from bootlegging to boxing. In the ring as a teenager, he earned wide respect as a lightweight slugger who could take it as well as he dished it out. By the Thirties he was working his way up through the crime syndicate ranks as a bookmaker, gambler, loan shark and fixer. He was a guy who always knew a guy who might know the right guy.

Diminutive but immaculately groomed, dressed always with sartorial splendor, he cut quite a figure. He was fastidious to a fault. He washed his hands perhaps 50 or 60 times a day. He took care to look after all the "little" people in his universe. He was a famously big tipper. And equally famous for enjoying life and for glamorous parties in glitzy nightclubs. Mickey liked to hang out with movie stars and other celebrities. Many came to like his brash humor, his quick wit, and the aura of danger that seemed to surround him. By the 1940's the formerly closed ranks of Los Angeles organized crime were pinched between incursions by well-financed Eastern mobsters and the increasingly difficult problem of finding the right people to bribe to stay in business. There was no shortage of cops and politicians willing to take a fixer's money; the problem, as Mickey lamented in his memoirs, was finding the right pockets to stuff. "There's no politics in Southern California you can deal with. It's anarchy."

Nevertheless Mickey got by with a little help from his friends. He donated heavily to Richard Nixon's first congressional campaign. He made a public show of his large contribution to Mayor Fletcher Bowron's reelection campaign, though Bowron, a reformer, didn't want the money and didn't want it known that he had *any* connection with Cohen.

In 1948, Mickey's world began to squeeze into fantastic shapes. He was in the newspapers so often that one wag, writing a column for the *New York Daily News*, called the series of unlikely misadventures surrounding Cohen the "L.A. Vicecapades."

One of the sources of his problems was the national crime syndicate, often called "the Mafia." With the 1947 death of Mickey's mentor, Bugsy Siegel*, of New York, Chicago, and, most recently, Las Vegas, Eastern mobsters wanted to "protect" Mickey's racketeering operations—in exchange for a hefty cut of his take. The Mob sent Jack Dragna to bring Cohen into line. When he resisted, Dragna put a price on his head.

At a time when many Los Angeles political leaders were either on the take or campaigning against those who were, Mickey's highly publicized exploits made him a natural target. The LAPD and the sheriff's office habitually called Cohen the "Number One Hoodlum of Los Angeles." Anyone perceived as a frequent associate of Cohen's was dubbed a "Mickey Cohen henchman." Mickey scoffed at such descriptions. "If I see a guy a couple of times or go out socially with him, all of a sudden he becomes my 'henchman.' What the hell is a henchman, anyway?"

As a front for his headquarters, which included a back room bookie shop, Mickey established an exclusive haberdashery, Michael's. Exclusive. Although he was generous about handing out ties and handkerchiefs to visitors, he rarely sold any of the goods, since that would have required reordering and restocking. On August 18, 1948, while Cohen was putting the finishing touches to his "haberdashery," an attempt was made on his life.

His entourage that day included Hooky Rothman, his right-hand flunky; Jimmy Rist, a utility gunsel; Slick Snyder, a shadowy "henchman"; and Jimmy "The Weasel" Frattiano. Frattiano, who decades later would become a noted "canary," was paying a courtesy call on Cohen and was accompanied by his wife and young son.

As the Frattianos departed, Mickey got up to wash his hands. As he did so, a man carrying a gun walked in the front door. Snyder, sitting at a desk, ducked behind it. The gunman rushed forward, firing. He hit Snyder in the arm before he was tackled by Rist. Rist wrestled the gun away but was shot in the ear. The gunman broke loose, but left his pistol. Mickey, who wasn't armed, barricaded himself in the bathroom, lying flat on the floor with his feet bracing the door.

Hooky Rothman had been outside and when he heard the shots he ran to the door. He almost collided with a second intruder, who was likewise carrying a shotgun. The second gunman fired, almost tearing Hooky's head off. Then both gunmen fled.

Sheriff's deputies arrested Mickey and all his men, including the store clerk who had been across the street eating dinner when the shooting started. They charged Mickey with killing Hooky, but the charges were dropped for lack of evidence. Cohen later said he knew who had ordered the hit—but he would settle the score personally.

One of Mickey's "henchmen" was pal and sometime business associate "Happy" Meltzer. Meltzer owned a jewelry store next door to Michael's. On January 15, 1949, LAPD vice-squad cops arrested Meltzer while he drove his Cadillac along Santa Monica Boulevard, on charges of carrying a gun without a permit. No weapon was found, but Meltzer stood trial anyway. In court, Meltzer's mouthpiece accused the arresting officers, Lieutenant Rudy Wellpot and Sergeant Elmer Jackson, of carrying out a vendetta against Cohen by arresting his pal, Meltzer. The attorney, who was on retainer to Cohen, rhetorically asked why two vice cops would want to punish Cohen.

Because when Wellpot and Jackson first approached Cohen about a "donation" to Mayor Bowron's campaign, it seemed to Mickey more like a shakedown. Cohen thought the cops were operating on their own, since Bowron wouldn't want any public association with him. So to foil that game, Cohen had been stubborn and public about donating to Bowron's campaign. In retaliation, Wellpot and Jackson started to lean on Mickey—or so suggested the defense counsel. Cohen was called as a witness. He testified he wasn't so sure the money had actually gone to Bowron's *campaign.* Then Cohen had a wire recording (the recording device that preceded tape) played in court: a secret conversation between Sergeant Jackson and a well-known Hollywood madame, Brenda Allen, suggesting police corruption.

Meltzer was acquitted on the gun charge, but the grand jury subpoenaed the recordings, which also featured LAPD Chief C.B. Horrall and Deputy Chief Joe Reed talking about what might have been bribes. Soon perjury indictments were handed down against Wellpot, Jackson and other vice squaders. They were acquitted, but an embarrassed Horrall and Reed resigned. Cohen never explained how he got the recordings. But his message was clear: If the cops wanted a game, Mickey could play hardball with the best.

In March, possibly as part of a public relations campaign, Cohen sent seven of his men over to Alfred Pearson's radio repair shop. Pearson had been in the news after he acquired the home of a 63-year-old widow, Elsie Phillips, when she failed to pay a $9 repair bill. He'd won an $81 default judgment against her, which forced a marshall's liquidation sale of her $4,000 house. Pearson bought it for $26.50.

Mickey's minions showed up on the sidewalk outside Pearson's place. They told him what they thought of him and what they'd do to him if he didn't return the house to Phillips. Pearson said he'd made a wire recording of their threats. The gunsels, unfamiliar with high technology, decided to take the whole recording machine with them.

In their haste to depart, they made an illegal U-turn and were stopped by traffic police after a two-block chase. During the chase a riding crop, pistol and tire iron were tossed from the speeding Cadillac. The cops took the seven men down to the Wilshire police station. There the watch commander, Lieutenant Clarence Swan, ordered them released.

But an amateur photographer named Roy Diehl took a photo of the seven men being frisked by the police and tried to sell it to the *Los Angeles Times*. Chester Hale, the night city editor, didn't recognize the men as Cohen's. He nevertheless asked Diehl to leave a few prints. A reporter saw the photos, and called Cohen. Cohen didn't want everyone to know about his special relationship with senior police officials. Mickey went to Diehl's home and bought the negatives for $20 "so he could kid the boys." Mickey then offered Hale $300 for the prints. But Hale wouldn't sell. Instead he went to the chief of police and asked if the police hadn't erred in giving Cohen's torpedoes their guns back.

The grand jury indicted Cohen and his men for conspiracy to commit armed robbery—they'd taken Pearson's recorder—assault with a deadly weapon and conspiracy to commit obstruction of justice. Lieutenant Swan and three other cops were also indicted on conspiracy to obstruct justice.

Mickey put up $300,000 bail to get his men back on the street. And then someone—Dragna seems likely—found a way to hurt Mickey's pocketbook. One of the men out on bail, Frank Niccoli, simply disappeared after telling his friends he was invited to dinner at Jimmy Frattiano's. (Frattiano later denied Niccoli had been invited.) Then another of the Pearson Seven, David Ogul, also disappeared. Neither of them was heard from again and Cohen was forced to forfeit $75,000 in bail because he couldn't prove they'd been killed. Fearing for their lives, the others turned themselves in to police. Later they were released on bond provided by men not on Dragna's hit list.

Mickey made Pearson a generous offer and bought Phillips' house from him. He returned it to the widow, amid appropriate publicity. When the conspiracy case came to trial, Cohen and his surviving men were acquitted by a jury of 11 women and one man. After announcing the verdict, the women jurors gathered around Cohen to embrace him. Some were crying.

But Jack Dragna still wanted Cohen dead. A few months later, someone put a dynamite bomb under the picture window of Mickey's Brentwood home. One of his "henchmen" found the bomb and disarmed it. Cohen had a radar security system installed.

On an evening in early May, just as Mickey arrived home, a man in a parked car across the street fired a shotgun at him. Cohen ducked down behind his Cadillac's dashboard, pushed the gas pedal and roared down the street. Unable to see where he was going, he soon ran the car up on a curb. But the gunman didn't pursue, and Cohen wasn't hurt in the collision. A neighbor found the shotgun on his front lawn the next day.

For months, almost everywhere Mickey went he was ostentatiously followed by cars of cops and more cars with reporters. It all but ruined his business, but Mickey was not going to let it interfere with his pleasure. So on the night of July 18, 1949, he went to Sherry's, a Sunset Strip nightclub. As usual, upon leaving Michael's haberdashery, he and his entourage were stopped and patted down for weapons by sheriff's officers acting on orders of County Sheriff Eugene Biscailuz. But strangely, by the time he got to the cabaret, Mickey's ubiquitous police escort seemed to have taken the night off.

With Cohen that night was his chief lieutenant, Neddie Herbert; bodyguard Johnny Stompanato; and Harry Cooper, a six-foot-six-inch investigator from the California attorney general's office. The attorney general was investigating LAPD Vice Squad corruption in Los Angeles. Cohen had been ordered to testify and Cooper was there to protect his life. At about 4:00 a.m. on the morning of the 19th, as Cohen and his party were leaving, two gunmen opened fire.

They fired police-style shotguns with "double-ought" buckshot, slugs with a diameter as big as a 25-cent piece, the sort of ordnance used by deer hunters. One hit Mickey in the shoulder. Another took Neddie Herbert in the small of his back. A third ricocheted off the stone door facing and made an eight-inch purple bruise on the hip of *Daily Mirror* reporter Florabel Muir. Then Dee David, former film actress and a friend of Herbert, was hit by smaller shotgun pellets. Big Cooper took a shotgun blast to the belly.

While the hail of lead continued, a wounded, five-foot-five-inch Cohen bodily carried the wounded Cooper into his own Cadillac and drove him along with Dee David to a nearby hospital. This probably saved Cooper's life. David, less seriously wounded, also recovered, as did Cohen. Herbert died of his wounds eight days later.

The gunmen had apparently spent hours in a stairwell behind a vacant lot across the street, munching sardine sandwiches while they waited. When daylight came, police found the abandoned shotguns, both still loaded, on a nearby street. Years later, Sergeant Stoker of the LAPD, who became the darling of the grand jury and the LAPD's most despised social leper for his testimony about police corruption, wrote that the "murderous attack had been made by members of the LAPD whose motive was to seal Cohen's lips." Stoker opined that top LAPD officials were afraid that Cohen, under increasing pressure from the attorney general's office, might turn state's evidence against those he had bribed.

But Jake Jacoby, a veteran newsman interviewed in 1985 for this book, said that the killers were mobsters and their real target was Herbert, whom they suspected was a stool pigeon.

The drama continued on August 23. That evening, as Mickey was serving dinner to four male reporters representing *Time, Life* and the *San Francisco Examiner*, police and a federal narcotics agent rang his doorbell. They wanted him to go immediately to Michael's to pick up a pair of handguns they said one of Mickey's men had purchased with an illegal permit.

Mickey had guests, and dinner on the table. The guns, he told the police, could wait until tomorrow. The police insisted. Mickey got a little hot. He told the detectives to leave his property, unless they had a warrant. And he called them a few names. Actually, he called them more than a few. Mickey could be quite creative when angry.

A week later he was arrested on charges of "swearing at an officer" and using language "unbecoming even to a gangster," specifics to a charge of disturbing the peace. The case went to a jury trial. Nine women and three men unanimously returned an aquittal.

On the morning of February 6, 1950, Mickey was saved by the radar alarm he'd installed. When it went off at about 3:00 a.m., he arose and looked out the bathroom window. He smelled something burning. He thought it might be rubbish. It turned out to be a fuse. On a bomb. A huge blast went off under the bedroom window of his palatial Brentwood home. The explosion, caused by an estimated 30 sticks of dynamite, was heard as far as 10 miles away. But the dynamite had been placed in front of a heavy concrete floor safe, which reflected most of the blast back into the street. The bomb opened a crater 20 feet wide and six feet deep, blew out every window in the house, as well as those in neighbors' homes, splintered the front door and knocked out a 10-foot section of his bedroom closet wall, ruining 40 of Mickey's 200 expensive suits.

When reporters arrived at the house, Mickey, ever the fashion plate, was cool and collected in monogrammed silk pajamas. "I wish I knew who the sons of bitches are who are doing this to me," he said. A few minutes later, pointing out the bomb damage, he quipped, "You know, I don't think I'm going to be able to rent this room now."

Later that year Mickey told the Kefauver Senate Crime Investigating Committee that although he owned a $200,000 mansion, two Caddies, a $16,000 armored car and employed two bodyguards, he hadn't gambled in years and he was broke. He said that "friends" had tided him over with loans of $300,000 over the preceding five years and that his principal business was a tailor shop. Senator Charles Tobey was incredulous. "Is it not a fact that you live extravagantly...surrounded by violence?"

"Whadda ya mean, 'surrounded by violence?'" he complained. "People are shooting at *me.*"

And they were shooting at his close associates. At 1:30 on the cold morning of December 11, 1950, Cohen's attorney, Sam Rummel, 44, was mounting the steps between the garage and the front door of his Laurel Canyon home when he was killed by a blast from a double-barreled, sawed-off shotgun. The gunman had evidently waited at the edge of the garage. As Rummel lay dying, his assassin tossed the murder weapon into the bushes and escaped. Rummel's body was found early the next morning.

"The Police Department is going to try to solve this case if it takes every man to do it," Chief William H. Parker told newspaper reporters. Parker had only recently been promoted to chief. His remarks were dutifully reported, but reporters had few hopes the killer would be caught.

Rummel had long been known as the "Mouthpiece of the Mob" because his clientele included not only Cohen but several of his more notorious associates, including "Happy" Meltzer and "Admiral" Tony Cornero. * It was Rummel who won acquittal for Cohen and his seven men in the radio shop assault and conspiracy case. Rummel had gotten Meltzer off on concealed weapons charges. Rummel had also won civil and criminal cases for the owners of legal poker palaces in the cities of Monterey Park and Gardena and he had several times defended police officers accused of taking bribes from notorious criminals. He was an outspoken critic of Mayor Fletcher Bowron and of the Los Angeles Police Department.

But he was notably silent about the operation of the sheriff's department. A few hours before he was slain, Rummel had met with two sheriff's officers, Captain Carl Pearson and Deputy Lawrence Shaffer. The officers paid a late-night visit to Rummel's downtown Los Angeles office, a visit that had lasted until nearly midnight. But neither came forward with this information until the day after Rummel's death, when they were identified by an operator in Rummel's office building.

Pearson held a desk job in the sheriff's department's records and communications section. But until the previous August, he had headed the department's anti-vice and gangster detail. Along with Shaffer he was the subject of a much-publicized investigation into the Guaranty Finance loan company.

Guaranty Finance, run by some of Cohen's associates, operated from a storefront on Florence Avenue, in county jurisdiction. Guaranty's "lending" was merely a front for a multimillion-dollar bookmaking ring, easily the biggest such operation in the county. Apparently sheriff's police had known its real function for some time, but it wasn't until an LAPD officer, Lieutenant James Fiske, "jumped his jurisdiction" and began to sniff around Guaranty that public attention was focused on the operation.

After Fiske's investigation, a senior sheriff's officer, Captain Al Guasti, telephoned LAPD Assistant Chief Joe Reed and told him to keep his men out of county territory. Friction between the two departments began to increase. This brought the California attorney general's office into the act. An investigation of Guaranty's books revealed a $108,000 police—or sheriff's department—payoff. Implicated in this payoff were Captain Guasti and his right-hand man, Captain Pearson. And rumored to be advising the Guaranty gamblers was attorney Rummel. All were brought before the grand jury.

Heat from the state investigation forced Guasti to retire; he was later convicted of perjury and sentenced to prison. Pearson was transferred from vice to an administrative job. After it was revealed that he'd met with Rummel only hours before the attorney's death, Sheriff Eugene Biscailuz fired Pearson and demoted Shaffer. But no one was ever arrested for the murder of Sam Rummel.

In 1951, when he was 37 years old, Mickey Cohen was indicted for evading $156,000 in income taxes. He was convicted, sentenced to five years and fined $10,000. He served less than four, and whiled away the time peddling influence to inmates in exchange for prison clothing, which he sold. Upon his release, he opened an ice cream parlor in Brentwood. In a back room, he continued to make book on sporting events.

In 1961, Cohen was convicted of evading income taxes on another $347,669. He paid a $30,000 fine and started serving a 15-year term in Atlanta Federal Penitentiary in 1962. He was attacked by another inmate in 1963 and had to undergo brain surgery, which left him about 50 percent disabled. He sued the federal government for damages, and in 1966 collected $115,000 plus $10,000 in legal fees. Cohen was paroled in 1972 and announced his intentions to "go straight." He told Mike Wallace on network TV, "I have killed no man that in the first place didn't deserve killing by the standards of our way of life."

Mickey Cohen lived his last years in a third-floor apartment in West Los Angeles. A neighbor, now a nursing supervisor in suburban Orange County, recalls that he had a steady stream of visitors, "tough-looking men in black suits came and went all the time," she recalls. "His bodyguard drove him around in a big white Cadillac." In good weather Cohen sunned himself beside the pool, always in pajamas and robe, usually sipping whiskey highballs from a small glass. "His bodyguard always brought an empty wastebasket and a box of toilet tissues, and every few minutes Cohen would wipe his hands and toss the tissue in the wastebasket."

Mickey Cohen died in Los Angeles on July 29, 1976.

LOCATIONS:
Thomas Brothers map reference: Page 33 at D4
Mickey Cohen was ambushed at Sherry's, a posh nightclub at 9039 Sunset Boulevard, near the corner of Wetherly. From downtown Los Angeles, go west

on the Santa Monica Freeway (I-10) to La Cienega Boulevard, then north to Sunset and west to 9039. The club is now called Gazzari's Rock Club.

Thomas Brothers map reference: Page 33 at D4
Michael's, a men's clothing store that Cohen used as a front for bookmaking and other racketeering, was at 8804 Sunset Boulevard, where Palm and Holloway come together. From Gazzari's, go east six short blocks. The building is on the right. The old two-story building is gone, replaced by a new multi-story structure in 1985.

Thomas Brothers map reference: Page 41 at C2
The Carousel, a Brentwood ice cream parlor where Cohen had a bookmaking operation in a secret back room, was at 11715 San Vicente Boulevard, on the corner of Gorham and San Vicente. That building is gone. On the site is a one-story beige stucco building with a green roof housing Engel Brothers Westside Pharmacy. Exit the San Diego Freeway at Wilshire, go west to San Vicente, and north to Gorham.

Thomas Brothers map reference: Page 41 at A3
Mickey Cohen's home in Brentwood was at 513 Moreno. From the Santa Monica Freeway (I-10) exit at 26th Street. Go north to Montana, turn right to Moreno, then left to 513, near the end of the third block, on the left.

Thomas Brothers map reference: Page 41 at C3
The pool apartment where Cohen lived at the end of his life was at 1014 Westgate, just north of Wilshire Boulevard. The building's exterior has been substantially renovated since Cohen's era, including a connecting wall to the building next door and the combining of two addresses into one. But the apartments themselves remain substantially the same. From the corner of Gorham, San Vicente and Barrington, go south on Barrington to Wilshire, turn west (right) to Westgate, then right to 1000, on the right side, at the corner of Kiowa.

Thomas Brothers map reference: Page 23 at E1
Rummel was killed in front of his house at 2600 Laurel Canyon Boulevard, Los Angeles. From Sunset Boulevard, go north on Laurel Canyon to just past Amor Road, about a hundred yards below the intersection of Mulholland Drive. The house is on the left.

*See Chapter 22, *Admiral Tony Cornero and the Battle of Santa Monica Bay* (1939).

Harvey Glatman posed as a kinky photographer. Photo: Courtesy of the Hearst Collection, USC Library.

28

THE MURDEROUS MOMMA'S BOY: HARVEY GLATMAN (1957-58)

He was a creep and a momma's boy—albeit a very bright one with an IQ of 130—a disturbed child who eased his passage through the pangs of puberty by fondling ropes and fashioning nooses to arouse himself. Harvey Glatman grew up in Denver, where as a teenager he perfected a new technique for meeting girls: snatching their purses, then returning them. As a kid he wasn't much to look at. As an adult he was equally undistinguished. Newspaper reporters usually called Glatman "nondescript." He was a skinny, poorly dressed and sallow-faced fellow with a large nose, thick glasses, limp dark hair and a shy tentative manner.

By 1945 Glatman was 17 and desperate to lose his virginity. So he drove to Boulder, Colorado, and stalked teenaged girls until he found one alone on the street. He stopped his car and waved a toy gun at her. He ordered her to take off her clothes. She screamed and ran. The police nabbed him soon afterward. His elderly, widowed mother's pleas for pity and understanding got him out on bail. Harvey promptly lit out for New York City. There he met a wide variety of women, young and old, and robbed them at gunpoint on darkened street corners. Glatman became known as New York's "Phantom Bandit."

Then he took up a new profession: burglary. He wasn't very good at it and was soon caught by police. Sentenced to five years in Ossining (Sing Sing), Glatman became a model prisoner and seemed to respond to regular psychiatric treatments until his release in 1951.

His mother paid for continuing visits to a psychiatrist. She paid for his move to Los Angeles. She paid for his training in TV repair. She put up money so he could open his own TV service shop. And for six years it looked like quiet, diffident bachelor Harvey Glatman was settling into an unexciting but useful role in society.

But Glatman was still a creep and a momma's boy, only now he was older and more experienced. And he was still trying to find a way past the frustrating impotence that always overtook him just on the verge of realizing sexual satisfaction. Because Harvey Glatman, almost 30 years old, was still a virgin. Beneath the diffident and untidy exterior, he was seething with suppressed rage. In 1957 it boiled over.

Glatman was looking for a woman, any woman, who could fulfill his lusty fantasies. Fantasies that involved roped and gagged women. Fantasies of passive, yielding women who would quietly obey his wishes, allow him to satisfy his sexual urges, allow him to do whatever he wanted, at his own pace. He wanted women who were nothing at all like his mother.

And by July 1957, Glatman had thought of a way to do it. Shy but intelligent, cowardly but patient, he had conceived a method of meeting women who would obey his desires. He would masquerade as a magazine photographer. He would find models whom he could convince to pose, bound and gagged.

Calling himself Johnny Glynn, he somehow obtained the address of young Lynn Lykles, a Hollywood newcomer from Florida. Despite his lackluster appearance, Glatman's magazine photographer story was good enough to get him in the door of Lykles' apartment. Her roommate, Betty Carver, allowed him entrance on the evening of July 30. But Lykles was out. Glatman/Glynn asked to look at her portfolio. He put it aside when he saw another girl's photo on the wall. The photo belonged to the third roommate, 19-year-old Judy Dull.

It was quite a photo—but Judy was quite a model. Although just 19, she was the wife of Robert Dull, a newspaper pressman at the *Los Angeles Times*, and the mother of a 14-month-old daughter. Married but estranged, because Robert objected to his young wife's career in modeling. He was unhappy about sharing her rare and exciting combination of voluptuous curves and blond little-girl innocence with photographers who paid her to pose nude. But her sexy looks and her willingness to oblige had quickly earned Judy a fervent following among cheesecake photographers. In just a few months, her star was rising. Judy Dull was bound for fame.

One look at her photo and Glatman/Glynn was mesmerized. He asked to see others, and roommate Betty reluctantly complied. He studied the photos with the intensity of a zealot who has lucked onto a warm trail leading to the Holy Grail. Yes, Judy was exactly the woman he was looking for. Betty asked for his telephone number, so Judy could call him for an appointment. Glatman mumbled something about being hard to reach by phone, since he was usually out shooting photos on assignment. But he asked for and got Judy's telephone number.

He called on the morning of August 1 as the three roommate/models were having breakfast. Judy was at first reluctant, because Betty's description of "Johnny Glynn" was far from glowing. But this was Hollywood, where people are often not what they seem, where movie stars shop in neighborhood supermarkets, where producers wear jeans and millionaires sometimes ride motorcycles. Since his studio was tied up, explained Glatman/Glynn, the photos he needed would be shot at Judy's place. Judy's hesitation evaporated. She wasn't a star, yet, and little things might lead to big things, and a job was a job. And she could meet him in the safety of her own home. Judy Dull accepted an appointment with Glatman/Glynn for 2:00 that afternoon.

When he arrived, Glatman seemed to be positively glowing with enthusiasm. He had solved the problem of a studio, he said. A friend had loaned him one, with all the lights and equipment required. Judy mentioned her hourly fee. He generously agreed without discussion. Betty asked him for a phone number where Judy could be reached and he scribbled one down for her. Judy had other appointments that afternoon and in the evening. Would the session take very long? Not long, said Glatman/Glynn. A couple of hours at most. Everything now seemed in order. Judy agreed to take the job. The fake photographer was almost beside himself with joy. In minutes they were out the door, toting a suitcase with Judy's cheesecake costumes and makeup into the hot, sunny August afternoon. He loaded this gear into his car, a decrepit black Dodge with Colorado plates, and drove off.

But not very far. The "studio" was a second-story apartment in an aging building on Melrose, on the fringe of Hollywood. It was Glatman's apartment. The living-room blinds were tightly drawn. In the middle of the floor were lights, tripod, camera, and other accoutrements of the photographic profession.

Glatman told his model to take off her dress and put on a skirt and sweater. When she complied, he picked up a loose coil containing several pre-cut lengths of white sash cord. Judy reacted fearfully. She wasn't into sadomasochism. She didn't care much for the bondage and discipline scene. Not to worry, soothed Glatman. His assignment was the cover of a detective magazine. A sweet and innocent girl kidnapped by a ferocious brute. She was bound and gagged, her features contorted with fear. That was his photo. And Judy, who hadn't been modeling long enough to know better, went along with the gag and allowed Glatman to tie her up.

"Not too tight," she cautioned, fearful of bruising valuable skin. But by this time Glatman was beyond caring. His knots were carefully tight as he tied her hands and feet, then bound her knees for good measure. He gagged her sensual mouth with a torn strip of cloth. He made her look terrified. It was easy. And then Harvey Glatman took some photos. Souvenirs, he would say later.

Still he wasn't satisfied. He wanted it to look as though she had been raped. He unbuttoned her sweater. He pulled her bra down, exposing her breasts to the camera. And he pulled off her skirt. And at that he abandoned all pretense of professionalism.

As Judy struggled and emitted muffled shrieks through the gag, Glatman put her on the floor in a supine position. He fondled her body, now clad only in panties, his hands growing bolder. But Judy cried and writhed and protested through her gag. This would not do for Glatman. He became impotent before *any* feminine resistance. But he was so close now, so close to realizing his sick fantasy, he couldn't allow anything to stop him.

He left the room. He came back with a gun, a black, small-caliber automatic. He was an ex-con, he told Judy. He wouldn't think twice about killing her if she gave him any trouble at all. He was going to remove her gag, but if she cried out he would shoot, warned Glatman. He took off the gag.

Judy tried to reason with him. She would do whatever he asked, if he just put the gun away. She couldn't report him to the cops, she told Glatman, because she and her husband were involved in a custody battle over their daughter. Her husband contended that modeling was immoral and so she was an unfit mother. If she went to the police, she would lose all chance of getting her daughter back. So, said a panicked Judy, she would do whatever Glatman wanted. If he would just put the gun away and untie her.

He pocketed the gun. But Glatman was in no hurry. His fantasy was having a beautiful, naked woman totally and absolutely in his power and now that he finally had one he was going to make it last as long as he could. So he carried his bound fantasy object into the hallway where he could keep an eye on her while he had a little something to eat. Then he cleaned up the living room. He stashed the lights and photo equipment in a closet. He moved his shabby furniture back to its usual locations. And he turned his attentions back to his prize.

She had a nosebleed, probably from rolling around on the floor trying to get free. Glatman got a pillowcase to staunch the blood. He put it carefully aside, another souvenir. Then he carried her to the couch. He removed her bonds, and bade her model for him again. After a few exposures, he put the camera away—and carefully laid his gun on the coffee table. He would not hesitate to use it, he told Judy, and then proceeded to rape her. After a short rest interval, he raped her again.

And then it was time to watch a little TV. They sat together like old lovers, casual with each other's nudity, and he stared at the tube while he fondled Judy and mused about what he would do next. He was afraid that Judy would turn him in. As an ex-convict, he knew all too well that the courts would not believe his alibis or excuses. He also knew what prison was like and he wanted no part of it again. Judy tried to reassure him. She would just take a cab home and that would be the end of it, she said. She begged him to believe her. She cried.

But Glatman was a *smart* creep, momma's boy and, now, rapist. He knew he couldn't leave his fate in the hands of Judy Dull, who had a straight-arrow husband. She knew where he lived, what he looked like, what kind of a car with Colorado plates he drove, and that he had served time in prison. As long as Judy was alive, he was in great danger. But he couldn't tell her that. He had to have her cooperation to get her out of the apartment without a struggle.

So he told her it was better if he took her to some remote location and released her. He would even give her money for bus fare. By the time she got back to civilization he would have a big head start on the law. Judy didn't much like the idea, but the alternative, as Glatman presented it, was worse.   He would shoot her right now, right here, if she put up a struggle.

Camera gear in the trunk, a gun in his pocket and Judy by his side, he headed east, out the new San Bernardino Freeway. Past Riverside he arched south on Route 60. At the Palm Springs cutoff he continued toward Phoenix. He stopped, somewhere between Thousand Palms and Indio, on a stretch of deserted highway.

It was midnight, and Judy shivered in the cold desert air as Glatman marched her toward the Southern Pacific tracks paralleling the road. Her hands were tied. His were full of camera, flash and a blanket. He wanted to take just a few more shots before releasing her, he explained. She lay face down on the red blanket while he roped her arms and ankles. She didn't react at all when he looped a cord between her ankles. Until he put the other end around her throat, then pulled it till her feet almost touched her head. She screamed when he put his knee in her back and hauled on the rope with all his strength. She screamed until she lapsed into unconsciousness and died with a whimper after perhaps five minutes of strangling.

Glatman, remorseful for his deed, apologized to the corpse of his victim. He roused himself, dragged her body behind a desert bush, scooped a shallow pit from the sand, and rolled her into it. He took the ropes off poor Judy Dull and he took her shoes. More souvenirs.

Judy's disappearance did not go long unnoticed. When she failed to make her other appointments on August 1, Betty called the number Glatman had given her. It was a machine shop, and nobody had ever heard of "Johnny Glynn." Betty called the county sheriff to report a missing person. So did Robert Dull, worried because he hadn't heard from his wife that day, an unusual event. Betty gave police a fragmented description of Glatman. The only thing they could turn up in weeks of investigating was that nobody but Betty had ever heard of a photographer named Johnny Glynn.

Johnny Glynn was gone. Glatman buried him with Judy Dull. And for seven months he resumed his shy and quiet life as a TV repairman. Until March 8, 1958. On that day Glatman became George Williams, a plumber.

That was the name he gave to Shirley Ann Bridgeford, a lonely divorcee of 24. The mother of two small children, Shirley was a slender, plain-featured woman still suffering the pangs of rejection after her fiancé broke their year-long engagement. She lived with her mother in Sun Valley. Urgently seeking a mate, Shirley had paid $10 for membership in a "lonely hearts" club in hopes of meeting a nice man who might marry her. Shirley was desperate.

But not nearly as desperate as Harvey Glatman. No longer a frustrated virgin, he was a merciless killer who had learned to find sexual satisfaction through sadistic torture. On the telephone he told Shirley they were going to a hoedown, to a Western-style dance. Shirley dressed accordingly.

But when Glatman showed up, he was dressed in his usual rumpled suit. After mumbled introductions, he led Shirley to his car. Scarcely had they met when he suggested a change of plans. He wasn't much interested in square dancing, he allowed, but the night was young. There was a nearly full moon and some spectacular scenery to look at while they became better acquainted. So, suggested Glatman, why not go for a ride? Mild-mannered and agreeable, Shirley said it was all the same to her.

The route Glatman chose took them south to Long Beach and then down the coast toward San Diego. Near Oceanside, almost 100 miles from Los Angeles, he turned off the coast road onto a dark side lane. He stopped the car. Overcome with sexual urges, he was eager to explore Shirley's body. Shirley was unwilling to allow intimacies with a man she'd just met. It was late, she suggested. It was time to go home. She grabbed the door handle and held on for dear life.

Glatman said he was hungry, that he'd find a drive-in and after something to eat he would drive her back. Instead he turned off into the dark and lonely mountains along Highway 395, and headed inland. He drove with one hand on the wheel and one groping for Shirley's chest, her thighs, her lap. She fought him off. He stopped the car and produced the black automatic.

He ordered her into the back seat at gunpoint. Even staring at a loaded gun she was loath to take her clothes off and Glatman had to tear them from her body before he raped her. Then he tied her up. He continued driving over the mountains toward the Imperial Valley.

In the arid vastness of what is now the Anza Borrego Desert State Park, he turned off the paved road onto a track called Butterfield Stage Road and early on the morning of March 9 he stopped the car in the middle of nowhere. He unpacked his camera gear and fetish ropes from the car and tugged a bewildered Shirley along, promising that all he wanted was a few snapshots. Glatman tied and gagged Shirley on the same red blanket on which he had killed Judy Dull. He took his ghoulish photos. He removed the gag. Even as she pleaded for her life, begging him to consider that her two small children would be orphaned, Glatman killed Shirley, exactly as he had garroted Judy Dull. He tore the labels from her clothes and kept her red panties as a memento. And he scooped out another shallow grave in the desert.

Shirley's mother had phoned the Los Angeles police when her daughter failed to come home. Police soon learned that "George Williams" was a phony name and that his lonely hearts address was a fake. Checking with the sheriff's office, they discovered a number of similarities between descriptions of George Williams and Johnny Glynn. He might well be the same man, they decided. But with nothing else to go on, the police were at a dead end.

Now that he knew how easy it was, how safely he could slake his lust with ropes and rape, Glatman couldn't wait to try it again. On the night of July 22, he did. This time he was "Frank Johnson." He dialed the number of a nude modeling service on West Pico Boulevard and asked to speak to Angela Rojas.

Angela Rojas was the *nom de guerre* chosen by Ruth Rita Mercado, 24. Of medium height, with long dark hair, Ruth Rita was from Florida, where she had created a sensation as a striptease dancer. Her main attraction was a phenominally cantilevered chest that she was not shy about displaying to eager amateur "photographers." For cash. In advance.

Ruth Rita accepted a telephone appointment with "Mr. Johnson" but took sick the moment she saw him standing outside her door. He tried again early the following evening, but she wasn't home. He killed a few hours swilling beer in a local bar, then returned to find the alluring Ruth Rita in a clinging sweater and tight capri pants. Wasting no time on formalities, he took out his little black automatic.

After forcing Ruth Rita upstairs to her bedroom he went through the rope-and-gag routine. Wearing rubber gloves, Glatman prowled around downstairs looking for something he could steal, before returning to his trussed-up sex object. Warning her against crying out, he removed her bonds and brutally raped her.

Now he had to find a way to get her out to the car. Ruth Rita unwittingly provided it. "My boyfriend will be over soon," she said. Glatman told her they were going for a ride. He had some sandwiches and drinking water. It would be a regular picnic, said Glatman. Ruth Rita thoughtfully offered to bring two bottles of brandy from her liquor cabinet and Glatman accepted before he hustled her down to his car. "You're a pretty good sport," said Glatman. "I'm gonna like you."

By a different route than on the previous occasion, Glatman arrived at the set of wheel ruts called the Butterfield Stage Road early on the morning of July 24. He turned the opposite way from where Shirley lay beneath a cactus and stopped in the great outdoors. He got out his fetish kit and camera, and for the entire day he and Ruth Rita partied. Glatman raped the unresisting model "four or five" times. In between they ate and drank, and Glatman tied and untied Ruth Rita, each time taking more pictures of her nude voluptuousness. About dark, he decided it was time to leave.

After a few miles, Glatman stopped the car. He told Ruth Rita he'd just take one more set of pictures. With flash. He got out the ropes and the red blanket. Ruth Rita shrugged and trooped off into the desert, walked calmly over the cooling sands to meet the same fate that had ended the lives of Shirley Bridgeford and Judy Dull. But Glatman didn't feel all that happy about it. Though he didn't have much feeling for his first two victims, Glatman thought he actually liked the woman he knew as Angela Rojas. After she gasped her last breath, Glatman took her watch, torn nylons, white slip and all her identification. More souvenirs. He noticed that the real name of the woman he'd strangled was Ruth Rita Mercado.

It was more than two weeks before anyone reported her missing. Even then the police had nothing to go by, no clues at all.

Harvey Glatman felt that he'd had such good use out of "Frank Johnson" that he decided to keep him around for a while. In October Johnson went to see a 20-year-old, semi-retired nude "model" named Diane at her Sunset Strip agency. He'd shot some photos of her before, in the safety of a public studio. Johnson invited her over to his studio to shoot some "calendar art." Diane had a hunch about the creepy guy who called himself Johnson and she begged off. She was retired from that end of the business, said Diane.

Glatman persisted. He came back the following evening, October 27. Diane wouldn't budge. But...she had a friend, Lorraine Vigil, just down from San Francisco and a little on the hungry side, who might not be so choosy. Hoping to be rid of Johnson, she telephoned Lorraine.

Lorraine was 27, a petite woman with black hair and a surprisingly full figure. By the time Glatman pulled up outside her home it was almost 10:00 and she was in heavy makeup and an evening gown.

Glatman never bothered to get out of his old Dodge. He just tooted the horn a few times. Lorraine made a mental note that he was rude—and climbed in anyway. Her fee was $15. Lorraine wanted it up front. She settled for $10 with a promise of the rest when the assignment was completed.

The shoot, said Glatman, was to be in his studio in Anaheim. Lorraine objected. She'd understood it was to be at Diana's studio. Glatman insisted and headed south on the Santa Ana Freeway.

The entire trip was made in silence. When they slid right through Anaheim, heading south, Lorraine began to feel real fear. She sneaked a glance at Glatman. In the spooky glow of headlights from opposing traffic his face had a look of ghoulish concentration. He was anticipating the rest of the evening. Whetting his appetite for the pain and terror he would soon inflict on Lorraine and the glorious ecstasy of release he would experience at the moment he strangled her. Just past Santa Ana he pulled off the freeway. They were in semirural Tustin, moving rapidly down Tustin Avenue.

Without preamble he pulled off the road. He broke his silence. "Flat tire," he said. And took out his gun. He would put a bullet in her breast if she didn't do exactly as he told her, said Glatman. He took out his rope and started to tie her hands.

That wouldn't be necessary, pleaded Lorraine. She would be quiet, she would do whatever he asked—but please don't tie me up, she begged. He hesitated, considering it. A passing car's headlights crawled up the pavement toward them, and Lorraine made her move. As the car drew abreast of them she screamed and beat on the window with clenched fists. The car never paused, nor did the one just behind it.

Glatman jerked the tiny woman to him, covering her mouth with his hand. He would strangle her here and now if she opened her mouth again, he warned. "I've had enough of you. I could tie you up but I really ought to kill you," ranted

Glatman. His declaration steeled Lorraine's resolve. He might kill her if she resisted—but he would probably kill her anyway. She grabbed for his gun and struggled furiously for it.

Both were scared to hear the gun go off. The bullet pierced her skirt, harmlessly grazing her thigh. Glatman seemed petrified. Lorraine's hand sought the door handle behind Glatman. And found it. With a mighty heave she pushed him backward. They landed in a heap. Once again she struggled for the gun. She had it. Glatman took it away. She bit his hand savagely and picked up the automatic. She pointed it at him and pulled the trigger. Nothing happened. The gun was jammed. She tried again.

The gun wouldn't fire, but it no longer mattered. Screeching to a halt in a cloud of dust was the motorcycle of Highway Patrolman Tom Mulligan. He held a service revolver in his hand. Harvey Glatman would rape, torture and strangle no more.

In his Hollywood apartment police found the grisly mementoes of his three previous victims. Enlargements of Judy, Shirley and Ruth Rita adorned the walls. In a closet were their driver's licenses and other I.D. Police put Glatman in a lineup. When friends of his three victims identified him, Glatman broke his silence. He confessed in excruciating detail, leading police to the desert gravesites.

He pleaded guilty. He asked his public defender to get him the death penalty. Judge and jury obliged: Harvey Glatman died in the San Quentin gas chamber on August 18, 1959.

LOCATIONS:
Thomas Brothers map reference: Page 33 at E4
Judy Ann Dull lived in an apartment at 1302 Sweetzer Avenue. Go east from La Cienega on Fountain to Sweetzer. It's the ornate, six-story, cream-colored stucco building on the northeast corner.

Thomas Brothers map reference: Page 43 at C3
Take Olympic Boulevard east from Crenshaw to Norton. Turn south on Norton to 1011. The one-story white-shingle bungalow with black tarpaper roofing and bars on the windows is the building Glatman lived in when he committed the murders of Dull, Mercado and Bridgeford, and where police discovered the grisly evidence that helped convict him.

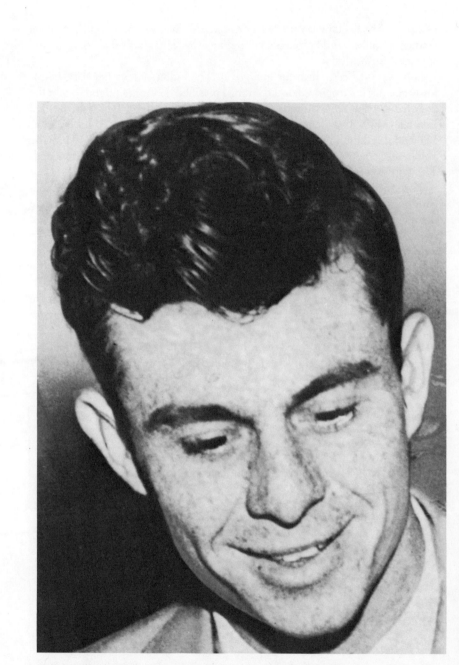

Carl "Alfalfa" Switzer: He lost a borrowed dog, then asked the owner to pay the reward. Photo: Courtesy of the Hearst Collection, USC Library.

29

CHILDISH QUARREL: THE SHOOTING OF CARL "ALFALFA" SWITZER (1959)

His baby pictures tickled generations of kids all over America and in half the world. A head taller than the rest of *Our Gang*, Alfalfa was a skinny kid with a yo-yo for an Adam's apple, a generous assortment of freckles, an irrepressible cowlick and a trained voice that could consistently sing off-key while he crossed his eyes and blew bubbles. Whatever the misadventures of the lovable, ragtag *Gang*, a banjo-eyed Alfalfa played them around a boyish screen crush on four-year-old   Darla. She responded in kind. The series was a colossal hit.

Between 1935, when he was eight years old, and 1942, when the no-longer-concealable end of adolescence ended his participation in the still-popular series, Carl W. Switzer played his Alfalfa role in 60 *Our Gang* shorts for Hal Roach. In 1955, along with Spanky, Buckwheat, Darla and Porky, he was introduced to a new generation when the *Our Gang* pictures were turned into a TV series, *The Little Rascals*.

But television had been an obscure, experimental novelty in 1935. Switzer and the rest had nothing in their contracts about TV residuals. They never got a dime of the millions the series earned from endless syndication.

Darla Hood gracefully retired from movies at age 14. Switzer hung out at the shabby fringes of the industry. He was a has-been who struggled for bit parts, a star who was washed up before he was old enough to drink. But drink he did. And brood. Switzer, known to his friends as "Alfie," refused to accept that there was no place for him in the Hollywood of the '50's.

219

Alfie had a few famous friends, among them Roy Rogers and Henry Fonda. He knew them, not from the sound stages, but from the backwoods. To eke out a living, Alfie had become a part-time hunting guide and sometime bartender. His friendship with Rogers got him two minor appearances on *The Roy Rogers Show* in 1956; Fonda helped steer him to obscure bit parts in *The Gas House Kids, Going My Way* and *Pat and Mike*.

He met, courted and married Kansas heiress Dian Collingwood in 1954. The marriage lasted four months. Hedda Hopper wrote its obituary: "Bear hunting and marriage don't mix."

By the end of 1958, things seemed a little brighter. He got a small supporting role in *The Defiant Ones*. While his paycheck was modest, his performance in the picture, which was scheduled for release in 1959, showed promise as a comeback vehicle.

But in the meantime Alfie had to earn a living. He borrowed a hunting dog from a friend, Moses S. "Bud" Stiltz, for a hunting expedition he was guiding. But the dog ran off and Stiltz, a welder, was upset. Alfie posted a reward for the animal: $35.00.

A few days later, a man called Alfie to claim the money. He delivered the dog to the tavern where Alfie tended bar. Much relieved, Alfie bought him a few drinks. The bar tab came to about $15.00.

In the next weeks the frustration that had dogged Alfie seemed to overwhelm him. He was 32 years old, broke or almost broke, and his long-awaited comeback was on hold until *The Defiant Ones* was released. Somehow he got it in his head that Bud Stiltz owed him the $50 he'd spent recovering the dog.

He called Stiltz and asked for the money. The welder didn't see things the same way. Alfie had borrowed his dog, and Alfie had lost the dog. If he'd had to spend money to recover the animal, that was Alfie's problem, not his.

But Alfie wasn't in the mood for logic. He wanted the money. He spent most of the night of January 22, 1959, with a pal, studio still photographer Jack Piott. Drinking and brooding and drinking, he developed a powerful hatred for Stiltz.

Late in the evening Alfie and Piott rang the doorbell of Stiltz's San Fernando Valley home. Piott flashed a studio prop department badge. "Open up, police!" he shouted. The door opened a crack, and the two visitors pushed their way in.

"I want the fifty bucks you owe me and I want it now," shouted Alfie.

"I don't owe you any fifty," screamed Stiltz. "You lost the dog, you pay." Alfie looked around the living room, and his eyes came to rest on a heavy clock under a glass dome. He grabbed the clock, swung it at Stiltz. "I'm gonna take $50 out of your face," he screamed. The clock struck above Stiltz's right eye and blood gushed. The swollen eye began to close.

The welder backed into the bedroom. Alfie followed. Stiltz opened the closet. He reached in and took out a .38 caliber revolver. Alfie grabbed for the gun. It went off, the bullet burying itself harmlessly in the wall.

Alfie shoved Stiltz into the closet and closed the door. He picked up the gun, laid it on the dresser and returned to the living room. "He's trying to kill me," he said to Piott, as he took a switchblade knife out of his pocket. He flicked it open.

He turned his head at the sound of Stiltz returning from the closet. He held the gun in his hand. Alfie brandished his blade. Stiltz fired a bullet that caught Alfie in the stomach. He died en route to the hospital.

"Alfalfa" died on the evening of January 22, 1959. Ordinarily, his shocking death would have been big news. It might have recovered a measure of the recognition he'd been denied during his adult life.

But the fickle gods of filmdom's fame had made other plans. Hollywood's most famous director, Cecil B. De Mille, died the same day, after a long illness. Prepared obituaries and celebrity tributes to De Mille's genius buried the death of Carl Switzer in relative obscurity.

Bud Stiltz was freed after a coroner's inquest ruled the shooting was justifiable homicide.

LOCATIONS:

Thomas Brothers map reference: Page 8 at C3
Switzer was shot at the Stiltz home in Mission Hills. Exit San Diego Freeway (I-405) at Devonshire. Go east past Sepulveda one block to Columbus Avenue, turn north (left). This is a pleasant residential street lined with many producing orange trees, remnants of the orchards that once dotted this community. The house at 10400 Columbus where Alfie Switzer died is a single-story tan stucco ranch house with a large white trellis.

Thomas Brothers map reference: Page 22 at C1
Carl Switzer lived at 5415 Sepulveda Boulevard, Van Nuys. Exit San Diego Freeway (I-405) at Burbank. Go south on Sepulveda to 5415, on the right side, just before Clark Street. The original property is long gone, replaced by a two-story stucco apartment building with a flagstone entranceway.

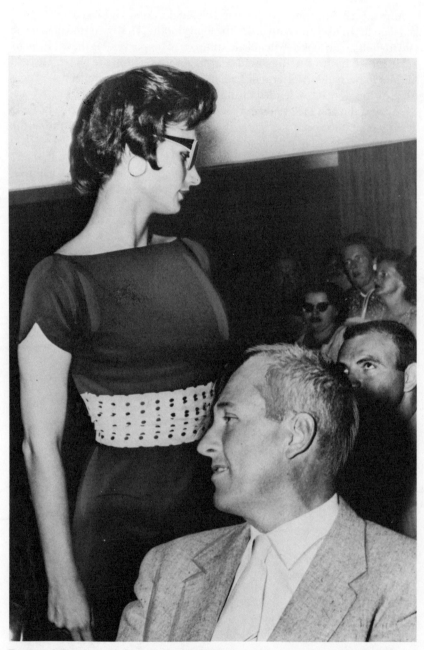

Bernard Finch and Carole Tregoff: They packed a murder kit and hid in the bougainvillea. Photo: Courtesy of the Hearst Collection, USC Library.

30

THE MURDER OF BARBARA (MRS. BERNARD) FINCH (1959)

Carole Tregoff was a ripe and leggy 23 and seemed to have found the fast track to realizing the California Dream. She had a good job, medical secretary to a rich and extremely successful Covina physician. And she had a muscular young husband, James Pappa. Carole exuded a sexy, glamorous glow, that attracted "cheesecake" photographers who paid her to model. Carole attracted many men, including her boss, Dr. R. (Raymond) Bernard Finch. She attracted him quite a lot.

In fact, Finch, 42, was crazy about her. They began sharing a succession of little love nest apartments. All rented under an assumed name, of course. Loving Carole was complicated.

One of the complications was Barbara, Finch's stylish blonde wife of 36. Slim, elegantly pretty, socially well-connected, Barbara had grown weary of her husband's indiscretions, weary of the whispered rumors that he sometimes performed illicit abortions for Covina's wealthy. But most of all, Barbara was weary of his violent rages and his cruel beatings. In 1957 the Finches agreed to a separation, though Barbara refused to speak of a divorce.

Free to come and go as he pleased, Dr. Finch pressed Carole to divorce her husband. In 1958, she did. Pappa felt victimized. He joined a growing number of patients who had accused Finch of malpractice, claiming he'd been crippled by botched knee surgery. And he looked up Mrs. Finch, with whom he shared what he knew about Finch's relationship with Carole.

Barbara saw red. Or perhaps green, the color of money. Under California law, her estranged husband's adultery gave Barbara cause to seek divorce on grounds of desertion. She could then claim their entire estate, valued at some $750,000, including half of a highly profitable medical clinic that the Finches co-owned with Dr. Frank Gordon. Barbara hired a private detective to get proof of her husband's infidelity. Then she started divorce proceedings.

That scared Dr. Finch, who faced heavy alimony and the prospect of pauperhood. So he hired John Patrick Cody of Las Vegas, Los Angeles and assorted jails. Cody was something of a lady's man, something of a petty thief. He was hired to make love to Barbara so Finch could later prove she had also been adulterous, which might even the score when they got to divorce court. But Barbara wasn't interested in Cody's advances.

So Carole Tregoff offered him $1,400 to shoot Barbara. "If you don't kill her, Dr. Finch will...and if he won't, I'll do it," she said, according to Cody's courtroom testimony. "Before you kill her, tell her the bullet came from Bernie," said Tregoff. Even so, Cody told police he never intended to kill anyone and by July 1959, Mrs. Finch was still alive. The lovers took things into their own hands.

Carole moved to Las Vegas and took a job as a waitress and Finch commuted from California. On the night of July 18, they drove to the Finches' West Covina home and brought along what prosecutors would later describe as a "do-it-yourself murder kit." It was an attaché case containing a length of rope, a butcher knife, ammunition for a .38 caliber revolver, two pairs of rubber surgical gloves, drugs, hypodermic syringes and needles. Finch later insisted this was what he always carried when making house calls.

Barbara Finch returned home at about 11:00 p.m. to find Carole and Bernard waiting on the front porch. There were some words, and then there were two shots and Barbara Finch lay dead with two bullets through her back. The Finches' 19-year-old Swedish maid appeared at the front door. She saw the doctor, gun in hand, standing over Barbara's inert body. She began to scream. And scream. She didn't stop until Finch banged her head against the door a few times. "I had to shut her up," he said.

Then the lovers drove the 250 miles back to Las Vegas in five hours and went to bed. Carole, unable to sleep, turned on the radio, only to hear the news of Barbara's death. She woke Finch. "Your wife is dead...what are you going to do?" she asked. He rolled over and went back to sleep. Police arrested both the following day.

In court, police theorized the "murder kit" was designed to kill Barbara Finch in several ways. They planned, said police, to inject an air bubble into Barbara's bloodstream in order to cause a fatal embolism. If this hadn't worked, they would have injected her with sodium seconal, a powerful tranquilizer. If she somehow managed to survive this, they planned to put her unconscious body behind the wheel of her Cadillac, then roll it over the cliff behind the Finch house.

On the witness stand, Finch told a jury that his wife had appeared with a .38 in hand. A struggle ensued; he wrestled the gun away from Barbara while Tregoff cowered, out of sight, in the bougainvillaea. Finch said the gun accidentally discharged when he threw it away, over his shoulder. In an already bizarre trial, Finch one-upped himself by descending from the stand to play his version of his wife's death scene to the jury. Kneeling on the courtroom floor, he repeated his version of his wife's dying words: "I'm sorry...I should have listened to you...I love you...take care of the kids...." Finch wanted the jury to believe his wife had apologized to her killer for her own murder.

The coroner's report proved otherwise. The fatal bullet had gone squarely between Barbara's shoulder blades and exited between her breasts. She had been shot while trying to flee.

Nevertheless the trial ended in a hung jury. So did a second. A third jury found Finch and Tregoff guilty of murder: he in the first degree; she in the second. Both received life sentences.

Moreover, their romance was obviously ancient history. Throughout the trial their chairs were scant feet apart, but they ignored each other, neither speaking nor making eye contact. Immediately after sentencing, Finch tried to kiss Tregoff. But she drew back, and his lips closed on empty air. During the long years of their confinement, Finch dispatched a steady stream of letters. She answered none. Carole Tregoff worked at a Pasadena, California, hospital for several months after her parole in 1969. A local newspaper story on this fact aroused a public outcry. Tregoff changed her name and found a similar job in a neighboring community.

Dr. Finch, released from prison in 1971, practiced medicine for a decade in Bolivar, Missouri. He returned to Covina in 1984.

LOCATION:
Thomas Brothers map reference: Page 92 at E2
Take the San Bernardino Freeway (I-10) to Citrus in Covina. Go south one mile to Lark Hill Drive. Turn left. The house is on the right at 2740 Lark Hill Drive at the top of a very long driveway that curves uphill. It's a one-story, mustard-colored ranch-style home. From the driveway is a spectacular view of Mt. San Antonio and of the tennis courts and swimming pool of South Hills Country Club. The bougainvillea where Tregoff claimed she hid has been replaced with less ostentatious foliage.

Nick Adams died of a massive dose of sedatives. Photo: Marc Wannamaker Bison Archives.

31

WHO KILLED NICK ADAMS? (1968)

He was Hollywood's quintessential outsider, a compact and scarred man, a fighter both on the screen and off. He came from the relentless poverty of Appalachia, a washed-up coal miner's son who Americanized his Lithuanian patronymic from Adamshock to Adams and who idolized James Dean. Deciding to become an actor, he went about getting "discovered" in the unorthodox style that was to become his trademark.

Nick Adams was still in the Coast Guard when Warners began shooting *Mr. Roberts* at their Burbank studios. One morning he arrived in uniform, just as a crowd of extras costumed as sailors were admitted to the lot. He walked in with them, unchallenged.

He won a bit part in *Rebel Without a Cause* and quickly became one of James Dean's closest friends. His grief was inconsolable when Dean was killed in an auto crash. His response was to become a "highway delinquent," arrested for reckless driving nine times in a single year. But he went on racing the ghost of James Dean.

Until he met actress Carol Nugent. And came up with a screen character, "Johnny Yuma." Johnny Yuma became *The Rebel*, a weekly television saga of an erroneously cashiered Confederate cavalry commander. With fists, knives, sixshooters, a lariat and a generous dose of compassion, he went around solving other people's problems. So for two TV years, Nick Adams of Pennsylvania and Jersey City was a very hot property. He married Carol and they started a family: Allyson Lee Adams was born in 1960 and Jeb Stuart Adams two years later.

Then the series was cancelled. The weekly paychecks stopped. Nick struggled to find bit parts and an occasional foreign feature film. The marriage unraveled: first a separation, then divorce. A bitter battle for custody of the children ensued. Nick won, but was enraged to learn that Carol's new beau was arrogating parental privilege by disciplining the children. Nick got a family court commissioner to issue an order: Henceforth, Carol could visit with her children but "not in the presence of non-related male adults."

About this time his career turned a new corner. Nick Adams found himself once more in demand. Returning from location work in Mexico, he had a few days at home before leaving for Rome to start work on a new film. Adams called his close friend and attorney, Erwin "Tip" Roeder, and they made a date for dinner on February 7, 1968.

But the Rebel never made it to dinner. Tip found this very strange; Adams was usually punctual. So Tip went to the house Adams rented in Coldwater Canyon. There he discovered his friend—dead.

Sometime the night before, Nick Adams had received a dose of paraldehyde, a powerful tranquilizer sometimes prescribed for extreme nervous conditions, or for treatment of alcohol dependency. His body was found sitting upright against the wall in his bedroom, clothed in blue jeans, shirt and boots. Less than two feet away was a telephone in working order. There were no signs of a struggle. The coroner's report indicated the equivalent of an oral dose of about 30 cc's of paraldehyde had somehow been ingested. That amount of paraldehyde was not enough to kill, but it had been taken in combination with "sedatives and other drugs," traces of which were found in his body.

Adams was never much of a drinker. None of his close friends ever recalled seeing him drunk. But a few months earlier while Adams was struggling for custody of his children, a doctor had prescribed a small amount of paraldehyde as a sedative.

Yet police found no trace of the drug anywhere in the house. There were no empty prescription bottles, no pills, nothing that might have once contained paraldehyde. In the coroner's expert opinion, the amount of the drug found in the body would cause instantaneous unconsciousness. But there were no syringes in or near the bedroom, no way in which paraldehyde could have been introduced into his body.

There are two ways that Nick Adams might have died: murder or suicide. If suicide, why were there none of the telltale traces usually found at death scenes? Why was there no note? No trace of the means by which drugs got into his body? And, having won custody of his children on his terms, having finally gotten a second chance at a film career, why would an observant Catholic take his own life just then? Did someone kill Nick Adams? Why? Who? Only the Rebel—or his killer—know the answers.

LOCATION:
Thomas Brothers map reference: Page 33 C2
Take Beverly Drive north from Sunset Boulevard until it becomes Coldwater Canyon. Continue north, then turn right at Cherokee, which has a traffic signal.

El Roble is the second street on the left. After making the turn the road forks; take the right-hand fork. The rented home where Nick Adams died on February 7, 1968, is the second house on the right, 2126 El Roble Lane, Trousdale Estates. It's a dead-end street.

Charles Manson: A near-illiterate with a messiah complex, his cult of lost souls practiced ritualistic murder. Photo: UPI/Bettmann Newsphotos.

32

BESTIAL ACTS BY A MURDEROUS MENAGERIE (1969)

In 1968 the Family left chilly San Francisco and moved to Southern California to the Spahn Movie Ranch, a decrepit collection of facades and weathered shacks among the stark boulders at the east end of the Simi Valley. The Family kept themselves in drugs, food and clothing by scrounging and by panhandling, but mostly by stealing. They lived communally, sharing virtually everything, including unlimited amounts of sex. But the lion's share always went to Charlie Manson, the head of the Family.

Charles Manson was 32, the bastard son of a teenage whore, an unkempt, bushy-bearded, diminutive man who stood only five feet two inches tall. He was intelligent, cunning, ruthless, cowardly. He was almost illiterate. He was a pimp, an inept but persistent car thief, burglar and forger. By 1969 he had spent more than 17 years behind bars, where he learned to enjoy sex with men as well as with women. But he was especially attractive to some very young women.

Young women like Patricia Krenwinkle, 21, who grew up in a happy, loving home. Patricia, who called herself "Katie," was a Blue Bird, a Camp Fire Girl, a Job's daughter. She joined the Audubon Society, sang in the church choir, had the benefit of a good education. She grew to adulthood, found a good job in a Los Angeles insurance agency. And threw it all away to run off with Manson the same day they met. Katie left her car, just abandoned it in a Manhattan Beach lot. She left the paycheck for her last working week. Left it all to become one of Charlie Manson's followers.

Susan Atkins, 21, was cut from different cloth. She had become a disciple of demonic satanism in her teens. She was working as a topless dancer when she met Manson, but she quickly abandoned this career for a new one. Very quickly Atkins became Manson's chief lieutenant.

Shortly after meeting Manson, 20-year-old Linda Kasabian deserted her husband Bob and their small children and stole $5,000 in cash from a friend. She gave it all to Charlie Manson as a sort of initiation fee. It seemed like the thing to do. But at the time, Kasabian had trouble perceiving reality, perhaps because she constantly took hallucinogenic drugs, including "about 50" doses of LSD. Linda joined the Family in July 1969, eager to prove herself to Manson.

Another of Manson's women was Leslie Van Houten, 19, a high school dropout and teenage runaway. Her pre-Manson friends described her as "a spoiled little princess" who frequently took LSD and other mind-altering drugs.

Charles "Tex" Watson, 23, was a nice-looking young man. During his high school days in Farmersville, Texas, he was an "A" student and a track, football and basketball star. He was usually cheerful, always a team player and a loyal follower. Under Manson's tutelage he became the most pitiless of killers.

Manson's eyes blazed with a hypnotic, unworldly fervor. He had learned ways to get others to do what he wanted. He used mind control techniques borrowed from Scientology and a mishmash of dogma from The Process and from other satanic cults. Manson created his own cult. He convinced the ragtag group of outcasts, drug-dependent dropouts, drifters and emotional cripples living as squatters at a decaying film ranch near Chatsworth that he was the Messiah. That his name, "Manson," meant "man-son," or "son-of-man." That he was the Christ—that he was God. That he was God and Satan.

Manson told his followers that he was the chosen instrument for an act of divine justice: the purification of the planet. In order to prepare the world for the coming of the Messiah, it was necessary to provoke war between blacks and whites, so that the ultimate victors, the whites, could exterminate the blacks. And in order to get that war started, Manson said, it was necessary to kill some white people—important well-known white people—and kill them in such a manner that their murders would be blamed on blacks. And so the war could begin. With such an important mission to carry out, Manson demanded obedience from his Family and demanded proof of their loyalty. So his followers showed their love for him and their faith in his twisted prophesies by murdering innocent strangers at his command.

But Manson's real goals were more ordinary. He wanted respect. He got plenty of blind obedience from his clan of followers. But after a time this wasn't enough. He wanted similar attention from the straight world. He wanted the rich and the famous and the respected to recognize his power. He wanted a world audience for his rambling monologues. More than wanted, Charles Manson needed that audience. He was possessed of an overpowering desire for recognition. One way of reaching that audience, he reasoned, was through music.

Manson played the guitar, though rather poorly, played it often. He had pretensions of vast musical talent. And he had written a song that he felt would soon be on everyone's lips if he could, somehow, bring it to public attention. The song had only two words: "you know," repeated over and over. Manson wanted to get this musical masterpiece before the right people. He cultivated a relationship with a successful musician and music teacher, Gary Hinman. Manson could be as ingratiating with someone he wished to cultivate as he was dictatorial with his Family. And Manson thought Hinman had something he wanted: connections to the music industry's power elite.

Gary Hinman was 34, lived in a splendid Topanga Canyon house, and for a time tolerated Manson. He even allowed Manson, with Susan Atkins and another follower, Robert K. Beausoleil, to live in his house. But Manson's expectations of instant success were delayed. Weeks passed. His impatience grew. Manson was not a man to be denied.

On July 28, 1969, Manson sent Atkins and Beausoleil to kill Hinman. But first they would try to find the $20,000 he had recently inherited, a sum they absurdly suspected was stashed somewhere in his home. For two days, alternately sleeping and torturing the bound Hinman, Atkins and Beausoleil tried to find this money, but the Family death squad departed without it. Beausoleil administered the coup de grace with a knife. They used some of Hinman's blood to scrawl *Political Piggie* on a living-room wall. They scrubbed the house of fingerprints, but neglected two, which soon led police to Beausoleil. He was arrested in Hinman's car on August 6. A bloody knife was concealed in the wheel well. Hinman's blood still stained Beausoleil's shirt and pants.

Manson was also cultivating Terry Melcher, who rented a house on a lovely, tree-encircled property in a remote part of Benedict Canyon. Melcher, the son of Doris Day, was acquainted with many music industry movers and shakers. Manson thought Melcher could help get him into the music business. So, with Tex Watson, Manson paid several visits to the house at 10050 Cielo Drive. Whatever his connections, Melcher did nothing to aid the musical career of Charles Manson. Manson decided to put the fear of God into him. The fear of Satan. The fear of Charles Manson. He would show Melcher that he was not one to be trifled with. He would kill some innocent people.

But first he had his minions rehearse their deadly art. The Family death squad garbed themselves entirely in black, and on several nights stealthily infiltrated abandoned buildings, along with some that were occupied. The Family called these rehearsals, "the Creepie Crawlies," and gave the same name to the black clothing they wore on these practice runs.

By the time Manson got around to dealing with Melcher, the night of August 8, 1969, Melcher no longer lived in the Cielo Drive house. Manson knew it. He had visited the place with Tex Watson on March 23. He'd seen some of the people who lived there at a distance. Manson wasn't too sure who they were. "Movie star types," he told his death squad. But the identity of his victims wasn't very important to him. In a surely unrivaled piece of demented logic, Manson wanted to show Melcher that he could destroy him by killing someone else who just happaned to live at his former address. Then Melcher would certainly come around. He would get Charlie Manson what he wanted. Or so Manson imagined.

The people living in the Cielo Drive house had rented it from owner Bruno Altobelli. And they were people who casually possessed the sort of riches and fame to which Manson aspired. One was Sharon Tate, 26, a film actress. Eight months pregnant, she was married to film director Roman Polanski, who specialized in quality horror films. One of these was *Rosemary's Baby*. On August 8, Polanski was in London, making a film.

Tate and Polanski lived with another couple. Abigail Folger, 25, was heiress to the Folger coffee fortune and worked as a Los Angeles County social services volunteer. Her boyfriend was the Polish-born writer and producer, 32-year-old Voyteck Frykowski, a friend of Polanski. Polanski told other friends that Voyteck was as long on charm as he was short on talent. But they were friends. Also visiting for the night of August 8 was Jay Sebring, 35, internationally known hairstylist to the rich and famous. He was one of Sharon's former boyfriends.

Sebring owned a lovely home farther up Benedict Canyon, a spacious and secluded house that he had only recently purchased. But after a series of spooky apparitions and strange, usually nocturnal sounds, Sebring began to believe the house was haunted. When he learned that it was the very house in which Paul Bern* had died in 1932 under mysterious circumstances and that several subsequent owners had come to strange and premature deaths, Sebring refused to sleep there. He sought shelter at the house Polanski had rented on Cielo Drive while he considered his options on what to do with his haunted house.

On the night of August 8, 1969, Manson gave Tex Watson a rope, a knife and a long-barrelled .22 caliber *Hi Standard Longhorn* revolver and told him to take Patricia Krenwinkle, Susan Atkins and Linda Kasabian to the house on Cielo Drive. Tex was to kill everybody. And Tex was to make it "as gruesome as possible."

The killers arrived about midnight and cut the telephone lines. Fearing that the sliding gate barring the driveway might be electrified, they climbed a rocky hillside to enter the property.

Watson first encountered 18-year-old Steven Parent, a student. He was behind the wheel of his white Rambler and was about to leave for home after a visit with his friend, caretaker William Garretson, 19. Garreston lived in the guest house, in a corner of the shrub-lined property so far removed from the main house that neither he nor his dogs heard anything of the mayhem that erupted as the Manson Family struck.

Young Steve Parent saw the gun in Tex's hand and begged for his life. "Please don't hurt me, I won't say anything," he pleaded. So Tex shot Parent four times with his pistol at point-blank range. Then he slashed his neck, just to be sure. Linda Kasabian's nerve failed. She remained outside as the others entered the house.

Inside the house the Family death squad woke Frykowski, then brought Tate, Sebring and Folger into the living room. To calm their victims they announced they were merely robbing them. They tied up Sebring. They shot him when he escaped his bonds. Frykowski was killed fighting for his life: shot, punched, pistol-whipped, and stabbed 51 times—stabbed long after he was dead. Folger tried to escape through the back door, but Krenwinkle chased her down. Tex stabbed her to death on the lawn. That left the obviously pregnant Sharon Tate, who begged her captors to spare her, to spare her unborn child. "Woman, I have no mercy for you," said Atkins. She stabbed Tate 16 times.

Afterward, the killers covered Sebring's head with a bloody towel, tied one end of a rope to his neck and snaked the other over to Tate's body. They draped a U.S. flag over a couch, and used Tate's blood to write the word "pig" on a door.

The death squad collected their weapons, walked out to their black Chevy, changed from their blood-spattered clothes to a clean set of "Creepie Crawlies" and drove off into the night. Tex found a ravine on the San Fernando Valley side of the hills and into it threw their bloody clothes and weapons. Except for Atkins' knife, which had unaccountably been left behind. They doubled back across the hills and stopped at a house above Sunset Boulevard on the Los Angeles side, where they appropriated a garden hose to wash the blood from their hands and faces. The elderly homeowners, wakened by their racket, drove them off.

The Cielo Drive murders made headlines the next day. Sharon Tate was beautiful and talented. Her star had been rising. But her bizarre death brought her more newspaper and TV coverage than she had ever had in life. Manson and his cult of some three dozen celebrated her death with an orgy, smoking great reefers of marijuana. Celebrated by planning another night of mayhem.

This time Manson himself deigned to lead his death squad, reinforced with the addition of Leslie Van Houten, 19, and Steve Grogan, 23. Dressed in ritual black "Creepie Crawlies," they cruised the silent streets of Los Angeles in the wee hours of that hot night of August 10, 1969, looking for another suitable group of victims. Manson low-crawled his way to the doors and windows of randomly chosen houses in wealthy neighborhoods, but found none suitable. Then, perhaps by chance, the gang found themselves in the Silver Lake district. Manson remembered a house there. He had once, long before, "done some acid" with its occupants. But they hadn't treated him with proper respect, he recalled. He would show them. He would murder the people who lived next door.

Next door were Rosemary and Leno LaBianca. They were wealthy, widely respected, loved by their family. They were solid members of the community.

Rosemary was 38 and owned a fashionable dress shop. Her husband Leno, 44, owned and operated a chain of Los Angeles grocery stores. Neither Manson nor his family had any idea who they were.

While the others waited in the car, Manson took a gun, climbed through a window of their house. He pointed the gun at the LaBiancas, tied them up with the ornamental leather thongs he wore around his neck and assured them that no harm would come. He took Leno LaBianca's wallet and went back out to the car to tell Tex, Leslie and Katie to kill the couple.

Manson told the trio that he and the others would find another house to invade. Instead they returned home, to the Spahn Ranch. En route they stopped at a gas station, where Manson told Kasabian to leave LaBianca's wallet in the women's room. He wanted someone to find it, to use the credit cards in it, to be blamed or at least implicated in their deaths. This ploy would muddy the waters.

At the LaBianca's Silver Lake home, Tex took Leno into the living room, tied his hands behind his back and strangled him with a lamp cord. Then stabbed him, and kept stabbing, while Leno screamed and howled in pain and fear. Tex left the knife in his throat, then covered his victim's head with a pillow case.

In the bedroom Krenwinkle and Leslie Van Houten were stabbing Rosemary LaBianca. They stabbed her 41 times, including 13 wounds made after she was dead. Another lamp cord was tied around her neck, another pillowcase put over her head.

The killers took the fresh blood of their victims and wrote "Death to all pigs" and "Rise" on the living-room walls. They added the words "Healter (sic) Skelter," written in blood on the refrigerator. Then the trio cleaned their fingerprints from the house. They all took hot showers, changed clothes and raided the refrigerator for a midnight snack. On the way out, Tex had an inspiration. He stuck an ivory-handled carving fork into Leno's lifeless stomach. He left it there. He carved the word "war" on Leno's abdomen.

It took Los Angeles police a while to connect the Hinman, Cielo Drive (Tate et al.) and LaBianca murders. By the time they did, the Family had scattered. Several members were in police custody on a variety of charges. One of them was Susan Atkins, now alias Sadie Mae Glutz, who told a cellmate some of what she knew about the Cielo Drive murders. She was overheard by another inmate, Virginia Graham. On November 26, 1969, Graham, against the advice of her husband, told authorities that the man they wanted was Charles Manson.

On August 16, Manson and several of his followers were arrested at the Spahn Ranch. Most, including Manson were released. On October 15, Manson and several others were again arrested in a raid on their camp near Death Valley. When Graham's tip provided the crucial clue to the puzzle, Manson was still in custody, as were Atkins, Van Houten, Kasabian, Beausoleil and Grogan.

"Katie" Krenwinkle was arrested at the Mobile, Alabama, home of her aunt. Tex Watson was collared in Collin County, Texas—by his own cousin, Sheriff Tom Montgomery. As the monstrous story of the Manson killings began to unfold, Watson's family used their considerable local political connections to complicate and delay extradition proceedings required to bring Watson back to California for trial.

But eventually he joined Manson, Van Houten, Krenwinkle, Beausoleil, Atkins and Grogan in the prisoner's dock. Manson and his cultists—including many who were not on trial—attempted to stop the wheels of justice with outrageous courtroom antics. For a time Manson, who had boasted to prison friends that, including the murders he was being tried for, he had killed or caused to be killed about 35 people, insisted on being his own attorney. It was probably the most bizarre criminal trial in California history.

While Kasabian was granted immunity in exchange for her eyewitness testimony, all the others were found guilty of first degree murder and sentenced to death. But when California's death penalty was abolished in 1972, their sentences were changed to life imprisonment, which calls for a minimum term of only seven years. Manson and all his fellow killers are now eligible for parole, have applied for it, have been refused. They will apply again.

LOCATIONS:
Thomas Brothers map reference: Page 32 F3
The house where Tate, Folger, Frykowski, Sebring and Parent were killed is outwardly still much as it was in 1969. Take Benedict Canyon north from Sunset in Beverly Hills. Go left at Hillgrove, then right at Angelo Drive to Davies Drive. Follow Davies until just before it ends at Cielo Drive, then right on Cielo. Bella Drive descends from the north and ends at Cielo. Just at this point is a private street on the right. Three mailboxes are here, but there are four houses on the street. The last house, at the very end of the private street—upon which it is not advisable to enter without an invitation—has no visible street number and is protected by a remotely controlled sliding gate. This is 10050 Cielo Drive, the former Polanski residence. A good view of the grounds may be had from across the narrow canyon at the top of Bella Drive, a public road.

Thomas Brothers map reference: Page 35 B2
In an apparent effort to escape the notoriety associated with the deaths of the LaBiancas, property owners have changed the number from 3301, the address at the time of the murders, to 3311. Take the Golden State Freeway (I-5) north from the downtown interchange, and exit at Glendale Boulevard. Only right turns are permitted. Take Glendale north a few blocks until it's legal to make a U-turn. Go south on Glendale and cross back over the freeway. Follow Glendale to Rowena, then go right three streets to Waverly. Go right on Waverly past a long wall protecting a convent. The first private residence on the left after the convent is 3311 Waverly Drive, the former residence of Leno and Rosemary LaBianca.

Thomas Brothers map reference: Page 35 B2
Gary Hinman was killed in his home at 964 Old Topanga Canyon Road. From the Ventura Freeway (U.S. 101) exit at Topanga Canyon Boulevard and go south through the canyon. Just below the summit turn right on Old Topanga Canyon for about 1.3 miles. The house, shaded by trees, is on the right side.

*See Chapter 17, *The Enigmatic Death of Paul Bern (1932).*

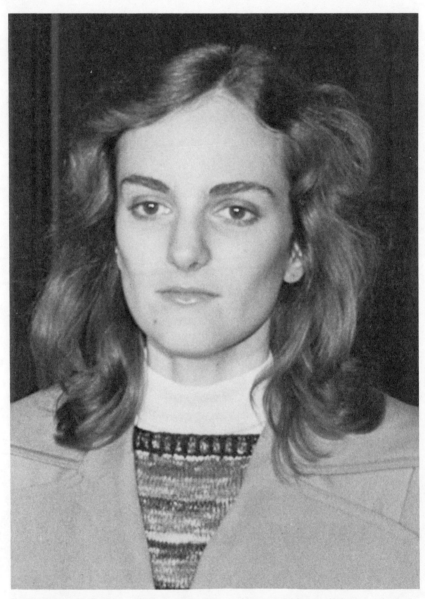

Patty Hearst: From socialite newspaper heiress to kidnap victim to urban terrorist. Photo: UPI/Bettmann Newsphotos.

33

PATTY HEARST AND THE SLA SHOOTOUT (1974)

Mel's Sporting Goods was a modest neighborhood store in Inglewood. No one there had ever heard of the so-called Symbionese Liberation Army (SLA) when members of this radical group kidnapped newspaper heiress Patricia Hearst, 19, from the Berkeley apartment she shared with her fiancé, Stephen Weed, on February 4, 1974. The SLA issued a series of bizarre ransom demands, including the distribution of $2 million in free food (paid for by her father, publisher Randolph Hearst, and the William Randolph Hearst Foundation) to San Francisco Bay-area poor. Then Hearst and her abductors vanished. Law enforcement could find no trace of the SLA.

While in captivity, Patty Hearst was subjected to weeks of mental conditioning by her captors. She was kept bound, blindfolded and gagged in a makeshift "sensory deprivation chamber," usually a locked closet, where she could hear, see, smell or touch almost nothing. At odd intervals her captors took her out of the closet. They alternately raped, threatened and beat her, while delivering lectures on their views of the "class struggle." Their objective was to brainwash Patty Hearst into a willing servant of their cause.

Weeks later, in a series of tape-recorded messages mailed to the media, Hearst identified herself as "Tania" and said she had joined the SLA. Soon she was photographed by a bank camera pointing an automatic weapon at a bank guard during the robbery of a suburban San Francisco Hibernia Bank branch office. More Bay area bank robberies followed. Sought by city and state police and the FBI, Patty Hearst and the SLA were not to be found.

Then on May 17, 1974, SLA members William and Emily Harris visited Mel's Sporting Goods, Inglewood. William, 29, bought $31.50 worth of heavy socks, sweatshirts and outdoor clothing. Soon afterward a clerk named Anthony Shepard saw him slipping extra socks up his sleeve. Shepard, a college student majoring in police science, followed him out of the store, attempted to apprehend him on the sidewalk. Harris was not going to be taken by an unarmed store clerk. He put up a fight, and the owner ran outside to help.

From a red-and-white van across the street, Patty Hearst opened fire on the store, spraying the storefront with 30 rounds of semi-automatic fire from a .30 caliber automatic rifle. Miraculously, no one was hit. The Harrises and Hearst escaped in the van.

The next day an informer told police that several members of the SLA were staying in a small stucco house at 1466 E. 54th St. Nearly 400 police and FBI agents surrounded the house while dozens of reporters converged on the scene. Police demands for surrender brought an immediate response: SLA members opened fire. A fierce firefight ensued. At least 5,371 rounds were fired from police pistols, rifles and shotguns.

Eventually police fired tear-gas cannisters into the house in an effort to force the occupants out. SLA "soldier" Nancy Ling Perry came out shooting and was cut down by a fusillade of police bullets. The others remained even after a tear-gas cannister set the house ablaze. They all died as it burned to the ground.

Police identified the bodies of SLA members:

Nancy Ling Perry (a.k.a. Fahiza), 26; *Angela Atwood* (a.k.a. Gelisa), 24; *Camilla Hall* (a.k.a. Gabi), 28; *William Wolfe* (a.k.a. Cujo), 23; *Patricia Soltysik* (a.k.a. Zoya), 24; *Donald Defreeze* (a.k.a. "General Field Marshal Cinque Mtume"), 30, leader of the SLA and the man who had engineered the kidnap of Patty Hearst.

Still at large, however, were William Harris (a.k.a. Teko), his wife, Emily (a.k.a. Yolanda), and Patty Hearst. The Harrises were eventually apprehended on September 18, 1975, convicted and sentenced to 25 years in prison. Both were paroled in 1984 in San Francisco.

Patty Hearst was also apprehended in San Francisco, a few hours before the Harrises. She listed her occupation on a police booking form as "Urban Guerilla." She was tried and found guilty of her part in the Mel's Sporting Goods shooting and given probation. She was also found guilty of the Hibernia Bank robbery and sentenced to seven years in federal prison. After a year she was released on bail pending an appeal. She returned to jail when her convictions were upheld. After such prominent citizens as William F. Buckley, Cesar Chavez, Ronald Reagan and San Francisco Mayor Joseph Alioto made appeals on her behalf, President Jimmy Carter granted executive clemency in January 1979. Hearst was released and later married her bodyguard, Bernard Shaw.

LOCATIONS:
Thomas Brothers map reference: Page 57 C5
From the Harbor Freeway take Imperial west. Turn south on Crenshaw. Mel's Sporting Goods store is no longer at 11425, but the storefront is still there.

Thomas Brothers map reference: Page 52 C4
From the Harbor Freeway take Slauson east to Avalon, turn north and go five short blocks to 54th Street. Turn left. On the south side of the street is a grassy vacant lot edged with palm trees. This is all that remains of 1466 E. 54th Street, the house where the SLA shot it out with the LAPD.

Sal Mineo receiving a congratulatory kiss in 1961 from actress Martha Hyer. Photo: UPI/Bettmann Newsphotos.

34

PREMATURE OBLIVION: SAL MINEO IS MURDERED (1976)

His father, Salvatore Mineo, Sr., was a Sicilian immigrant who earned his living as a coffin maker. His son was a tough, wild kid growing up in a dead-end Bronx neighborhood. He was expelled from school at age nine. Before puberty he masterminded and orchestrated a theft that netted $5,000; he was later caught by police. Most of his family wrote him off before he exorcized the demons of adolescence. It was widely predicted he'd wind up with a knife in his guts.

Salvatore Mineo fooled them all. Given the choice of reform school or performing arts high school, he chose theatrical training and promptly set out to dominate the stage as completely as he had dominated the street gangs of his childhood. A few years later he opened on Broadway in *The Rose Tattoo*, which starred Maureen Stapleton and Eli Wallach. Next he was Yul Brynner's crown prince in *The King and I*. And in 1955 he played sensitive, switchblade-wielding Plato in *Rebel Without a Cause*. His performance earned him the first of his two Academy Award nominations. The same year he got an Emmy for his role in *Dino*, a *Studio One* TV drama. Sal Mineo was 16 years old and his future seemed limitless.

He became a legend of the Fifties. Each week, upward of 5,000 fan letters poured into the studio addressed to Mineo. He couldn't appear in public without being mobbed by young women. He got a juicy part as Dov Landau in *Exodus*, and a second Academy Award nomination. Though he didn't pretend to have much of a singing voice, he nevertheless made a hit single, *Start Moving*, which earned him a gold record. In the Fifties, anything with Sal Mineo's name on it was gold.

But not in the Sixties. Suddenly there were few roles for pretty, slender, olive-skinned juvenile delinquents walking the thin red line between mayhem and vulnerability. And soon he was no longer quite so young, no longer quite so vulnerable. No longer so desirable. No longer bankable. By 1965, despite his enormous talents, Sal Mineo was over the hill at age 26.

He formed his own production company, but it soon sank into oblivion. Mineo returned to Broadway and to West Coast theaters, where he was critically acclaimed. But he bombed at the box office. He took lesser parts in *Krakatoa, East of Java* and in *Escape from the Planet of the Apes.*

By 1976 he was 37 and still struggling for a comeback. Though he maintained many of his Hollywood friendships—most notably with director Peter Bogdanovich—his standard of living had declined. He was struggling just to make ends meet. Gone were the sleek foreign sports cars. Mineo now drove a blue Chevette with plenty of mileage on its odometer. The expensive home he'd bought his parents in Mamaroneck, New York, was sold; the family needed the money. Unable to keep up the mortgage payments, he lost his own luxurious house in the Hollywood Hills.

He moved into a modest West Hollywood apartment. Palimony attorney Marvin Mitchelson, who also represented Mineo, was a part owner of the building on Holloway Drive, just below the Sunset Strip. It is a quiet area during the day, but it adjoins a neighborhood that at dusk becomes a parade field—and sometimes a battleground—for drug dealers, pimps and prostitutes from all shades of the sexual rainbow, as well as muggers and thieves.

And there he lived while *P.S. Your Cat Is Dead* was in rehearsal. It was a play that had done well in San Francisco, and Mineo and costar Keir Dullea hoped it would refocus Hollywood's attention on their careers when it opened in Los Angeles the last week of February 1976.

Mineo enjoyed a good rehearsal on the evening of February 12. At about 10:00 p.m. he parked his Chevette in the open-ended carport beneath his apartment. One of his neighbors—Marvin Mitchelson's mother—was preparing for bed. Suddenly she heard a man's voice cry out. She heard screams. Sal Mineo shouting, "No! My God! No!" Another neighbor, Ray Evans, heard the screams, heard Mineo calling for help. And he rushed to his rescue. Some witnesses reported a man fleeing the scene. He was a white man, they said, and he drove a small yellow car.

Evans found Mineo crumpled on the carport's concrete floor. He had been stabbed several times. His chest was covered with blood. A heavy blade had pierced his heart. In the minutes it took for paramedics to arrive he slipped into death.

Who killed Sal Mineo? And why? The police were baffled. The purveyors of gossip and rumor whispered about a homosexual love affair gone sour. About a doublecrossed drug deal. About an aborted robbery.

None of these was true. Though the man who killed him turned out to be a robber, he hadn't taken Mineo's valuables. If the actor had homosexual lovers—and perhaps he did—they weren't involved. And Sal Mineo used no drugs. For years his death was just another anonymous murder, with few clues.

But someone had killed Sal Mineo, and there were two people who knew who. One was Lionel Ray Williams, a 19-year-old pizza deliveryman. He was a violent, sadistic thug, first arrested at age 14, arrested thrice more before reaching age 18. By 1976 Williams was a burglar and robber and he had committed at least 10 robberies within a few miles of Mineo's apartment. This brutal man bought a five dollar hunting knife and had its likeness tattooed on his arm. For no particular reason at all he stuck that knife into Sal Mineo's heart.

When he came home that night, covered with blood, he casually told his wife, Theresa, "I just killed this dude in Hollywood." More than a year later, in May 1977, Theresa Williams went to the police. At first they didn't believe her. They had apprehended Williams on suspicion of robbery a few days after Mineo's death. He'd offered to give information on the murder in exchange for leniency on the robbery rap. But he'd told police that Mineo's killing had involved drugs, and they'd chosen not to believe him. Moreover, Williams was a black man, and his car wasn't yellow.

But Theresa Williams insisted. A detective took her description of the knife to a sporting goods store and bought a similar one. A pathologist tried it in the fatal wound, which had been preserved with a portion of Mineo's body. The blade fit perfectly.

Lionel Williams wasn't hard to find. He was doing time in Michigan for check forgery. A prison snitch revealed that Williams had bragged to cellmates about Mineo's murder. He had demonstrated his knife-wielding style while showing other convicts how he'd done it.

It took almost three years, but in January 1979 Williams went on trial for the murder of Sal Mineo and for 11 robberies in West Hollywood, Beverly Hills and the Wilshire district. Though he was a black man, he was very light-skinned. On the night in question he'd been driving a yellow Dodge Colt that belonged to someone who owed him money. The jury found him guilty of second degree murder and of 10 robbery counts. Lionel Williams was sentenced to 51 years in state prison.

Though they were a generation apart, the young Sal Mineo and the young Lionel Williams had much in common. Both grew up wild on mean city streets, surviving by grit and guile. One became a celebrity—an idol for his generation—however briefly. The other went to prison. In a strange way, the prophesies of Sal Mineo's childhood had in the end come true. It was as if he'd been condemned to die with a knife in his guts, and despite all the hearts he had gladdened, despite all he accomplished in a brief lifetime, he couldn't elude his fate.

LOCATION:
Thomas Brothers map reference: Page 33 D4
Take Sunset Boulevard east from Doheny. At Palm, Sunset bends northward;

continue straight ahead and the street becomes Holloway. Continue to the middle of the block to 8563, on the left. Sal Mineo was stabbed to death in the carport below the three-story apartment building, four doors west of Alta Loma. It's a cream-colored stucco building with small balconies and a long stairway with wrought-iron railings.

Kenneth Bianchi: One of two "Hillside Stranglers," his cruel murders terrorized the city for months. Photo: UPI/Bettmann Newsphotos.

35

HILLSIDE STRANGLINGS BY KENNETH BIANCHI & ANGELO BUONO (1977-78)

In the 121 days between October 18, 1977, and February 17, 1978, the bodies of 10 young women and girls, nearly all of them raped and most strangled, were found on hillsides in the northeastern part of Los Angeles County. During that period, and for months afterward, an almost palpable fear hung over the streets of Los Angeles. Many women lived in almost constant dread of the nameless monster—the media soon dubbed him "the Hillside Strangler"—who lurked out there, somewhere.

The Hillside Strangler became a leading topic of conversation. Frightened women refused dates with recent acquaintances or called police to report weirdo boyfriends they suspected of being the Strangler. Many women postponed or canceled evening travel, or asked husbands, fathers or trusted male friends to accompany them on the most routine nocturnal errands.

Serial murder is not a peculiarly Los Angeles phenomenon, nor is it even an especially California crime. Yet those who slay random victims have found Los Angeles, and particularly the Hollywood area, a rich hunting ground. Day or night, the streets are full of hustlers, drug dealers, pimps and hookers of all imaginable sexual persuasions. Thousands of transients of all ages—but especially the young—pass through this part of the city annually. Many are adolescent runaways; some are adult dropouts. Few seem to have close friends or relatives in the community. Often their death is the first indication to relatives that the victim was even in Los Angeles.

So, over the years, a parade of serial killers has stalked through the public's consciousness. There was Vaughn Greenwood, the "Skidrow Slasher." Starting on December 8, 1974, he slashed the throats of nine men, most of them derelicts, in and near Los Angeles. The object of the city's biggest manhunt since the Manson madness of 1969, he was eventually convicted of eight murders, and sentenced to life in prison.

There was the killing spree of the so-called "Trash Bag Murderer," which began on Christmas Day, 1972, and ended, 28 mutilated, homosexually assaulted bodies later, in December 1977, when Patrick Kearny, 38, a bearded, bespectacled and avowedly homosexual aerospace technician pleaded guilty to 21 of the 28 murders. His dismembered victims were placed in plastic trash bags and left in garbage bins or on the shoulders of roads all over California.

In 1979 police apprehended William Bonin, Gregory Miley and James Munro on suspicion of killing at least 22 men and young boys around the Los Angeles area. A fourth suspect, Vernon Butts, committed suicide after being arrested. Accomplices Miley and Munro agreed to accept life imprisonment in exchange for a guilty plea and testimony about Bonin's savage acts. Bonin picked_up his victims while they were hitchhiking and with his accomplices held them in the back of a van where they were tortured for days. Since most victims were strangled and their tortured, and often mutilated, nude bodies dumped on or near freeways, the media inevitably began calling Bonin the "Freeway Strangler." Bonin was convicted of 10 L.A. murders, plus four in nearby Orange County, and strongly suspected of at least a score more at locations all over the state.

Douglas Clark was dubbed the "Sunset Slayer" because he cruised Sunset Boulevard to select his victims. He liked to shoot out the brains of prostitutes, especially *while* he was having sex with them. Convicted of six murders in 1983, he was sentenced to death. An accomplice, nurse Carol Bundy, was sentenced to 52 years in prison.

Three or four people are murdered every day in Los Angeles County. In an average year, this amounts to upward of 900 killings. Perhaps 25 of them die by strangulation. So 10 stranglings in four months was only a little higher than average. But the nude bodies turning up on hillsides all seemed to bear a common stamp. Moreover, all the victims had been killed elsewhere and the *manner* in which the bodies were carefully put where they would be easily discovered conveyed a chilling message to police.

Unlike the Trashbag Murderer, Skid Row Slasher, Freeway Strangler, Sunset Slayer or other Los Angeles serial killers, the Hillside Strangler seemed to want each victim found quickly. At the same time, the Strangler also took special pains to clean up each corpse, to deprive investigators of the kinds of physical evidence that might shed light on the death scene and ultimately lead to the murderer. To veteran investigators, the killer seemed to be saying that he knew more about crime-scene investigations than the police. He even seemed to be taunting them. The bodies of his sixth and seventh victims, two young schoolgirls, were taken to Elysian Park, very near the vaunted L.A. Police Academy. Another victim, Jane King, was carefully laid out on a hillside, her spread-eagled legs forming a "V" that neatly framed City Hall and Parker Center, LAPD headquarters.

Shortly after these episodes, police publicly acknowledged that the killer, whoever he might be, was "a good student of police operations," and was perhaps someone who had been rejected for police duty. In fact, the man who would one day confess to the killings had applied for LAPD reserve status and in connection with this had gone on two "ride-alongs" during the very period when his victims' bodies were turning up on hillsides.

The Strangler's victims were found in both Los Angeles city and county jurisdictions, and in Glendale. A special, interagency, Strangler Task Force was created, numbering at its peak some 130 investigators from LAPD, the sheriff's office, and Glendale PD. The task force was assigned use of a massive computer. Before the investigation ended more than 10,000 clues, the overwhelming majority of them worthless, were logged into its memory banks.

Deputy LAPD Chief Daryl Gates assumed personal charge of the hunt for the Hillside Strangler. Nearly every week for months, Gates called a press conference to report some promising development. Frequently he announced that the case would soon be solved. On two occasions, suspects were arrested, and each time Gates solemnly informed the media that it was a "promising" arrest. Both suspects were subsequently released. On a third occasion a dead man was named as a "promising" suspect.

But when the murders stopped in the early spring of 1978, the trail, never very warm, cooled rapidly. Nearly a year passed. The LAPD seemed stymied. The Strangler Task Force was scaled back and many of the more senior investigators went back to their old assignments. It began to look as though the Strangler would never be found.

Although they didn't know it at the time, Strangler Task Force investigators had at least twice spoken to the killer. The clues that would unravel the enigma of the Hillside Strangler were already stored among the vast chunks of data within their very own computer. But the police computer simply *stored* information. It spit out what it was asked to find, nothing more or less, and the cops might never have known where to start looking had it not been for a late-night call on January 13, 1979.

The caller was a homicide cop on the Bellingham, Washington, force. He had just taken into custody a man suspected of the rape and murder of two young women there. The victims, said the Washington cop, had been strangled. The crime scene had been located; the killer had done a thorough job of cleaning it up. The bodies had been put into one victim's car, and the car abandoned.

The suspect was Kenneth Bianchi, 27, formerly of Los Angeles. The sketchy details provided by the Bellingham police included a Los Angeles address, listed on his driver's license as 1950 Tamarind. By coincidence the sheriff's officer taking the call was a former member of the Strangler Task Force. The address jumped out at him. It was a Hollywood apartment building called the Tamarind Terrace, and it was the last address to which Kimberly Martin, a prostitute associated with Climax Outcall Service, could be traced. Martin, 18, was the Strangler's ninth victim.

Now that the police knew what to ask the computer, Bianchi's name surfaced in connection with clues number 6111, 6458, 7598 and 7745. These disclosed that Bianchi owned a set of handcuffs and a police badge (actually, a California Highway Patrol shield, perhaps stolen from the set of a TV drama series CHIPS); that he matched the composite description of the unknown suspect; and that he had applied for police duty but been rejected by both LAPD and the Sheriff's Department. In addition to Kimberly Martin, he was linked to two other Strangler victims, Cindy Hudspeth and Kristina Weckler, through a former address. Bianchi had formerly lived at 809 E. Garfield, Glendale. Weckler lived in another apartment in the same courtyard building. At the time of her death, Hudspeth had lived across the street. Sergeant Frank Salerno, LAPD, and Dudley Varney, a Sheriff's Department investigator, flew to Bellingham the next day.

When he first met Bianchi, Bellingham's police chief, Terry Mangan, had come away with a good impression of the man. He was tall, just under six feet, a well-muscled man of 180 pounds, with a neat mustache, dark permed hair, and traces of skin once ravaged by acne on his neck. Bianchi was employed by Whatcom Security, his name was on the list as a prospective member of the Bellingham PD, and he was in training for the Whatcom County Sheriff's Reserve. He was doing an outstanding job as a security guard.

Chief Mangan was a former Roman Catholic priest, and had once served as police chief of Torrance, California. There he had made the acquaintance of a nun who eventually became a school principal. One of the Strangler's victims was a student in that school. After her death the nun had introduced Mangan to the victim's father, who had begged for his help in finding the killer. So Mangan had become somewhat familiar with the Strangler's imprint.

When Karen Mandic, 22, and her roommate, Diane Wilder, 27, were found strangled in Mandic's hatchback Bobcat, Mangan and others saw parallels between those murders and the Strangler's Los Angeles killings. Thorough police work soon turned up enough evidence to make Bianchi a prime suspect in the Bellingham stranglings. It was Bianchi who had lured Mandic to a temporarily vacant house by offering her $100 for an evening of housesitting, while, he said, the building's security system was being repaired. It was Bianchi who had lied to his boss and to Kelli, the woman he lived with, about his whereabouts that night. It was Bianchi who had warned Mandic not to tell anyone about her housesitting job. She nevertheless told her boyfriend, a Western Washington University campus cop, and passed along Bianchi's curious warning about revealing her whereabouts.

In his home, investigators found, Bianchi had a box filled with diplomas, among them *Master of Science* from Columbia University and *Doctor of Psychology* from the National Psychiatric Association of America. Bianchi was also, according to a diploma, a *Certified Sex Therapist*. This was very curious for a man who earned his living as a smalltown rent-a-cop. When Bellingham police began to check the diplomas, they discovered that every one of these sheepskins was bogus. Ken Bianchi was a pathological liar.

And a thief. The basement of his home was filled with stolen goods: chain saws, telephones, canned goods, jackets and new tools. And there was a small cache of used women's jewelry. One of the items was a ring that was later identified as belonging to Yolanda Washington. Washington, a 19-year-old waitress and sometime prostitute, was allegedly the first victim of the Hillside Strangler. (Some authorities believe that two or even three other women killed prior to Washington were also the Strangler's victims, though these crimes remain officially unsolved.)

Bianchi knew from his police science studies that bodies alone usually yield up little physical evidence. That was why, in Los Angeles, the clothing, jewelry and personal effects were removed from the victim's body, and why bodies were always dumped far from the death scene. He had done a fairly good job of cleaning up the Bellingham murder scene. But not good enough. Exercising extreme thoroughness, the city's small forensic crime team managed to come away with several telltale clues. Two pubic hairs that microscopically matched Bianchi's were found, one on the sheet in which authorities wrapped Diane Wilder's body when it was removed from the car, the other on a stair in the murder home. And three hairs brushed from Wilder's body matched three taken from Bianchi's head. Nylon fibers found on the victim's clothing matched those taken from Bianchi's shirt, pants and his lint brush, and all these matched samples from the death-scene carpet.

At Bianchi's home, police found a note with victim Karen Mandic's name on it, and at her house a note with Bianchi's name. They also tracked down eyewitnesses who remembered seeing Bianchi's security truck on the night of the killings on the dead-end street where the bodies were found. Another eyewitness placed him at the death scene, a house on Bayside Drive. Near his place of work, the guard shack where Bianchi was arrested, investigators found victim Diane Wilder's coat. The small-town cops of Bellingham did a marvelous job of collecting physical evidence. By the time they were ready to indict him, the only question seemed to be how Bianchi would plead.

Incredibly, Bianchi denied all involvement. He told wonderfully convoluted stories. As each of his lies was contradicted by physical evidence, another lie was exposed. He had, for example, told Kelli, the mother of his infant son, that the reason for his many unexplained absences from his Los Angeles job was that he was being treated for cancer, and had to visit the doctor's office for long radiation therapy sessions, which made him sick for hours afterward. He had wanted to spare her the heartache of knowing about his illness, said Ken Bianchi. And when the cops had exposed all his lies, when they finally got to the bottom line, Bianchi reached into himself and pulled out his last defense.

Not for nothing had this man with an IQ of 116 spent years reading psychology texts. Not without some understanding of psychological phenomena had he for months passed himself off as Dr. Robert Johnson, a shrink in Los Angeles. When the accumulation of damning physical evidence was so great that there was no longer a possibility that anyone else could have strangled the two Bellingham women, Bianchi looked his accusers in the eye and said he just didn't remember killing anyone. He told the same story to his attorney, Dean Brett. He told it to psychologists sent in by police. He told it to Dr. Watkins, a University of Montana psychology professor and internationally recognized authority on hypnosis and "dissociative reaction."

Dissociative reaction is a psychiatric term for the mental process of blocking out control over one's actions. It accounts for certain types of amnesia and also for the controversial phenomenon of multiple personalities residing within a single mind. Through hypnosis, Bianchi's other personalities identified themselves.

Dr. Watkins was introduced to Bianchi's supposed mindmates, beginning with another being named Ken, a thoughtful, cautious, often depressed and puzzled entity. There was also Billy, the liar and thief, the schemer who forced Bianchi to call himself "doctor," to write away for bogus credentials, to tell his mate—and his mother—that he had cancer when he didn't. There was an unnamed being, which Dr. Watkins called "ISH" or "internal self-helper," who was powerless and deceitless, but always present. And there was Steve Walker, evil and foul-mouthed, a rapist, murderer and sadist. It was Steve Walker, who had, along with Bianchi's cousin, Angelo Buono, killed all those women in Los Angeles, as well as the two in Bellingham.

To the consternation and amazement of Washington authorities, Bianchi convinced two of six shrinks that he was in fact a multiple personality and probably insane. Yet some of those examining him, as well as most of the Bellingham cops, were convinced that it was all an elaborate charade—as when, in his supposed trance, he recounted his formative years, when he had invented his mindmates as a refuge from an almost impossible adolescence.

Bianchi recounted a chilling childhood in Rochester, New York, a time filled with bone-numbing headaches and blackouts. The saga started with his illegitimate birth to a 17-year-old barmaid, followed by adoption by a woman who was soon widowed. He told about having his hand held to a red-hot stove as prophylaxis against stealing again. He told about being forced to wear his mother's sanitary napkins when he became a bed wetter. He told about being laced into his late father's shoes to attend his funeral.

But when investigators went back to Rochester they found no one who knew about headaches or blackouts. They found nobody, including his mother, who would confirm that he'd worn sanitary napkins, had had his hand intentionally burned, or had worn his father's shoes to his funeral, which had occurred when Kenneth was 13. What they found were plenty of people who remembered Bianchi very well and remembered him as an unrivaled liar.

The Whatcom County authorities knew they were looking at a long, expensive and problematical trial. Four out of six psychiatrists would testify that he was to some degree crazy. Any jury pondering Bianchi's mental state would have the benefit of 5,000 pages of psychiatric interviews, 50 hours of videotapes during which Ken, "Billy," the "other Ken," "Steve" and "ISH" all took turns performing, and a 2,000-page document that had to rank among the most convoluted and contradictory confessions of all time.

So when Ken Bianchi—the real one—said he was ready to deal, Whatcom County was ready to listen. Bianchi wanted to escape Washington State's death penalty: hanging. He would do some time, but he wanted the possibility of parole. And he wanted to serve his time in California, where the prisons are more convivial than the one in frigid Walla Walla. In return, Whatcom taxpapers would be spared millions of dollars in trial costs, and Bianchi would testify against his cousin, Angelo Buono, in Los Angeles.

Bianchi got everything he wanted. There was no trial, just a guilty plea and a sentence. And no sooner was Bianchi whisked off to California than he reneged on his pledge to help convict Buono.

Angelo Buono: Bianchi's cousin, he was convicted of nine of the Hillside Strangler murders. Photo: UPI/Bettmann Newsphotos.

Angelo Buono had been under surveillance for months, ever since he was implicated by Bianchi's mindmate, "Steve Walker." Buono was 44, a second-generation American of Sicilian ancestry, a tough, often crude, curly-haired man with huge hands and long, sinewy, almost simian arms. He was dark and just above average height at five feet 10 inches tall, and had lots of female friends, many younger than his son, Peter, who was serving in the Marine Corps.

Buono owned an automotive upholstery business, operated from a converted garage behind his home in Glendale. He flew an Italian flag from a pole atop his house, and he flew it 24 hours a day. At night it was illuminated by a spotlight. In the house Buono kept his gun collection, which included five rifles, a pair of .45 caliber pistols, and a Thompson submachine gun.

As Bianchi had explained in his convoluted Bellingham confessions, he and Buono had lured most of the girls and women they raped and murdered into Buono's official-looking car by masquerading as vice cops, complete with a fast display of police badges. So the victims, whether streetwalkers, schoolgirls, waitresses or aspiring actresses, climbed into Buono's car without resistance. They were then taken to Buono's Glendale home where they were bound, gagged, sadistically tortured, raped and/or forced to commit oral copulation on one or both men, and eventually strangled with strong white cord used in Buono's upholstery business. In one case the strangling, according to Bianchi, took place in the car after the victim had been raped.

Now that sentence had been pronounced and Bianchi was able to contemplate the day in September 2005 when he would be only 54 years old and eligible for parole, his story began to loop back on itself. Now that there was nothing worse that could happen to him, he began to make himself the kind of witness that no district attorney wants to put on the stand.

In his first confession, ostensibly under hypnosis, Bianchi told Dr. Watkins, the Montana psychologist, that he had walked into Buono's home and surprised him in the act of killing a woman. But in the fall of 1979, Bianchi told Bellingham police that he, himself, strangled the first victim, Yolanda Washington, in the back seat of Buono's car while his cousin drove. Then in late 1980 he told Los Angeles reporters about a letter he'd earlier written to Dr. Ralph Allison, a University of California, Davis, pyschiatrist. In the letter and to the reporters Bianchi maintained that he *never* personally killed any of the Strangler's Los Angeles victims.

At about the same time, Veronica Compton, a 24-year-old woman Bianchi had met while in the Los Angeles jail, went to Washington and tried to murder a young woman, to kill her by strangulation in a manner similar to the Southern California murders. The copycat style was a transparent attempt to convince authorities that the real Strangler was still at large. Compton was convicted of attempted murder.

There was much, much more. In Bellingham, Bianchi claimed that Buono had started strangling Lissa Kasstin, victim number three, and that he had finished the job. But at his preliminary hearing in Los Angeles, Bianchi testified that he himself started the strangling and Buono finished it.

Bianchi first said that he had enticed his seventh victim, Kristina Weckler, 20 an Art Center student and his neighbor, from her apartment by inviting her to a party. But later he told investigators he had knocked on her door, identified himself as a cop, and told her he wanted to question her about a traffic accident involving her car.

After raping and sodomizing her at Buono's house, said Bianchi, he and his cousin first injected her with air in an effort to cause a fatal embolism. When that failed, they injected her with a combination of caustic household cleaning agents, which caused her to go into convulsions. Bianchi said he then put her head into a plastic bag and used a hose to bring gas from the kitchen stove. They secured the bag around her neck with the usual white cord. Ultimately the cause of her death was strangulation.

In the case of Outcall prostitute Kimberly Martin, Bianchi told Washington authorities that he strangled her. At his Los Angeles hearing he insisted that Buono had done so, but on cross-examination he again said that he himself had killed her.

There were many other inconsistencies. In addition there was conflicting testimony given by the parade of witnesses who testified about some of the 10 Strangler killings.

When Los Angeles police investigators began to probe into how Bianchi had managed to come up with his bogus psychology credentials, they discovered that far from being an imaginary alter ego, invented in his adolescence, Steve Walker was a real human being. It was unemployed Steven Walker, doctor of educational psychology, who had sent his authentic credentials to a man calling himself Dr. R. Johnson, after Johnson advertised for an associate. Johnson used Walker's legitimate papers to forge his own. Johnson, of course, was Kenneth Bianchi. His multiple personality show was nothing more than a sustained and superb acting performance.

Los Angeles District Attorney John Van De Kamp wondered if he could convict Buono on Bianchi's confusing testimony. Or if he could convict him *without* using Bianchi at all. It was a bedeviling puzzlement to Roger Kelly, the deputy district attorney actually prosecuting the case.

Hanging over Kelly's head was the possibility that if he presented such conflicting and sometimes confusing testimony, it might result in a hung jury, at a long, expensive and highly publicized trial. Thus there would be another long and expensive repeat trial. Or worse, using Bianchi's incredible testimony might even result in a "not guilty" verdict. And once a jury had spoken those words, Buono could never be tried for the same crime again.

On July 6, 1981, Bianchi dropped the last straw on Kelly's plate. In the morning he insisted, under oath, that he knew absolutely nothing about the Hillside Strangler at all, except what he had seen in the newspapers and on TV or read in police reports after he was arrested in Washington. In the afternoon session, Bianchi went into excruciating detail concerning his own participation in the deaths of several Strangler victims.

Van De Kamp decided he couldn't take a chance on using Bianchi's testimony against Buono in a court of law. So on July 31, 1981, following Kelly's recommendation, Van De Kamp asked Superior Court Judge Ronald George to drop the murder charges against Buono for "lack of evidence."

The request triggered a firestorm of outraged protest. Nevertheless, Roger Kelly's evaluation of his principal witness, Bianchi, was that no jury would believe his testimony. Four credentialed doctors of psychology or psychiatry had said he was insane. Bianchi's behavior in custody, the multiple-personality episodes, the way in which his story kept changing from day to day and week to seek, the testimony of people who had known him for years as a nonstop liar—it was all too much.

"I don't think Kenneth Bianchi knows *what* he knows anymore—if he ever *did* know," said Kelly. "In my opinion there is nothing, no credible evidence independent of the direct evidence of Kenneth Bianchi, that connects Angelo Buono with those killings! Before we filed to dismiss, I tried to isolate just one of those murders which would hold water without Bianchi—and I couldn't." Without Bianchi, reasoned Kelly, there was nothing solid enough to convince a jury that Buono was anything except Bianchi's cousin.

Judge George didn't buy it. A week went by and George, a politically ambitious man but an extremely knowledgeable legal scholar, produced a 36-page legal opinion that castigated District Attorney Van De Kamp's office for failing to build a case. His ruling also spelled out damning items of evidence and testimony which he said had been ignored by the prosecution "for reasons not apparent to this court." Never shy about personal publicity, Judge George had invited the news media into his chambers throughout the trial, and when he delivered his bombshell report he was repaid tenfold with rapt media attention.

George invited the California attorney general's office to prosecute the case, and within days Attorney General George Deukmejian agreed to take over prosecution. He assigned assistant attorneys general Roger Boren and Michael Nash to the task. For two months they pored over the mountain of evidence accumulated by their predecessors. Gradually their prosecution seemed to acquire the aura of a holy crusade. They were determined to convict Buono.

On November 16, 1981, after 10 months of pretrial proceedings, jury selection for the trial of Angelo Buono began. Amid huge enlargements of grotesque crime-scene photographs of Strangler victims, the prosecution presented its case. The strongest physical evidence presented were tiny fibers taken from victim Judy Miller's eyelid and from the body of Lauren Wagner. Bianchi had testified that he and Buono used masking tape and upholstery stuffing to blindfold victims. Microscopic analysis of the different fibers revealed that they were similar to material used in Buono's upholstery shop and found in his home. The defense countered with the fact that the fibrous materials were common items and were found in many places.

In addition to physical evidence, the prosecution seemed to delight in introducing the sensational details of Buono's sex life. Their strategy was to portray him as a sadistic abuser of women, and to that end a procession of prostitutes and other former Buono lovers testified. Buono liked to perform anal sex and was given to using dildos, but refused to lubricate them, said witnesses. Some of the Strangler's victims had been anally raped. Buono loved to pinch and bite his lovers—some of whom were in their lower teen years—and he enjoyed oral sex which he performed in ways calculated to induce choking and even strangulation in his sex partners. It was a kinky show, and the media loved it.

In a bizarre twist to an already bizarre case, investigators had located 27-year-old Catherine Lorre, daughter of the late film actor Peter Lorre.* According to Bianchi, in 1977 he and Buono had stopped Catherine on a Hollywood street. Flashing badges, they identified themselves as police. At that moment, Lorre was a candidate for rape, torture and strangling. But when asked to produce identification, she showed not only her driver's license but a photo of herself sitting on her father's lap. She told the bogus cops that she was the late actor's only child. Fearing that a celebrity's child would get much more police attention than the sort of anonymous victims they had been killing, Bianchi let Catherine go. In court she clearly identified both Bianchi and Buono. Bianchi testified that Buono had made the initial approach to Lorre, but Lorre said it was Bianchi. Nevertheless, she placed both Bianchi and Buono at the scene.

Buono refused to testify in his own defense, although he never wavered, both publicly and privately, from his assertion of innocence. After deliberating 19 days, on Monday, November 14, 1983, the jury returned with the first of many verdicts. Angelo Buono was found guilty of nine murders. He was found not guilty in the death of Yolanda Washington, the Strangler's first victim. In the penalty phase, jurors did not recommend the death penalty, to Judge George's public consternation. Thus ended the longest criminal trial of a single defendant in American history: two years and two days.

Buono was sentenced to life in prison without possibility of parole. Furious, he fired his court-appointed attorneys because he had wanted a death sentence. But not because he wanted to die; death sentences carry with them an automatic appeal process directly to the Supreme Court, bypassing the Court of Appeals. Buono's appeal process will likely take many years. The trial transcript alone, which must be analyzed, runs to over 56,000 pages of testimony. He is serving his sentence in Folsom Prison.

Judge George, ruling that Bianchi had violated his plea bargain, could not increase the sentence of the Washington court, but he could make things somewhat less comfortable for the convicted murderer. Instead of serving his

time in the comparative comfort of California, Bianchi was returned to the cold
confines of Walla Walla, Washington. In 1984 Bianchi legally changed his
name, first to Anthony D'Amato, and then a second time, to Nicholas
Fontana.

Early in 1982, not long after the trial, California Attorney General George
Deukmejian was elected governor. In the same election, Los Angeles District
Attorney John Van De Kamp became attorney general. Deukmejian appointed
his close associate and former attorney general office aide Robert Philibosian to
Van De Kamp's former post as L.A. district attorney. Philibosian promptly
transferred Deputy District Attorney Roger Kelly to the county's equivalent of
Siberia: Compton.

Deukmejian appointed prosecutors Roger Boren and Michael Nash to
judgeships.

LOCATIONS:
Thomas Brothers map reference: Page 25 D4
Bianchi claimed that most of the Hillside Strangler murders were committed at
Buono's home, an upholstery shop at 703 E. Colorado Street, Glendale. The
front house was demolished; the shop remains in the rear. From the Golden
State Freeway (I-5) exit at Colorado, and go east. The site is on the left (north)
side of the street, just past Glendale Avenue.

Thomas Brothers map reference: Page 25 D5
Bianchi earlier lived at 809 E. Garfield, where his neighbor was Kristina
Weckler. He returned to this small courtyard apartment house to lure her from
her apartment. From Buono's former upholstery shop on Colorado, go west to
Glendale and south to Windsor. Turn left; then go right on Mariposa, then left
on Garfield. The building is about two-thirds of the way down a very long block,
on the left. On the right, across the street, is 800 Garfield, where victim Cindy
Hudspeth lived, though she was not abducted form her residence. Bianchi
claimed it was coincidental that she had lived across the street.

Thomas Brothers map reference: Page 34 D2
Kenneth Bianchi lived in the Tamarind Apartments at 1950 Tamarind, during
several of the slayings. Exit the northbound Hollywood Freeway (US 101) at
Gower, make an immediate right and right again on Franklin. Tamarind is the
second street on the left. The apartments are near the end of the street, on the
right side.

*In 1936, Peter Lorre spent several days listening to courtroom testimony and
studying the facial expressions of serial murderer William James. James tortured
and killed at least two of his wives. See Chapter 19, *The Rattlesnake Murderer:
Robert James (1936)*.

Stanley Mark Rifkin: He used his knowledge of computers to steal
$10.2 million from Security Pacific Bank. Photo: UPI/Bettmann Newsphotos.

36

STANLEY RIFKIN AND THE BIGGEST BANK ROBBERY (1978)

It was the largest bank robbery in U.S. history. It took only a few minutes. No alarms went off, no guns were drawn. For days, no one even noticed. And the man who did it might have gotten away with the perfect crime and enjoyed the rest of his life in the luxury of a Rio de Janeiro villa. Except that he seemed determined to bask in the recognition his feat had earned him, seemed far more interested in fame than fortune, more interested in attracting attention than in keeping his freedom.

Stanley Mark Rifkin was 32, a short, soft, chunky bachelor and a highly accomplished computer programmer. He grew up in Sun Valley, at the east end of the San Fernando Valley, in a solidly middle-class family, thoroughly inculcated with traditional values: hard work, education, thrift and moderation.

Rifkin was smart. At Francis Polytech High he earned near-perfect grades and wielded a sharp pen as editor of the student newspaper.

Unfortunately, being smart was not quite enough. He developed an attitude problem during his high school years. He began to display open contempt for fellow students and for teachers, whom he described as "menials." A journalism instructor later described him as "rigid, uptight, egotistical." Rifkin thought he was a superior being. He thought that ordinary rules did not apply to someone of his genius. When nobody seemed to agree, he became, by turns, angry, morose and withdrawn.

And then suicidal. He spent three months in the psychiatric ward of L.A. County Hospital after swallowing an entire bottle of aspirin.

From high school he went to the Northridge campus of California State University, where he focused on computer science. He did well, although sometimes he had trouble working with others who couldn't follow his rapid mental processes.

After graduation, he worked at several computer jobs, honing his skills as a programmer and putting aside a little money. In 1975 he eased into his own business. On the advice of his attorney, Gary Goodgame, he incorporated as a consulting firm. Operating from an office in his San Fernando Valley townhouse, he gradually hired four associates.

Then came an offer of a job with a San Diego firm that paid $35,000. It was more than he was making from his own operation and there was no risk of failure. He decided to accept.

Until he got an idea. A notion so outrageous that when he confided it to his best buddy from college, an Internal Revenue Service auditor, the IRS man laughed until tears came to his eyes. It was, the auditor thought, a wonderfully funny joke. He hadn't realized that Stan had quite so sharp a sense of humor. But it was no joke to Rifkin. In October 1978, he embarked upon an ambitious and unprecedented scheme.

The key to Rifkin's scam was his almost unlimited ability to come and go from one of the most sensitive areas at the downtown Los Angeles headquarters of Security Pacific Bank. The bank had several times hired him as a consultant to write or troubleshoot computer programs for their massive mainframe data processing machines. One of his projects was to create a backup system for the bank's wire transfer computers. After weeks on this project, he came and went form the bank's wire transfer room and no one paid him much attention.

Having studied the details of the wire transfer system, Rifkin understood it intimately. And he had learned how easy it was to be inconspicuous and blend into the background. In short, Rifkin had found a way, at extremely low risk to himself, to quickly and easily penetrate what the bank believed were formidable security barriers.

So on October 25, wearing a three-piece suit and carrying a briefcase, he got into his Datsun 240Z and drove to the 55-story skyscraper that housed the bank's worldwide headquarters. He parked in the underground garage, took an elevator to the lobby. Nearby were more banks of elevators. With a half dozen passengers he rode in anonymous silence. He left the elevator and boldly entered the wire transfer room. Selecting a young man at a corner computer terminal, he told him that he was a consultant hired by the Federal Reserve in Washington, D.C., to help Security Pacific solve problems with its wire transfers.

The young man was very glad to see Rifkin. He had a multitude of complaints about the computerized system. Rifkin listened patiently, taking careful notes. And when the man turned his head for a moment, Rifkin quickly wrote down a nine-digit number and a four-digit number.

The numbers were codes which were scribbled on worksheets festooning the wall of the computer cubicle. The numbers were Rifkin's reason for putting on this charade in the wire room. After investing an hour, he glanced at his watch, thanked the computer operator, and said he was through for the day. He wanted to pull his heist at a time when operators were likely to be rushed and perhaps a little careless. He would make his move a few minutes before closing time. He had about 10 minutes to accomplish his mission.

Rifkin walked out of the wire room almost unnoticed. He rode an elevator down to the lobby. In a vacant telephone booth, he fed a dime into the slot. He dialed the number of the wire transfer room he had just left.

A bank check is a piece of paper that serves as an I.O.U., a promise to pay. Someone writes a check and gives it to someone else, perhaps a grocery store, in exchange for goods or services. The store sends the check to the bank upon which it is written and is then credited with the appropriate amount of money. The same amount is removed from the account of the check's writer. Today the money is usually posted electronically and recorded on a computer tape.

Security Pacific maintained a $700 million balance with the Federal Reserve Bank, using those funds for the same purpose that individuals use their own checking accounts: to pay their bills. But instead of writing out a check, the bank simply sent an electronic message to the Federal Reserve. The Fed electronically transferred the money from the sender's account to the receiver's. Customers with very large balances made the same kind of transfers over the bank's computer system. For convenience, they routinely arranged them by telephone. For security, the bank required a coded number, changed daily. Anyone with the right nine-digit number could effect the transfer of almost any sum from the bank to any other account served by the Fed's electronic system.

From his phone booth, Rifkin was connected to a woman with a pleasant voice in the wire transfer room. Identifying himself as "Mike Hansen" of the bank's international division, he gave an authentic-sounding office number and a four-digit code.

There was an agonizing pause, as the woman checked the number. Inwardly, Rifkin squirmed, but only a little. If the number was wrong, if he'd made a mistake, the woman would just hang up. There would be no way to trace him. No harm, no foul, no police. No jail.

"Okay," said the pleasant female voice.

Masking his relief behind a voice that sounded almost bored, the thief instructed the wire transfer room to sent $10.2 million to the Irving Trust Bank in New York, and thence to a Swiss bank. He spelled its name: "W-O-Z-C-H-O-D, Wozchod." Then he read off the account number.

The clerk, who said her name was Lupe, seemed a little confused. Rifkin painstakingly talked her through the sequence of the transaction, but she still had trouble. He suggested she get some help.

A male voice came on the line. He asked for whom the order was to be debited. "Coast Diamond," said Rifkin. The male clerk asked for an interoffice settlement number and Rifkin knew he was home free. He started to read off the nine-digit number he'd copied in the wire room minutes earlier. "106131537," he started to say.

Rifkin never finished. After five digits, the clerk interrupted. "We need a 107 or a 109 number," he said. A little flustered, Rifkin read the nine-digit number again.

But the male clerk insisted. A 107 or a 109. Not a 106. Coolly, Rifkin said he'd double-check the number and call him back. Perhaps he'd have to make it tomorrow, since it was getting close to quitting time. He was just a smidgeon away from aborting the whole scheme. "If you can get a number tonight, we'll wait for you," said the male clerk. "Ask for Lupe."

Rifkin hung up and thought for a minute, trying to locate his mistake. Then he realized that he had gotten the right code number, but he'd used the wrong interoffice code. The number he'd scribbled down was for a domestic cash letter, not an international transfer.

He knew how to get the right number. Dropping another dime, he dialed the international banking department. Now he said he was calling from the wire room and that he'd garbled a code number on an international transfer that had started with the digits 109. What was that interoffice code again?

Rifkin was sweating now. The receiver was damp in his hands. But a dispassionate male voice supplied the numbers and he wrote them down in his little notebook and hung up. Once again he called Lupe in the wire room.

He read her the 109 code plus the last six digits of the number he'd copied from the worksheet. He heard the distinctive tapping of the terminal keyboard, and then Lupe came back on the line to tell him that everything was fine. She'd typed the money transfer order into the Federal Reserve's system, and the order had gone through. Rifkin mumbled perfunctory thanks and hung up.

The bank's money was on its way to Zurich. Rifkin was rich. He had stolen $10.2 million, and nobody knew it! He himself could hardly believe it. Hurrying to beat the rush-hour traffic, he recovered his car from the subterranean garage, and sped off toward the airport.

But before catching his plane to Switzerland, Rifkin had to send a telegram to a Russian diamond merchant.

On the long transatlantic flight, the rotund Rifkin sipped champagne and thought about how clever he had been. When he first began to consider ripping off Security Pacific, he saw himself faced with the problem of what to do with the money. Large sums moving between banks leave paper or electronic trails. Sooner or later—and probably sooner—someone would start looking for $10 million. Cash in small denominations was untraceable, but $10.2 million would be a huge and bulky amount, too much to carry.

So he'd gone to his Beverly Hills attorney and friend, Gary Goodgame, and explained that in his role as a consultant, he represented a "Fortune 500 company" that wanted to make payoffs discreetly in the Middle East. What sort of untraceable commodity, asked Rifkin, could his "client" use for this purpose?

Diamonds, said Goodgame. Diamonds that were not so large that they would be memorable, and not so small that they would become bulky in quantity. Goodgame recommended his friend and old USC classmate, Lon Stein, a commodity broker, to handle the transaction. On Rifkin's instructions, Stein had gone to Geneva and met with officials of *Russalmaz*, the state-owned Soviet diamond monopoly. Stein examined some $40 million worth of Soviet diamonds, selecting only those between 3.0 and .3 carats.

But despite the Russian's prior assurances, Stein had been unable to find quite as many of the right stones as Rifkin required. He had only been able to come up with $8.145 million worth. Subtracting that and Stein's commission from the $10.2 million in Rifkin's account, that left $1.855 million. So Stein tried to call Rifkin, a man he'd never met, in Los Angeles. To his surprise, he learned that nobody had seen him for days. Rifkin seemed to be missing. The San Diego electronics firm that was expecting him to start work called the police and made a missing persons report. Stein told the Russians to put the leftover cash into the Geneva bank account of another diamond merchant, a trusted friend.

The diamond courier who arrived at the posh Geneva offices of *Russalmaz* was a short, chunky, bespectacled man in a rumpled three-piece suit. A pale man who seemed fatigued, nervous and hesitant. He was shown to the office of Alex Malinin, head of the Swiss branch of *Russalmaz* and a KGB agent. He had come for the diamonds, explained Rifkin, and, after a false start, he correctly recited the 10-digit code number that identified him as the right man. But the diamonds were not here, explained the ever-affable Russian. That wasn't quite how things were done. Nobody should have to carry such valuable goods on their person. It wasn't safe. So the thoughtful Swiss had made it illegal. The diamonds had been sent by bonded courier and armored car to the customs area at the airport.

Watching this little exchange, without knowing the courier's name or recognizing his face, was Lon Stein, who had moments earlier helped Malinin polish off a whole bottle of the best Russian vodka. They were celebrating the largest sale of Soviet diamonds in history. A sale so important to the Russian diamond industry that Malinin himself had written the news release describing it.

But, drunk or not, Malinin had the good sense to check the courier's passport, and to check the code number before giving him a numbered claim check. He would present the claim check at Swiss Air's terminal customs office and exchange it for the diamonds.

Rifkin's first look at his loot was in the bedroom of a large suite in a chic Luxembourg hotel. Unwrapping his package, he stared unbelieving at almost four pounds—9,000 carats—of diamonds. There were more than a quarter of a million individual stones. He held them up to the light and let them slip through his fingers, and he marveled at what he had done.

And worried about what he would do next. His careful plan had unfolded a step at a time. At each new step there was always an opportunity to back out with minimal risk. But now the deed was done. Now he had 9,000 carats of untraceable diamonds and Security Pacific was out $10.2 million. Surely they would have missed it by now, he thought. Surely they would be looking for him. And worst of all, his mother would be worried sick. He had called her every day of his adult life, until the previous Wednesday, when he had boardedthe plane. Now she hadn't heard from him at all and must be frantic.

Standing there up to his wrists in Russian diamonds, Rifkin realized that he could never go back to his humdrum life as a computer consultant. Somehow his little townhouse and the few thousand dollars he'd saved by dint of extreme frugality were now meaningless.

Suddenly the enormity of what he'd done began to sink in. What if his old friends from high school and college could see him *now*! What would they think, he wondered. How would they react to the chubby kid, the nerd's nerd, who had pulled off the biggest bank heist in American history? There was only one way to find out, decided Rifkin. He'd have to go home.

Home this time was the luxurious and exclusive L'Ermitage, arguably Beverly Hills' most prestigious hotel hideaway. Rifkin checked into a suite, telephoned attorney Goodgame, and slept off his cumulative double jet lag beneath scented sheets.

The next morning, October 30, Goodgame, just off a plane himself after returning from a Hawaiian vacation, knocked on the door of Rifkin's suite. After ordering a room service breakfast, Rifkin got down to details. He handed Goodgame a detailed list of legal actions necessary to dissolve his corporation, Stan Rifkin, Inc. The company, said Rifkin between bites of caviar omelet, was no longer going to be part of his life. Goodgame was a little surprised, but he methodically set about filling in spaces on the previously prepared forms. Rifkin silently signed each.

Just before the meeting broke up, Rifkin decided he had to tell *somebody* about the diamonds. So he told Goodgame. Told him that he'd been involved as a bagman for his fictional Fortune 500 client, that he'd been hired to deliver a fictional bribe to a Middle Eastern figure, and that he had simply stolen the diamonds.

Goodgame thought it was a joke.

So Rifkin got up and went to his suitcase and returned with a small envelope bound by a rubber band. he removed the band and filled an ashtray with glittering diamonds. Goodgame picked at a few. Glass. They must be glass. Stanley Rifkin was no jewel thief, thought Goodgame. The whole thing's a joke.

No joke, insisted Rifkin with a grin. And then he laid all his cards on the table. "I made an unauthorized wire transfer of $10 million from Security Pacific."

Goodgame was stunned. How could the shy, roly-poly man he'd once helped form a computer consulting corporation be capable of all that? It didn't figure.

Rifkin soberly assured him that it was true. He had paid Stein his commission; now he was headed "off to places unknown." In a burst of generosity, he gave Gary Goodgame three small diamonds. He wasn't worried that Goodgame would turn him in. Their conversation, he was sure, had been privileged. It was an attorney-client conversation; Goodgame could not divulge what had been said. Stan Rifkin was smart.

That same afternoon Rifkin the computer expert became Rifkin the gem merchant. Starting with Van Cleef & Arpels, he made the rounds of better Beverly Hills jewelers. At each he discreetly offered to sell a few stones and at each he made a sale. He took the checks to the jewelers' own banks, where he exchanged them for cash. The next morning, Tuesday, October 31, Rifkin drove to Burbank Airport in the valley, where he caught a plane for Rochester, New York.

The very smart Stanley Rifkin was sure that his attorney Gary Goodgame was bound by attorney-client privilege. Attorney Goodgame knew it wasn't so. As Rifkin flew east, Goodgame sat down on a hard chair in an austere meeting room on the 17th floor of the Federal Building near the Westwood campus of UCLA.

Across the table was Special Agent Robin Brown of the FBI's white-collar crime unit. Brown, an accountant by training, at first had a hard time believing what Goodgame was saying. The elegantly attired Beverly Hills attorney was trying to tell him that Security Pacific Bank had been robbed of $10 million by fraudulent wire transfer. They spoke for more than two hours. During that time it crossed Brown's mind that if there had indeed been a theft, the bank would surely have notified the FBI by now. He was also mindful that he didn't know this attorney and that it was Halloween.

But when Goodgame produced the three diamonds Rifkin had given him, Brown put his doubts aside.

The next day he interviewed three of Rifkin's former employees, and Rifkin's mother. All they could tell him was that a week earlier he had vanished.

On Thursday, November 2, Special Agent Brown sat down with Senior Vice President and General Auditor Walter Fisher in a tastefully appointed conference room at Security Pacific's downtown offices. The genial banker listened carefully. It was an incredible story Brown told: Swiss banks, Russian diamonds, phony computer consultants. Very interesting, said Fisher, then shook his head. If someone had stolen $10 million of the bank's money, surely *he* would have known it by now. It was an interesting story, but such a theft was highly improbable.

So Brown told his story again. And he asked Fisher for a favor. Maybe there was nothing to the story. But would the bank indulge him just this once by checking their records? A few hours later, Security Pacific's management realized for the first time that the bank had been robbed eight days earlier.

In a Rochester hotel room Rifkin stared at his own face on the TV and realized for the first time that he was a wanted man. His dismay was tempered by the fact that the FBI had proclaimed the heist the biggest bank robbery in the country's history. He was wanted, thought Rifkin, but he was also famous. It was starting to snow outside, but Rifkin, worrying, checked out of his hotel. He caught a cab to another hotel and checked in. An hour later without ever having unpacked, he checked out again, and took another cab to another hotel, and checked in again. At dawn he headed for the airport.

The FBI knew he was in Rochester because minutes after the TV broadcast an attorney named Paul O'Brien had telephoned. O'Brien reported that Rifkin had, earlier in the day, asked him to help set up a New York City brokerage firm to sell diamonds that Rifkin had recently acquired in a swap for some West German land. O'Brien had accepted the offer, and with it $6,000 in cash as "earnest money."

Somehow Rifkin slipped through the Rochester police cordon and caught a plane for Chicago. At O'Hare he telephoned a buddy in San Diego, Dan Wolfson. Wolfson had seen the TV broadcast, too. Rifkin asked him if he could hide out at his place for a few days, just until he gave himself up. Wolfson agreed.

In San Diego, Rifkin telephoned Paul O'Brien in Rochester. The deal was off, said Rifkin. Would he please return the $6,000 by sending it to a post office box in Carlsbad, California? Sure, said O'Brien. Rifkin gave the box number to O'Brien. O'Brien gave it to the FBI agent standing next to him.

The FBI woke the postmaster in Carlsbad to get the name of the person who rented the post office box. And early the morning of November 6, Special Agent Brown knocked on the door of Wolfson's apartment. A sleepy Stanley Rifkin meekly surrendered.

Rifkin was charged with four counts of wire fraud, but while he sat in the San Diego federal jail, a Los Angeles district court judge noted that the arrest warrant did not bear the name of Rifkin's accuser, Goodgame. The arrest was flawed; possibly the government's whole case was imperiled. A legal struggle began between Rifkin's lawyer, Robert Talcott, and the U.S. attorney's office. The government was willing to drop two of the four counts; it would cost him a 10-year sentence. It seemed like a good deal to Talcott. It seemed like an eternity to Rifkin. He turned them down. The U.S. attorney's office began to wonder if their damaged case was enough to convict Rifkin of anything.

But while Rifkin's family and friends were trying to raise $200,000 in cash needed to get Rifkin out of jail, he was hatching a scheme: another theft by wire plan. The catalyst was his cellmate, who offered to introduce Rifkin to a banker on the take. Once he was free on bond, Rifkin wasted no time making the contact his cellmate had set up.

He met with financial consultant Joe McAfee on a Beverly Hills street corner. Walking and talking, they discussed the details of the new scam. Rifkin said that he now realized diamonds were too clumsy. The time he'd use bearer bonds. Rifkin described how the new theft would be accomplished, how they would split the money and where they would cash the bonds.

And at all times during this conversation, FBI agents in an Air Force spotter plane were circling overhead at 8,000 feet, watching the meeting through binoculars. Special Agent Joseph Sheehan, who had played the role of Joe McAfee, had been equipped with a concealed wireless microphone. The tape recording made from that device was enough to indict Rifkin for conspiracy to commit wire fraud. He was arrested the next morning at a Marina del Rey boatslip, where he was waiting for the "banker" to show up.

A few days later Rifkin agreed to plead guilty to two of the first four counts in return for the government dropping the conspiracy charge.

Security Pacific recovered about $6.4 million of Rifkin's loot. Most of the rest was lost because his rough handling of the diamonds reduced their value. The gems were auctioned off. On Mother's Day, 1980, the May Company Department Stores held a special sale of jewelry produced from some of the Rifkin stones.

Attempting to tighten security, Security Pacific Bank eliminated the use of telephone wire transfers. Computer terminals installed for this purpose in branch banks make it more difficult to transfer funds. It now requires relatively sophisticated computer skills. To train some of their employees in these new skills, the bank will have to employ outside experts. These are sometimes known as computer consultants.

On March 28, 1979, Rifkin was sentenced to eight years in prison. He began his sentence at the federal Terminal Island facility near Long Beach. In the spring of 1981 he was transferred to Lompoc, and was paroled in 1982 after serving 3.5 years. In 1985 he was hired in Washington, D.C., by the American Association for the Advancement of Science. Hired as a consultant, to help improve operations of an internal computing system, used for many chores, including payroll and accounting.

"We were very pleased with his performance," said Carol Rogers, the AAAS's spokesperson. It was almost the exact phrase that Rifkin's former client, Security Pacific Bank, had once used.

LOCATIONS:
Thomas Brothers map reference: Page 44 C3
Security Pacific Bank's world headquarters is the 55-story building at 800 Sixth Street, corner of Figueroa. Exit the Harbor Freeway (I-110) at Sixth; the bank is on the southeast corner.

Thomas Brothers map reference: Page 33 C6
L'Ermitage is at 9291 Burton Way, Beverly Hills. Exit the San Diego Freeway (I-405) at Wilshire, go east to Santa Monica, then north on Santa Monica and right at Burton Way. The hotel is on the northeast corner of Elm. Rifkin gave three diamonds to Goodgame in suite 304.

Frederick Jerome Thomas murdered Sarai Ribicoff on a Venice street. Photo: UPI/Bettmann Newsphotos.

37

THE RANDOM KILLING OF SARAI RIBICOFF (1980)

Los Angeles defies geographic conventions. So, speaking not geographically but philosophically, in 1980 Venice was the crossroads of the city. Venice was nothing so much as L.A. writ small: multiracial, multisocioeconomic, multiethnic, multilingual, multisexual preference, it was home to a parade of day-trippers and heavy-duty youth gangs. At once glitzy suburb, inner-city slum and tightly knit small town, Venice was outrageously hip and beach-town conventional, upscale pretentious and meanly desperate. Some gladly paid $50 for a meal; others pushed angel dust or peddled their post-juvenile bodies to make the rent. If Venice streets were occasionally dangerous, everyone acknowledged they were also safer than most parts of town.

So when Sarai Ribicoff was gunned down along a busy Venice thoroughfare, the upscalers of Los Angeles, the citizens with jobs and money and futures, grieved mightily. Some few grieved for Sarai. Most grieved because it proved what everyone feared but no one had wanted to know: No one and no place in L.A. was safe any more.

Sarai was 23, 15 months out of Yale, and those who knew her said she was intense and ambitious, and that she burned with the fervor of righteous causes and had gotten off to a good start in her first year as a staff reporter for the *Herald Examiner*. Sarai grew up in more than comfortable circumstances. She was the niece of Connecticut Senator Abraham Ribicoff and the daughter of a prominent Hartford attorney, Irving Ribicoff. As respected and cultured as any family in America, the Ribicoffs were leaders of the liberal movement. No one had done more to champion the causes of the poor and the disadvantaged. The causes, as newspaper editorials would remind the public conscience in the days and months to come, included the urgent causes of blacks.

On the night of November 12, Sarai Ribicoff went to dinner with John Shoven, 33, a professor of economics at Stanford. They dined at Chez Hélène, an expensive French restaurant not far from Sarai's apartment. They ate a leisurely dinner, and as they prepared to leave about 10:00, Sarai remarked that she had enjoyed the evening immensely. They stepped into the chill of Washington Boulevard, and into a nightmare.

Frederick Jerome Thomas was 21, a high school graduate and functional illiterate, baron of the Venice angel dust (PCP) pushers, a leader of the Crips—L.A.'s biggest and baddest soul street gang—a man who used almost as much PCP as he sold. A big, tough and angry thief, burglar and street robber. He was born in Texas and came to California at age five, after his father abandoned the family. Thomas was all those things and one more. Thomas was black.

Anthony LaQuin McAdoo was another sort. He had never been arrested, never been in serious trouble, never known to use drugs. Black and 19 years old, a head shorter than Thomas, he was another semiliterate graduate of Venice High, a young man struggling for pocket money by working a series of temporary jobs, manual labor of the meanest sort. And then his car broke down, and without money to fix it, McAdoo was reduced to riding the bus. In Los Angeles a car is the minimum index of manhood. A man who must ride the bus to find work is not a man. McAdoo threw in with Thomas for the evening so he could get enough money to fix his car.

These four people met once only, on the street in front of Chez Hélène. Thomas, waving a 9mm automatic, just strolled by, McAdoo at his side. Shoven had never experienced anything that might have remotely prepared him for the encounter. He hadn't yet begun to comprehend what was happening. He took Sarai's hand and moved out into the street, hoping "there might be traffic." They started to cross the street. Thomas McAdoo came after them, circling, looking, making a quick inventory of Shoven's heavy gold watch, of the small gold pendant with a diamond chip hanging from a gold chain around Sarai's neck.

They circled and they continued across the street and waited in the deep shadow of an unfenced lawn. Halfway out, Shoven reversed course, and headed back for the safety of the restaurant. The robbers ran them down. The frightened couple never got farther than the sidewalk.

Thomas leveled the 9mm at Shoven's middle. "This is for real," he said. He said it again. "This is for real." He said it twice more, four times in all. His message was unmistakable. Shoven didn't quite get it. As McAdoo removed his wallet, which held about $200 in cash, Shoven asked him not to take his credit cards and I.D.

Thomas shoved Sarai down onto the sidewalk. She was saying something about not having a purse. Thomas cocked the pistol, and the sharp *click* sent a freezing finger up Shoven's spine. McAdoo relieved him of his watch. He watched in disbelief as Thomas put the barrel of the pistol to Sarai's back. And pulled the trigger. A single shot echoed off the concrete and Sarai struggled to speak, to breathe, to live. Thomas bent low over his victim then fired twice more into the dark. Clutching his booty—Sarai's pendant—he sprinted away, McAdoo close behind.

Shoven went into the restaurant for help, but by the time paramedics arrived it was too late. The bullet had gone clean through Sarai. Both lungs were pierced, as well as her heart. She drowned in her own blood.

A close examination of the crime scene produced a strange clue: a bloodstain just below Sarai's knee. Her blood was Type A. The thin stream was Type O. The blood trail led away into the darkness.

Next door in a crêpe restaurant's kitchen worked Oscar Benitez, 22, a Salvadoran. He heard the shots and followed the fleeing men into the darkness. A few blocks away, Benitez saw them duck into a large, nearly abandoned brown stucco building on Fifth Avenue. Although he was an illegal immigrant, Benitez knew his duty as a citizen and as a human being. He went to the police with his story. They followed the blood trail to a second-story apartment, but there was no one home. Shoven's empty wallet was found in the garbage-littered courtyard. (Benitez was later rewarded with a grant of legal immigrant status.)

The police also checked nearby emergency rooms—and got lucky. Thomas had gone to the Marina Mercy hospital. The same bullet that killed Sarai had ricocheted off the sidewalk and nicked his arm. By midnight Thomas was in custody. McAdoo turned himself in the next day, accompanied by his mother.

And now the city found itself gripped by near hysteria. The *Herald Examiner* ran an editorial: "We Are Frightened (We Suspect You Are Frightened Too)," said headline. The text ended with a statement and a question: "Sarai Ribicoff, 23, Los Angeles County victim number 2008. Who will be next?"

The newspaper, frequently associated with local liberal causes, began carrying a black box on the front page, ticking off the number of days since Sarai's death. It carried that box until Thomas and McAdoo were tried and convicted. Reporters on the *Herald Examiner* did a little digging and learned that the previous April, Thomas had been arrested with four ounces of PCP in a grape-juice can tucked into his pocket. The district attorney's office had never bothered to prosecute. The newspaper, and many of its readers, wanted to know why.

McAdoo's attorney, Curtis Shaw, a flamboyant black whose practice was normally limited to movie deals, wanted his client off the stage before the rising indignation of the white mob could only be satisfied by blood. So when

McAdoo was offered a deal to turn state's evidence—a sentence of 25 years, with the possiblity of parole in 17—Shaw convinced him to take it and avoid what seemed a strong possibility: death in the gas chamber.

A captive Thomas was hostile and unrepentant. He refused to plead guilty, and during the 15 months of pretrial and trial, rarely spoke, even to his court-appointed attorney, Richard Hirsch. In court Thomas once slyly gave "the finger" to a *Herald* reporter who stared at him. Hirsch had his hands full, but he did his best. And it was enough. By a narrow margin, the jury that convicted Thomas of first degree murder refused to take his life. He was sentenced to life in prison, without possibility of parole.

He was saved, partly, by the testimony of McAdoo. In the seconds before Thomas pulled the trigger, said the prosecution witness, he was trying to rip the gold pendant from Sarai's neck. And she resisted. She struggled to keep her property and was murdered for this. And so, according to what they later told reporters, all seven women jurors voted to spare Thomas' life. Sarai's mother, Belle, was horrified. "Have we reached the point as a society where someone who struggles with an attacker becomes responsible for his own murder?" she cried. Around Belle's neck was a pendant nearly identical to the one for which her daughter died. Belle had given Sarai the pendant upon her graduation from Yale.

Afterward some jurors said they had also considered Thomas' age and the fact that he had no previous convictions. His April PCP arrest didn't count; he'd never been tried on that charge.

Anthony McAdoo, Thomas' partner in crime, was a neighborhood youth with no previous criminal record. Photo: UPI/Bettmann Newsphotos.

The death of Sarai Ribicoff was in some ways the death of a certain kind of Los Angeles innocence. It dried up the shallow pool of white sympathy created by the police shooting of Eulia Love, a black housewife who had waved a kitchen knife at police. It was an event that seared the souls of limousine liberals, polarized an already uneasy affluent white community, and focused the nation's attention on a Los Angeles crime rate that for the first time exceeded that of New York.

In this climate of fear actor Sylvester Stallone, businessman Arthur Kassel, and other investors started the Beverly Hills Gun Club, and some of those who had once worked overtime for gun-control legislation came to learn about choosing calibers for maximum stopping power and how to shoot quickly and accurately. In the six months after Ribicoff's death, the number of California women applying for tear gas permits jumped from 26,000 to 341,000. More than half of them lived in or near Los Angeles.

LOCATIONS:

Thomas Brothers map reference: Page 49 C4
Chez Hélène, the Venice restaurant outside which Sarai was slain, is at 1029 W. Washington Boulevard, Venice. The present establishment is called Rockenwagner. Go west on the Marina Freeway until its end. Turn right on Lincoln to Washington Boulevard, then left. Follow the street as it curves to the right. The restaurant is in a two-story rococo building with red tile roofing, on the right side of the street near the corner of Broadway. Across the street is Westminister Avenue School. Two doors west is LaGrange Aux Crepes, where brave Oscar Benitez worked.

Thomas Brothers map reference: Page 49 C4
From Rockenwagner turn right on Broadway, then left on Fifth Avenue a short distance to 919, the house to which McAdoo and Thomas fled. It's a 26-unit built as a 60's urban renewal project. By the night of Ribicoff's murder, the semiabandoned structure was the focus of neighborhood drug trafficking.

John Belushi: Too much pressure, too many temptations.
Photo: AP/Wide World.

38

JOHN BELUSHI STRIKES OUT ON A SPEEDBALL (1982)

John Belushi, 33, was a rotund comic, a TV and film writer, a multi-talented performer and sometime blues singer idolized by millions of TV and film fans for his "Killer Bee," "Samurai Warrior," "Cheeburga Counterman" and "crazed blues man" roles.

Belushi lived with his wife, Judy, in New York, but made frequent, often extended trips to Los Angeles on business. There he began to develop a second set of friends, colleagues, and professional acquaintances—and a widening circle of Hollywood groupies. Some of them supplied him with drugs.

When Belushi came west, he usually preferred the fading opulence and very private atmosphere of the Château Marmont Hotel in West Hollywood, where he rented a detached bungalow with a private entrance for $200 a day.

In March of 1982 Belushi was under intense, unremitting pressure to alter and finish a film script, a script already rejected by Paramount executives. To save Belushi's face, they had said it required "extensive rewrite." It was an intensely humiliating experience to Belushi's fragile ego, and he was unwilling to admit the script couldn't be saved with more work. But at the same time, Paramount was encouraging him to drop the first script altogether and to write instead a comedy script loosely based on a sex manual, *The Joy of Sex*. It would be, they insisted, as big a hit as his 1978 *Animal House* film. But it was made plain to Belushi that if he failed again his considerable bankability at the studio would be greatly diminished.

When Belushi was under this kind of pressure he often fell into a self-destructive behavior pattern that had developed over the years. He would stay awake for days at a time, using cocaine both for its temporary euphoria and to help him stay awake. But the quality of his work suffered. Falling further and further behind in his work, becoming increasingly dependent on drugs, using larger and larger doses, he became childishly stubborn and petulant. He lived from drug dose to drug dose, and the tide of paranoia rose within him. By March 4, 1982, he was out of control.

Cathy Evelyn Smith was who he wanted that day. Cathy Smith, a Canadian woman of 34, once a backup singer for Gordon Lightfoot, had become a sort of inner-circle groupie, a woman who seemed to enjoy basking in the reflected glow of stardom. Arrested in 1981 for possession of heroin, she was John Belushi's best connection to the drugs he craved.

Though he was now a wealthy man, Belushi's freespending tendencies—those close to him felt he could easily spend all he had on drugs—were checked by his manager, Bernie Brillstein, who doled out small sums of cash as Belushi required and oversaw payment of his business expenses. On March 4, Belushi tried to beg or con $1,500 from Brillstein, money he said he needed for a new guitar he wanted to buy. Brillstein knew he'd only spend it on drugs, so he said no. Belushi was able to borrow from his friends and also wheedled money from his wife. It was widely rumored that someone in the film studio supplied him with drugs that were charged to the production company as overhead.

Later that day Belushi finally caught up with Cathy Smith at the home of April Milstead, a mutual friend. He and Cathy injected themselves with several doses of cocaine mixed with heroin, a combination called a "speedball," over a period of about 30 minutes. They left in Belushi's rented Mercedes. Belushi gave her $300 to buy some more heroin, and she dropped him off at the home of Tino Insana, a friend with whom Belushi was collaborating on another script. Insana didn't do drugs and didn't like what they did to other people. Smith returned with the heroin, and the pair moved on to the home of Nelson Lyon, another friend, where they shot up more speedballs.

From there Belushi went to his favorite private club, On the Rox, where he called Tino Insana. He wanted to get together the next day and work on their script. Insana didn't think Belushi would be up to that kind of demanding work. And he was uncomfortable with the notions Belushi was developing of what the script should be like: He wanted to show actors shooting up with real drugs, on camera. Nevertheless, Insana reluctantly agreed to meet Belushi the next day.

At Rox Belushi shared some cocaine with a piano-player friend. Later, when Smith returned, the three of them went into the club's grubby office and shot up. Smith did the preparations, then injected them all. At about midnight, actor Robert DeNiro came by the club. Belushi asked him to stop by his Marmont bungalow after the club closed at 2:00 a.m.

At closing time Belushi was in the parking lot. Leaving in his car, he saw someone selling drugs, and stopped to buy $100 worth of cocaine. On the way back to the Marmont on Sunset, with Smith driving, Belushi felt ill. He asked her to stop. He opened the door and without leaving the car, threw up in the gutter, heaving and gasping. Back at the bungalow he had to be helped into the room by Smith. He immediately went to the bathroom and vomited again. He told Smith it was the greasy food he had eaten at the Rox. Belushi and Smith left the bungalow, returning a short while later.

Waiting for them was comedian Robin Williams. He had just spoken by telephone with DeNiro, who said the party would continue at Belushi's bungalow. Williams had immediately driven over to the hotel. But he didn't stay long. He was uneasy with the grubby room, which was littered with wine bottles. Uneasy with Cathy Smith, in whom he perceived a hard edge that was alien to his experience. And he was uneasy with the way Belushi was fading in and out of consciousness, passing out after snorting some cocaine, then coming right back awake a few seconds later. Williams left, feeling that he didn't fit in with this degenerate scene.

Robert DeNiro arrived soon thereafter, but he, too, didn't stay long. Just long enough to snort a few "lines" of Belushi's cocaine. He left the way he came, through a sliding glass door at the rear of the bungalow.

Soon Belushi told Smith he felt cold. He turned up the heat. He ordered everyone else to leave. The only other guest, Nelson Lyon, departed—after Belushi borrowed $10 from him.

From a pocket Belushi produced more cocaine, which Smith mixed with heroin, making yet another speedball. She injected herself with the mixture, then Belushi. He got up, stripped, took a shower. Smith washed his back. Then he got into bed, joined by Smith, and they sat up, talking about the various deals and projects Belushi was involved with. Belushi complained again of the cold, and Smith tucked him under the blankets, and again turned up the heat.

Smith went into the next room to write a letter to an old friend in Toronto. She wanted to borrow Belushi's car so she could return to her own apartment. She asked Belushi if he was hungry, but got only a mumble in reply. Later she heard coughing and wheezing coming from his bedroom, and deep choking sounds. Pulling the covers back, she asked Belushi if he was all right. He complained of congestion in his lungs after swallowing a little of the water Smith brought him.

At about 10:15 on the morning of March 5, Smith checked Belushi again. He seemed to be sleeping soundly, snoring. She left in his car, after putting in her purse the drug paraphernalia they'd been using. She drove over to a bar in Santa Monica to bet $6 on a horse.

At about noon, Belushi's physical trainer, Bill Wallace, came over with a typewriter and tape recorder Belushi had asked for. Letting himself in with a key, he found Belushi huddled in the fetal position under the blankets, his head under a pillow. Belushi wasn't breathing. Wallace tried CPR, he tried mouth-to-mouth resuscitation, he tried everything he knew. But nothing would bring John Belushi back from the dead. There would be no more rewrites on his life's script.

A few weeks later, in a Toronto interview with the *National Enquirer* (for which she was paid $15,000), Cathy Smith admitted she had injected Belushi with several speedballs the night of his death. "John supplied the coke, I supplied the heroin. I was Florence Nightingale with the hypodermic," she said. But she later claimed she was under the influence of alcohol and drugs at the time of the interview, and furthermore her remarks had been taken out of context. She was indicted by a Los Angeles grand jury on 13 counts of administering dangerous drugs.

After surrendering to Canadian authorities, Smith fought extradition proceedings for nearly three years. In January 1985, Smith made a deal with Los Angeles authorities. She agreed to waive extradition in return for a reduced charge. The deal apparently fell apart after she arrived in Los Angeles and she will be tried on second degree murder charges.

LOCATION:
Thomas Brothers map reference: Page 33 3E
Follow Sunset Boulevard in West Hollywood to the Hotel Marmont, 8221 Sunset Boulevard. Entrance is on Marmont Lane, the second street west of Crescent Heights on Sunset's north side. Follow the road as it curves around the hotel, then go right on Monteel. Past a brushy area a few yards down Monteel is a carport, then two identical bungalows, units B-4 and B-3, then a second carport. The bungalows are behind locked wrought-iron gates. Belushi died in unit B-3.

Vicki Morgan: While mistress to one of the President's inner circle, she had everything. Photo: AP/Wide World.

39

POWER, LUST & DESPAIR: THE BRUTAL END OF VICKI MORGAN (1983)

She was beauty and glamor, money and power, corruption and perversion, grandly crafted public image and sordid secret life; she made a bold, exciting run along the edge of convention before being overtaken by a sudden, sickening unraveling into despair and penury—and a brutal, senseless death. In a peculiar way, her story typifies the compellingly attractive but ultimately destructive Möbius Strip that circles the heart of Los Angeles.

At 17 Vicki Morgan was alluring. Tall, slender and bosomy, with sensuously full lips, she turned male heads, young and old. Strolling her insouciant walk down Sunset Boulevard in the spring of 1970, she caught the eye of a dirty old man.

A rich, powerful, perverted 53-year-old man named Alfred Bloomingdale. Heir to the Bloomingdale's Department Store fortune, and founder of Diner's Club, Bloomingdale lived a public life that seemed like the pot of gold beneath the far rainbow of the rosiest American Dream. Not just rich but *filthy* rich, he'd enjoyed a long and outwardly tranquil marriage to Betsy, a handsome society matron who was a close friend of Nancy Reagan. Thus Alfred became a buddy of Nancy's husband, Ronald, or Ron, as Al Bloomingdale called him. Ron was an actor who had become governor of California. But Ron and Al and some of their other rich friends—the so-called "Kitchen Cabinet" of informal advisors that had Reagan's ear—had big plans for Ron. Between wealth and charisma, Reagan became President of the United States in 1980.

But that was well after that afternoon when a bewitched Al Bloomingdale followed Vicki Morgan down Sunset and into the Old World Restaurant. And struck up a conversation. And demanded her phone number before he could leave. "He was so persistent, I had lunch with him," said Morgan.

Within a week she had been inducted into Bloomingdale's secret and phantasmagorical world of leather and chains, featuring Al as sadistic dungeonmaster. Along with as many as three other women at the same time, Vicki took off her clothes so that Al could bind and whip her. Thus aroused, he had sex with Vicki, then with other women, all the while being encouraged and caressed by the "slaves." Other sex games at the Bloomingdale hideaway explored the infinite permutations possible with multiple partners.

Soon Vicki "found herself falling in love" with Bloomingdale. She became his mistress, a liaison which continued, with brief interruptions at the outset, for a dozen years.

One of the brief interruptions was an affair with another man, which resulted in the birth of her son, Todd, in 1971. Later that year she became pregnant by Bloomingdale. An abortion soon followed.

And then came the best years of Vicki's life. Bloomingdale paid her rent, gave her spending money, and helped launch an exciting if ultimately flaccid movie career. He spent a lot of time with her, considering his other obligations to the president, to his wife, and to his myriad business dealings.

In the final months before Bloomingdale succumbed to cancer in August 1982, his illicit relationship with Vicki became even stronger. Denying to himself the futility of his struggle against impending death, Bloomingdale began planning a new enterprise, a nationwide chain of pizza parlors. In July, Betsy Bloomingdale discovered the carefully hidden truth about her dying husband's relationship with Vicki Morgan. Betsy had her evicted from the house Al had rented for her.

And then Al died. Hardly was he cold when the lawsuits were filed. Vicki wanted $10 million in palimony. Although the couple never lived together, Vicki claimed that she had tried to cure Bloomingdale of his "Marquis de Sade" complex. She also wanted the $10,000 a month that she claimed he promised to pay her for "personal services," and she wanted a half interest in Bloomingdale's prospective pizza chain, since, she alleged, that was what Bloomingdale had promised her in return for her business advice. That's what Vicki Morgan wanted.

What she got was an avalanche of sensational publicity, heavy legal expenses and a shortcut to the oblivion of the grave.

In September 1982, Superior Court Judge Christian Markey heard the palimony case. Vicki claimed her relationship with Bloomingdale was that of "business confidante, companion and mistress." The judge said it was a relationship based mostly on sex and therefore the palimony precedents of *Michelle Triola Marvin v. Lee Marvin* were not relevant. So no trial and no palimony millions. Not a dime.

Vicki's two other claims were less easily resolved. They would be tried on their merits, in due time, as the court's calendar permitted.

Meanwhile Vicki, now 30 years old and without specific job skills or the sort of experience that lends itself to executive employment, had a more basic problem: survival. Evicted from the house that Bloomingdale built, she and son Todd moved from one friend's place to another for a few weeks. Early in 1983, she rented a condo in Studio City from *Los Angeles Times* calendar section editor Robert Epstein for $1,000 a month.

By June of 1983 things were looking down for Vicki Morgan. Still unemployed, her lawsuit inching forward through the cluttered court calendar, she was desperate for money. She sold the Mercedes Benz that Bloomingdale had given her. Still unable to hack the rent on her own, she took a roommate, a gay man she'd known for about four years.

Marvin Pancoast was 33, an admitted homosexual who had worked as a clerk at the William Morris Agency. He had a long history of mental problems. And he, too, was unemployed.

Vicki and Marvin were surely the odd couple. Since her teen years she had been the pampered plaything of a very rich man, a woman who participated in the kinkiest of sexual shenanigans. He was a confused and mentally unbalanced homosexual, a veteran of the gay bar and massage parlor circuit who had for many months worked closely with the cream of internationally famous show-business figures. And both of them were broke.

Vicki was imperiously distant with Marvin. He was not attracted by her still considerable charms and he couldn't come up with his share of the rent money. She was used to fawning, obedient men who showed their appreciation for her sexual attractions. The odd couple quarrelled frequently. Finally, early in July 1983, Vicki, almost totally broke and feeling the strain of an uneasy relationship with Pancoast, made plans to move in with a girlfriend in Beverly Hills. Pancoast, at least temporarily, would go to Thousand Oaks. Vicki called Elephant Movers, in West Hollywood, and arranged for them to move her belongings. They were scheduled to come on July 7. First thing in the morning.

Vicki was a slinky, sexy woman. Among the mighty, many men would have killed for the privilege of sharing her home. But by the night of July 6, Pancoast had had all he could stand of her. "I was tired of being her slave boy," he said later. He was thinking of strangling her in the living room.

But Pancoast changed his mind. Instead, he waited for her to go to sleep. After midnight, he rose, adjusted the lighting in the living room, turned up the stereo so that the neighbors couldn't hear any of the sounds that would soon be coming from Vicki's bedroom. Then he took one of Todd's wooden baseball bats, walked into Vicki's bedroom and beat on her head and chest for several minutes.

At about 3:20 on the morning of July 7, Pancoast walked into the North Hollywood division police station and asked to speak to a homicide detective. "Why?" asked the desk sergeant.

"I just killed someone," said Pancoast.

The brutal death of Vicki Morgan sent shockwaves through Hollywood. Some of them bounced off Washington, D.C. On July 11, Los Angeles attorney Robert Steinberg announced that he'd seen three video tapes depicting Morgan, Bloomingdale, and a number of unnamed "top government officials" engaged in sadomasochistic sex orgies. The tapes, claimed Steinberg, contained "things of high risk to the national security of the country." He said that the people involved "would definitely embarrass the President, just like Mr. Bloomingdale did."

The announcement stunned the city and fueled wild speculation that Morgan had been killed to silence her, that Pancoast, with a history of mental illness going back to 1969, was merely an unresisting pawn, or had been framed by powerful interests that wanted Vicki Morgan dead. The tapes, said Steinberg, were proof that high government figures were involved.

But where were the tapes? On July 12, Steinberg said they'd been stolen from his office. The next day, porno publishing king Larry Flynt announced that he'd made a deal with Steinberg. He would pay Steinberg $1 million for the tapes. But Steinberg had never appeared to conclude the transaction and later denied ever speaking to Flynt.

Pancoast pleaded not guilty by reason of insanity. On September 14, 1984, after a short trial, he was convicted of murder in the first degree. The jury also found him sane. He was sentenced to a term of 26 years to life and will be eligible for parole in 1997.

In May 1985, Steinberg agreed to a plea bargain with the district attorney's office. He agreed to plead "no contest" to misdemeanor charges of criminal contempt. The charge of filing a false police report was dropped. The district attorney would have had to prove the disappearance of an object that only Steinberg claimed to have seen, a conundrum of double negatives he did not wish to attempt unraveling. The tapes, if they ever existed, have never turned up.

LOCATIONS:

Thomas Brothers map reference: Page 23 D4
Vicki Morgan died in a rented condo at 4171 D Colfax Avenue, Studio City. Exit Ventura Freeway (US 101) at Laurel Canyon, go south to Moorpark, east to Colfax, south to just before the concrete flood control channel.

Thomas Brothers map reference: Page 33 D4
The Old World Restaurant where in 1970 Bloomingdale first spoke to Morgan, is at 8762 Sunset Boulevard, on the corner of Sunset and Palm. Exit the Hollywood Freeway at Highland, go south to Sunset, then west to Palm.

BIBLIOGRAPHY

Anderson, Clinton H. *Beverly Hills Is My Beat*. Englewood Cliffs, N.J.: Prentice-Hall, 1960

Anger, Kenneth. *Hollywood Babylon*. Phoenix: Associated Professional Services, 1965.

Austin, John. *Hollywood's Unsolved Mysteries*. New York: Ace Star Publishing, 1970.

Bowman, Lynn. *Los Angeles, Epic of a City*. Berkeley: Howell-North Books, 1974.

Caughey & Caughey. *Los Angeles: Biography of a City*. Berkeley: U. of California Press, 1976.

Chisholm, Joe and Cohn, Alfred. *Take the Witness*. New York: Frederick A. Stokes, 1934.

Churchill, Allen. *A Pictorial History of American Crime, 1849-1929*. New York: Holt, Rinehart & Winston, 1964.

Cini, Zelda and Crane, Bob. *Hollywood, Land & Legend*. New Rochelle, N.Y.: Arlington House, 1980.

Cohen, Mickey. *Mickey Cohen, In My Own Words, As Told to John Peer Nugent*. Englewood Cliffs, N.J.: Prentice Hall, 1975.

Colby, Robert. *The California Crime Book*. New York: Pyramid Books, 1971.

David, Andrew. *Famous Criminal Trials*. Minneapolis: Lerner Publications, 1979.

Duffy, Clinton T. *88 Men and Two Women*. New York: Doubleday, 1962.

Dunlap, Carol. *California People*. Salt Lake City: Peregrene Smith Books, 1982.

Ehrlichman, John. *Witness to Power*. New York: Simon & Schuster, 1982.

Fogelson, Robert M. *The Los Angeles Riots*. New York: Arno Press & The New York Times, 1969.

Gaute, J.H.H. and Odell, Robin. *The Murderer's Who's Who*. New York: Methuen, 1979.

Giesler, Jerry. *The Jerry Giesler Story*. New York: Simon & Schuster, 1960.

Godwin, John. *Murder USA*. New York: Ballantine Books, 1978.

Halpern, John. *Los Angeles, Improbable City*. New York: E.P. Dutton, 1963.

Hynd, Alan. *Murder, Mayhem & Mystery*. New York: A.S. Barnes, 1958.

Jackson, Joseph Henry. *Bad Company*. New York, Harcourt, Brace & Co., 1939, 1940.

Jacobson, Lauri. *Hollywood Heartbreak*. New York: Simon & Schuster, 1984.

Kilgallen, Dorothy. *Murder One*. New York: Random House, 1967.

Kunstler, William. *First Degree*. New York: Ocean Publications, 1960.

Longstreet, Stephen. *All Star Cast, an Anecdotal History of Los Angeles*. New York: Thomas Y. Crowell, 1977.

Lukas, J. Anthony. *Nightmare, the Underside of the Nixon Years*. New York: Viking Press, 1976.

Mayer, Robert. *Los Angeles, a Chronological & Documentary History*. Dobbs Ferry, N.Y.: Oceana Publications, 1978.

Mayo, Morrow. *Los Angeles*. New York: Alfred A. Knopf, 1932, 1933.

McWilliams, Carey. *Southern California Country*. New York: Duell, Sloan & Pearce, 1946.

Muir, Florabel. *Headline Happy*. New York: Henry Holt & Co., 1950.

Nadeau, Remi. *Los Angeles, from Mission to Modern City*. New York: Longmans, Green & Co., 1960.

Nash, Jay Robert. *Almanac of World Crime*. New York: Anchor Press, Doubleday, 1981.

———. *Among the Missing*. New York: Simon & Schuster, 1978.

———. *Bloodletters and Badmen*. New York: M. Evans and Co., 1973.

———. *Look for the Woman*. New York: M. Evans & Co., 1981.

———. *Murder, America*. New York: Simon & Schuster, 1980.

———. *Murder Among the Mighty*. New York: Delacorte Press, 1983.

Noguchi, Thomas. *Coroner*. New York: Pocket Books, 1983.

Parker, Frank. *Caryl Chessman, the Red Light Bandit*. Chicago: Nelson-Hall, 1975.

Rice, Craig. *Los Angeles Murders*. New York: Sloan & Pearce, 1947.

Robinson, W.W. *Lawyers of Los Angeles*. Los Angeles: Los Angeles Bar Association, 1959.

Rolle, Andrew F. *California, A History*. Arlington Heights, Ill.: Harlan Davidson, 1978.

Root, Gladys and Rice, Cy. *Defender of the Damned*. New York: Citadel Press, 1964.

St. John, Adela Rogers. *Final Verdict*. New York: Doubleday, 1962.

Schessler, Ken. *This is Hollywood*. Los Angeles: Ken Schessler Productions, 1984.

Sifakis, Carl. *Encyclopedia of American Crime*. New York: Facts On File, 1982.

Sjoquist, Captain Arthur W. *Los Angeles Police Department, 1869-1984, A History*. Los Angeles: LAPD Revolver & Athletic Club, 1984.

Stoker, Charles. *Thicker 'N Thieves*. Santa Monica: Sidereal, 1949.

Street-Porter, Janet. *Scandal*. New York: Dell, 1981, 1983.

Van Winkle, Marshall and Wolff, H. *Sixty Famous Cases*. Summertown, Tenn.: Book Manufacturing Co., 1956.

Wagner, Diane. *Corpus Delecti*. New York: St. Martin's Press, 1986.

Walker, Bill. *The Case of Barbara Graham*. New York: Ballantine Books, 1961.

Wambaugh, Joseph. *The Onion Field*. New York: Delacorte Press, 1973.

Warren, Viola Lockhart. *Dragoons on Trial*. Los Angeles: Dawson Book Shop, 1965.

Webb, Jack. *The Badge*. Englewood Cliffs, N.J.: Prentice-Hall, 1958.

Willard, Charles Dwight. *The Herald's History of Los Angeles City*. Los Angeles: Kingsley-Barnes & Neuner Co., 1901.

Young, Betty Lou. *Pacific Palisades, Where the Mountains Meet the Sea*. Los Angeles: Pacific Palisades Historical Society Press, 1983.

INDEX